RENEWING SOCIALISM

RENEWING SOCIALISM

Democracy, Strategy, and Imagination

Leo Panitch

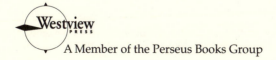

A Member of the Perseus Books Group

Copyright © 2001 by Westview Press, A Member of the Perseus Books Group

Westview Press books are available at special discounts for bulk purchases in the United States by corporations, institutions, and other organizations. For more information, please contact the Special Markets Department at The Perseus Books Group, 11 Cambridge Center, Cambridge MA 02142, or call (617) 252-5298.

Published in 2001 in the United States of America by Westview Press, 5500 Central Avenue, Boulder, Colorado 80301–2877, and in the United Kingdom by Westview Press, 12 Hid's Copse Road, Cumnor Hill, Oxford OX2 9JJ

Find us on the World Wide Web at www.westviewpress.com

Library of Congress Cataloging-in-Publication Data
Panitch, Leo.
  Renewing socialism : democracy, strategy, and imagination /Leo Panitch.
    p.   cm.
  Includes bibliographical references and index.
  ISBN 0-8133-6458-2 (cloth); 0-8133-9821-5 (paper)
  1. Socialism.   2. Democracy.   3. Globalization.   I. Title.

HX73 .P35   2001
320.53'1—dc21
                                                                          2001026071

The paper used in this publication meets the requirements of the American National Standard for Permanence of Paper for Printed Library Materials Z39.48–1984.

10   9   8   7   6   5   4   3   2   1

For Sam and Colin,
comrades in renewing socialism

Ring the bells that still can ring
Forget your perfect offering
There is a crack in everything
That's how the light gets in.

        —Leonard Cohen, "Anthem"

What has happened has happened. The water
You once poured into the wine cannot be
Drained off again, but
Everything changes. You can make
A fresh start with your final breath.

        —Bertolt Brecht, "Everything Changes"

To make the thief disgorge his booty,
To free the spirit from its cell.
We must ourselves decide our duty,
We must decide and do it well.

        —Eugene Pottier, "The Internationale"

CONTENTS

ACKNOWLEDGMENTS

I owe the idea for this book to a suggestion made several years ago by Stephen Bronner. In presenting my thoughts on what is required to move toward the renewal of socialist politics, I have drawn especially on my essays in the annual volumes of the *Socialist Register*: "The Contemporary Meaning of Revolution in the West" (1989) for Chapter 1; "Perestroika and the Proletariat" (1991) for Chapter 2 (which also draws somewhat, as does the Introduction, on my contributions to the *Socialist Register 1992* on the "New World Order" and to the forum on "Socialism after Communism" in *Studies in Political Economy* 38, 1992); "Liberal Democracy and Socialist Democracy: The Antinomies of C. B. Macpherson" (1981) for Chapter 3; "The Political Legacy of the Manifesto" (with Colin Leys, 1998) for Chapter 4; "Globalization and the State" (1994) for Chapter 5; "Reflections on Strategy for Labour" (2001) for Chapter 6; and "Transcending Pessimism: Rekindling Socialist Imagination" (with Sam Gindin, 2000) for Chapter 7. For allowing me to use these writings for the *Register* here, I am grateful to Tony Zurbrugg of Merlin Press, and especially to Sam Gindin and Colin Leys, to whom I dedicate this book, for their comradeship and inspiration, as well as their generosity, over so many years. There are, of course, many others whose comments, criticisms, and encouragement at various points were helpful, and I especially want to acknowledge David Abraham, Greg Albo, Amy Bartholemew, Tony Benn, Geoff Bickerton, Fred Bienefeld, Eric Canepa, David Coates, Robert Cox, Stephen Gill, Steve Hellman, Gerard Greenfield, Marion Kozac, Liz Maestres, Marsha Niemeijer, Margie Mendell, Harry Magdoff, James O'Connor, Frances Fox Piven, Sheila Rowbotham, Herman Rosenfeld, John Saul, John Saville, Donald Swartz, Hilary Wainwright, Rosemary Warskett, Reg Whitaker, Ellen Wood, Alan Zuege, and, not least, my dear departed comrades on the *Register*, Ralph Miliband and Martin Eve. The ideas and arguments presented in this book were considerably enriched over many years by my students at York University in Toronto; among them, Ruth Groff deserves particular acknowledgment here for her advice and editorial help in preparing this manuscript, as does Bob Marshall for preparing the index. I also want to thank my students, especially Jason Schulman and Kevin Ozgencin, at the CUNY Graduate Center in 1998–1999 as well as the participants in the guest seminars I gave that year at the Brecht Forum, Columbia University and New York University, where many of the ideas in the last two chapters were discussed. Among all the very helpful people at Westview, I owe a special thank-you to Geof Garvey for his excellent copy editing, and to Leo Wiegman for his encouragement, advice, and guidance. Finally, to Melanie, Maxim, and Vida, I can only once again express my deepest appreciation for their love and support.

The quotations on the epigraph page are from Leonard Cohen, "Anthem," from the album *The Future* (Leonard Cohen Stranger Music, Inc., 1992); Bertolt Brecht, "Everything Changes," from *Bertolt Brecht Poems*, edited by John Willett and Ralph Mannhiem (London: Eyre Methuen, 1979); and Eugene Pottier, "The Internationale" (American version) from *The Big Red Songbook* (London: Pluto Press, 1977).

Leo Panitch

Introduction

Does it make any sense to speak in terms of socialist renewal of the beginning of the twenty-first century? The massive anticapitalist protests from Seattle to Prague to Quebec that captured the world's attention at the beginning of the new millennium attest to the fact that the spirit of revolution, one of the central facets of political life over the previous centuries, is hardly a thing of the past. If "the revolutionary spirit of the last centuries, that is, the eagerness to liberate and to build a new house where freedom can dwell, [which] is unprecedented and unequaled in all prior history"[1] properly begins with the bourgeois revolutions of the late eighteenth century, few would dispute that this eagerness for fundamental social transformation was in very large part carried into the world of the twentieth century by socialism's revolutionary aspirations to transcend the capitalist order itself. It was socialism that expressed the past century's struggle for liberation from the paradoxical freedom of the bourgeois revolution, that is, from the competition and exploitation upon which capitalist social relations are founded; and it was socialism that embodied the aspiration to build a fully democratic, cooperative, and classless society where freedom and equality might realize rather than negate the sociability of humankind.

Yet by the end of the century, what could be said to remain of the socialist project? The answer appeared self-evident to many people in the 1990s in the face of the ignominious collapse of Communist regimes in the East and the utter loss of radical purpose on the part of Social Democratic parties in the West. The question of what the very concept of socialist change might any longer mean in terms of objectives, social forces, or agencies, let alone in terms of methods or immediate or long-term possibilities, elicited, if not sheer disdain, then at least uncertainty and confusion, hesitation and pessimism. That there should no longer be significant political organizations oriented to fundamental social change in the context of the inequalities and irrationalities of global capitalism defined the tragedy of the modern Left by the end of the twentieth century.

Yet, at the same time, it has in recent years been impossible to miss a growing frustration at the lack of political alternatives to parties and governments dedicated to the capitalist order, and a sense that something must be done about this. "There is no alternative" began as a campaign slogan of the New Right. Today, in the wake of the depredations and irrationalities of neo-liberalism, it is heard as a constant lament on the left. In this context, it is increasingly clear that there is some point, after all, to continuing reflection on the contemporary prospects of socialism.

To be sure, such reflection must be sober and careful. It must be mindful of past failures and disappointments, but it must above all look to the future even as it reexamines the past. For the main point of the exercise, as Marx once put it, is that of "finding once more the spirit of revolution, not of making its ghost walk about again."[2] Indeed, in so far as people looking for how to build new political institutions oriented to achieving socialist ideals are made despondent by the failure of the Communist and Social Democratic parties in the twentieth century, or are paralyzed by the fear that they will be replicated all over again, it may help to overcome these debilitating sentiments if we recall to what extent the old party institutions and their practices were a product of their time and place. We may think of socialism in terms of ideals and principles, theories and goals; but in so far as we think of socialism as *politics*, we need to think of it historically, as political projects embodied in and articulated through particular institutions at specific points in time. Conceived this way, the question of the future of socialism may also come into clearer focus.

The mass Socialist parties that in so many countries had stepped onto the political stage by the early twentieth century were something entirely new: never before had subordinate classes been able to fashion for themselves relatively enduring mass political organizations. Of course, the changes wrought by capitalism itself—not only the invention of new forms of exploitation and inequality, but also the dissolution of old social bonds and local parochialisms; the creation of new conditions of life through industrialization and urbanization; the development of new forms of associational autonomy from the state—provided the conditions for this remarkable political development. These working-class parties came to represent, practically speaking, the socialist project, but they could not but reflect, to a substantial degree, in their organization and ideology the conditions specific to capitalism in their time. The Second International at first provided a common umbrella internationally, but in the aftermath of the split that occurred with World War I (presaged earlier in great debates over strategy and organizational form) there emerged the two institutional wings which dominated socialist politics in the twentieth century: Communism and Social Democracy, each of which came to rely heavily, in their very different ways, on the power of the state. The predominance of these two formations in the politics of the Left for most of the remainder of the century was part of a more general "freezing of party alternatives" often commented upon in the comparative study of political parties.

It was abundantly clear long before the 1990s that the institutions that emerged as the particular embodiments of the socialist project at the beginning of the twentieth century had run their historical course. From a historical materialist perspective, taking into account the tremendous changes that occurred over the course of the century in social, economic, political, and cultural conditions, could it really be expected that the party-political instruments founded at the beginning of the century would continue to be viable expressions of the politics of socialism at the end of the century? Their claims to be the universal and eternal institutional representations of socialist principles should never have been taken too seriously: these claims in good part reflected inflated ideological attempts at reinforcing support for their immediate tactics and particular strategies. Although they presented themselves as the unique embodiments of socialism, they were historically conditional expressions thereof, by no means fixed forever in time's eye.

Already in the 1960s there had been a very strong sense on the "New Left" that both Communism and Social Democracy had become embedded in sclerotic institutions which in their different ways stifled political and intellectual creativity. As a member of that 1960s generation, I think it is fair to say that very few people I knew who embraced socialist values and ideas did so because they were inspired by the Soviet example. On the contrary, we became socialists *despite* that example, indeed, explicitly rejecting it as a model. That example was constantly thrown up in our faces by those who objected to our socialism, and we responded not by defending authoritarian Communism, but by expressing a conviction that a democratic socialism was still possible to conceive and worth committing ourselves to struggle to achieve. Although we were inspired by courageous and tenacious anti-imperialist and national liberation struggles sometimes led by third world Communist leaders and movements, such links as any of this had to Soviet Communism were rarely the object of our admiration.

The Marxism we turned to as a mode of analysis in this context was most emphatically not Soviet Marxism. It was a renewed Marxism fashioned by those who had pointed ways out of and beyond, and usually explicitly broken with, that suffocating orthodoxy. Claims that the particular kind of authoritarian Communist system built in Russia was the only possible outcome of Marx's ideas were not taken too seriously; indeed, such arguments could be seen as a mirror image of the claims that Soviet party leaders themselves made. Joseph Schumpeter, himself no Marxist, once put this in proper perspective: "There is, between the true meaning of Marx's message and bolshevist practice and ideology, at least as great a gulf as there was between the religion of the humble Galileans and the practice and ideology of the princes of the church or the warlords of the middle ages."[3] The point retained its validity, whether it needed put to a Stalinist apologist in earlier decades or to a post-modernist critic in recent ones.

Some among that 1960s generation who became socialists went off in search of a purer Marxism-Leninism. They gathered together under the rubric of relatively tiny revolutionary parties of Trotskyist or Maoist persuasions and affiliations of various sorts. But certainly most of the socialists I knew sensed that the problem with the Communist parties went deeper than a Stalinist or post-Stalinist deviation, that elements in the thought and practice of Leninism, Trotskyism, and Maoism were themselves highly problematic; and that the very discourse of Marxism-Leninism was debilitating, intellectually narrowing, and politically marginalizing. Indeed, while we embraced Marxism for its potential to help us understand the capitalist societies we lived in, we also recognized at least implicitly, and often explicitly, that Marxism offered relatively few conceptual handles with which to understand the nature of authoritarian Communist societies themselves.

It was the hope, perhaps even the expectation, of most socialists of my generation that what would eventually come to replace this system of authoritarian Communism would be some version of democratic socialism. In this sense, Prague 1968 was almost as important in our political formation as Paris 1968. But our socialism was hardly conditional upon an expectation that a democratic socialist outcome was inevitable in the Soviet Bloc. What impelled us toward socialism, rather, was our experience with and observation of the inequalities, irrationalities, intolerances, and hierarchies of our own capitalist societies—in both their global and their domestic expressions. The frustrations with Social Democratic governments which were unable to—or worse, did not even try very hard to—effect substantial change were in this context our main concern. But this is *not* to say that romantic illusions of imminent revolutionary upheavals were nearly as common among the 1960s generation as sometimes now appears in retrospect. To the contrary, the readiness with which Gramsci's distinction between East and West was taken up at that time reflected a widespread recognition that the conditions for insurrection were simply missing in more developed capitalist countries. What primarily came under challenge by the 1960s were the specific ideological and institutional forms of Social Democratic and Communist party politics, and the conventional parliamentarist and bureaucratic modes of representation and administration which they had come to represent.

In the West, Social Democracy's lack of popular mobilizing capacity proved especially debilitating in the transition from the postwar welfare state era to a new era of neo-liberal globalization marked by a successful series of right-wing assaults against reforms won in the earlier era. Yet it was during this very period of transition from one era of capitalism to another that so many activists of the 1960s generation, acutely aware of the limitations of Social Democracy as well as the old and new versions of Leninism, turned to building the "new social movements" which had such a strong social and political impact in the last few decades of the twentieth century. These movements, in part because they learned from the failures of the old politics, certainly proved that mobilization was still possible and that reforms were still winnable. But the failure to develop new party political alternatives on the left was nevertheless registered in every election; and it has been increasingly registered as well in the constantly fraught attempts at keeping movement coalitions going from issue to issue and event to event. Increasingly social movement activists have been faced with the question once again of what prospects there are for the emergence of new political institutions that will carry an anticapitalist political project into the twenty-first century.

There are still no easy answers to this. While conditions of acute exploitation, market irrationality, and intermittent crisis are everywhere manifest, albeit often in new forms, it is nevertheless also true that the cultural, economic, and social profiles of the working classes out of which the old institutional expressions of socialist politics developed initially are radically changed. The issue is not that working classes are less homogeneous than they used to be, and hence that the political expression of class is now impossible. The working classes were never homogeneous. The relevant question—and it *is* a very difficult one—is whether and how political solidarity may be reorganized and rejuvenated in light of the diversity of the working classes and the very significant changes they have undergone. There have always been tensions on the left between those who sought to reinforce solidarity by ignoring this diversity and by resisting change, and those who emphasized the need to transform the working classes in and through the recognition of diversity and the process of change. There can be no question that the experience gained from the new social movements will now have a major influence on any new attempts at socialist renewal, above all our understanding that the transformation of social relations should never have been conceived in undifferentiated class terms, but as encompassing multiple relations of domination as these are inscribed in systems of production, reproduction, administration, and communication.

There has, in fact, already been a marked shift in socialist thinking which lays greater stress than ever on the goal of changing social relations, as broadly outlined above, through economic and political democracy. This has reflected a rejection of the domination inscribed in technocracy and corporatism as embedded in Communism's central planning agencies and also in the institutions that managed Keynesian-style capitalism. This is not to say that planning is no longer important for socialists. The possibility of strategically coordinating economic decision making will seem important indeed to those millions who are made to suffer anew amid the repeated crises of overaccumulation and financial speculation that today's intensified capitalist competition brings about. And the virtues of such coordination, indeed the necessity of it, for preventing the destruction of nature, becomes more and more manifest each day. We know that command economic planning driven by an authoritarian statist industrialization strategy, and a type of Social Democratic indicative planning which was itself subject to the laws of private capital accumulation, both proved unable to plan in accordance with ecological sanity. Given the disappointing trajectory of the Green party in Germany, moreover, there does indeed increasingly appear to be room for a new type of socialism that understands how successful struggles to limit the exploitation of nature, like successful struggles to limit the exploitation of labor, impose direct or indirect costs on capital which also induce economic crises under capitalism. Socialists can build upon this analysis to make a strong case for democratic economic coordination aimed at reconciling human needs for material goods and services with the reproduction of nature.

That said, contemporary socialists cannot claim to have a foolproof blueprint for a new type of political and economic democracy. It often occasions impatience that this is so. In fact, there has been no shortage of more or less attractive models advanced over the past few decades, as we shall see. But such models cannot be persuasive unless they are connected to the establishment of the political means of realizing them, i.e., the creation of new political institutions which would mobilize and educate not only for economic democracy but also for a transformation of conventional modes of representation and administration within the state. Especially relevant here as well are the participatory themes sounded by the New Left of the 1960s. The disdainful dismissal of this theme by Social Democratic and Communist parties, indeed their resistance to attempts at greater internal political democratization, meant that popular alienation from bureaucratic administration and ersatz representation was left to fester, and this helped pave the way for market populism both East and West. Yet, as the evidence accumulates that markets are themselves full of discrimination and power, the limitations of market populism present new opportunities for rebuilding socialist politics.

In looking to such opportunities it will be important not to revive new versions of the old breakdown thesis, whereby expectations of severe capitalist crises are made to do the hard work of socialist strategy and struggle. Of course, such economic crises of greater or lesser severity as are on the horizon will provide opportunities for the Left to develop new forms and strategies that qualitatively enhance its capacities. Out of the long crisis of 1873 to 1896 emerged the European mass working-class parties and trade unions; during the course of the Great Depression of the 1930s, the models of industrial unionism in North America and of Social Democratic governance in Scandinavia were cast; it was amidst the renewed economic crises of the 1970s and 1980s that the new social movements developed. But we must also bear in mind that it is through crises that capitalism historically has tended to recover its dynamism; where and when it is unable to do so, and where no viable socialist alternative or at least few means of democratic defense exist, the consequences are always appalling.

This book's discussion of all these themes is partial insofar as it is mainly undertaken from the perspective of the particular situation of the Left in the advanced capitalist countries. And it needs to be said immediately that it is precisely the limitations of this experience, as much as anything else, which reinforces the need for a renewed internationalism. The importance of this will be addressed at many points in the pages that follow, not least in relation to establishing strategic cohesion for resisting the neo-liberal agenda and developing international means for controlling capital. It needs to be noted, however, that the Left's internationalist focus today is sometimes unfortunately advanced at the expense of deriding or at least giving up on the struggles that remain so necessary at the level of the nation-state, and indeed at subnational levels. This is a false polarization of strategies, not least because even a capitalism that is fully extended in its global reach still relies on nation-states more than on any other structures for its preservation and reproduction. Progressive policy interventions in relation to international institutions and issues, moreover, must still be made, and will continue to be made for the foreseeable future, primarily via the representatives of nation-states. To put aside thinking about how to renew the struggle for socialism at the national level, in the name of a global socialism to match a global capitalism, is mere romanticism.

What is especially required of a new internationalism is the sharing of experiences regarding the difficulty of transforming the local and national state even when radical governments come into office. This is sorely needed if new socialist movements, in the South as well as the North, are to emerge which finally are capable of changing the administrative apparatuses so that they become representative and accountable and oriented to providing the means and resources for as much decentralized and popular decision making and resource allocation as is compatible with democratic planning for common societal problems. The renewed socialist project must not be about more state versus less state, but about a different kind of state. The two main institutional expressions of the socialist project in the twentieth century came to rely on the bureaucratic state as an instrument of allocation, regulation, and coercion to such a degree that the main purpose of socialism, the development of a popular capacity for collective self-determination, was undermined rather than enhanced. But it is important to recognize that the problem is not easily solved by techniques of direct democracy such as referenda (much less will it be solved by proportional representation alone, as many on the left sometimes imply today). A left populism which engages in the pretense that the people inherently know what to do ignores the passivity and deference which lifetimes of exclusion and atomization breed. Rather than assume that communities of active, informed citizens are waiting to be called from the deep, the first task of a democratic socialism, in remaking the state, no less than movement building, is to actively facilitate the creation of democratic capacities. This must start with promoting the capacity of isolated individuals to discover common needs and interests with others in various diverse aspects of their lives, and then encouraging the formation of collective identities and associations and the development of the institutional means and resources to determine collectively how their needs and interests might be fulfilled. Socialism's promise is precisely that of unleashing creative human capacities through a "developmental democracy," to use C. B. Macpherson's apt term, which capitalism and the state stifle. What is needed now is the emergence of institutional expressions of socialist politics which put front and center the immense task of discovering forms of public representation and administration which are developmental in this sense.

Socialists today can have no illusions about the speed with which they may be able to achieve a really significant advance in the fulfillment of their aims. Patterns of advance will vary greatly from one country to another; and there will be setbacks as well as victories. But the gloom in which so much of the Left has been plunged in recent years is very short-sighted. For wherever one looks, there is ferment, with grievances expressed, demands made, rights affirmed. Some of it assumes profoundly unhealthy forms; but a good deal of it is progressive and increasingly speaks an anticapitalist language which is well in tune with socialist aspirations. To be sure, the difficulties involved in developing new socialist institutions and practices must not be underestimated. The new generation of socialists that came to maturity in the advanced capitalist countries in the 1960s and early 1970s were in the following quarter-century unable to forge new political instruments of any comparable range and salience to the old sclerotic ones whose mistakes they often pinpointed so acutely and criticized so mercilessly. But a quarter-century is, historically speaking, a short period of time; compare it to the half-century that separated the defeat of Chartism and the revolutions of 1848 from the rise of the new mass unionism and Socialist parties toward the end of the nineteenth century. Moreover, the instability, let alone the social costs, of capital's current global romp will make the vesting of such massive power in an inherently undemocratic private domain, rather than in a potentially democratic public domain, ever more salient as a political issue. Democratic socialism was never inevitable, but it certainly remains historically relevant.

In any case, we should at least try not to mix up our mortality with the issue of the realization of socialism. Marx's underestimation of the longevity of capitalism is but the first of many mistakes that rest on this understandable but unfortunate error. Many of the people on the left who feel despondent today, and take seriously the talk about the death of socialism, are only acknowledging that their death is likely to come before socialism does. But socialism need not come in our lifetimes for us to be politically relevant as socialists. The point of socialist politics is about ordinary people developing themselves through the process of engaging in political life. The first question a socialist should ask is whether existing political institutions serve a framework for doing so rather than repressing it. As long as we can muster the strategic creativity and imagination to develop alternative political institutions that will in fact be developmental, we are contributing to making socialism possible. That other socialist intellectuals were coming to this conclusion by the end of the twentieth century is one small, if encouraging, sign that an era of socialist renewal may be on the horizon.[4]

The chapters that follow take up, from various perspectives, all the themes raised in this introduction. The first chapter explores the contemporary meaning of revolution and reform in the West, beginning by stressing not only the appropriation of both terms into the rhetoric of the ruling classes, but the need for the Left to take seriously the reality of the continuing revolutionary character of the capitalist class, as evidenced in the current era of competition which drives technological innovation. But if it is competition which determines the revolutionary nature of the bourgeoisie, as Marx's *Manifesto* also understood, it is organization that determines the revolutionary possibilities of working classes; and the chapter goes on to draw the lessons that can be learned from the failure to realize socialism's revolutionary promise in the West through an analysis of this organizational dimension, in particular as it was expressed in Social Democratic parties and the "politics of compromise" they advanced. Chapter 2 then takes up the limitations of the Communist revolutionary experience. Although arguing that these limitations were already foreshadowed at the birth of the Soviet Union, the main focus is on how these limitations were exhibited in the dying days of that regime, drawing in particular on personal observations gleaned from intensive discussions with Russian workers and trade unionists shortly before Mikhail Gorbachev was overthrown and the Soviet Union was dissolved.

After quoting a close adviser to Gorbachev to the effect that it is now incumbent on the Left in the West to find ways to advance the socialist project, the second chapter ends by asking whether we are up to the task. This is what Chapter 3 begins to assess through an examination of the failure of radical intellectuals in the West in the past to sufficiently take responsibility for the improvement of Marxist political theory, and especially of its theory of the state in any transition to socialism, rather than utilizing Marxism primarily as a means of explaining the limitations of the liberal democratic capitalist order. This argument is particularly advanced through an appreciation and critique of the work of C. B. Macpherson. Chapter 4 goes on to argue that the defects of Marxist political theory in this respect has been one aspect of the legacy of the *Communist Manifesto*, while at the same time demonstrating, via a survey of key facets of the current global capitalist conjuncture, the continuing richness of that legacy taken as a whole. Indeed, one of the greater ironies of the socialist experience is that it was especially after the demise the Communist regimes that the remarkable relevance of the *Manifesto* for developing an agenda for the renewal of socialism in our own time really became clear.

It is the full globalization of capitalism in our time that especially makes it so, and Chapter 5, in the context of a critique of the widespread misunderstanding of globalization as an irreversible process associated with the alleged withering away of the state by a transnational capitalism, turns to a sober examination of the limitations of those strategies so far advanced on the left as a means of coping with globalization. Particularly stressed here is the need for a new type of socialist internationalism, yet one which is founded on building solidarities to advance a shift in the balance of social forces within each state to the end of facilitating democratic socialist goals. If this is to happen, the salience of class will have to be brought more centrally back into the analysis and strategy of the Left. This is the remit of Chapter 6, which emphasizes the continuing importance of labor for any project of socialist renewal, while stressing at the same time that this can only be realized through refounding, reorganizing, and democratizing existing labor movements. This must be done in a manner that not only incorporates both the diversity and issues represented by the new social movements, but ensures that the capacities of working people, so stunted under capitalism, are developed to the furthest extent possible through their own organizations. Only this can make the socialist dream realizable.

But it is first of all necessary to dream. It is the task of getting people to think ambitiously once again that is the immediate challenge before the Left today. To transcend a debilitating political pessimism, Chapter 7 contends—to make "the defeated man try the world again," as Ernst Bloch[5] put it in the darkest days of fascism's advance—it will be necessary to rekindle socialist imagination through a revival of utopian thought. This means not abandoning Marxism, but rather reviving what Bloch called its visionary "warm stream" alongside the "cold stream" of political economy;[6] and perhaps even adding a new layer to Marxist theory to help socialists appreciate that in addition to analyzing the accumulation of capital we need to figure out how to foster the accumulation of capacities. The book ends by outlining ten dimensions for a renewed socialist vision to promote the indispensable process of capacity building that socialist renewal must really be about.

We can see through the cracks in the edifice earlier generations of socialists tried to build—"that's how the light gets in." We can make "a fresh start" with every new breath. Through socialist renewal it will be possible for "the spirit of revolution" to flourish anew. What will remain to be seen, of course, is whether we finally can "do it well."

Notes

1. Hannah Arendt, *On Revolution* (New York: Viking, 1965), p. 28.

2. Karl Marx, *The Eighteenth Brumaire of Louis Bonaparte* (New York: International Publishers, 1963), p. 17.

3. Joseph A. Schumpeter, *Capitalism, Socialism and Democracy*, 5th ed. (London: Allen & Unwin, 1976), p. 3. Originally published in 1943.

4. In contrast with the intellectually lazy and uninspired "renewal of Social Democracy" envisaged by Anthony Giddens in *The Third Way* (Cambridge, UK: Polity, 1998) or the three disappointing "real utopias" discussed at length in the concluding chapter of this book, I am thinking in particular of *Return of Radicalism: Reshaping the Left Institutions* (London: Pluto, 2000) by Boris Kagarlitsky; *Spaces of Hope* (Berkeley: University of California Press, 2000) by David Harvey; and *Whose Millennium? Theirs or Ours* (New York: Monthly Review Press, 1999) by the late Daniel Singer, who did so much to try to keep the spirit of revolution alive through the dark decade for the Left that closed the twentieth century.

5. Ernst Bloch, *The Principle of Hope*, translated by N. Plaice, S. Plaice, and P. Knight (Cambridge, Mass.: MIT Press, 1986), p. 198.

6. Ibid., p. 148.

1

Rethinking Revolution and Reform in Capitalist Democracies

There must be something in every socialist, from the very values involved in wanting socialism at all, wanting a revolution to bring about socialism rather than just wanting a revolution, that continually pulls towards precisely the compromises, the settlements, the getting through without too much trouble and suffering. . . . It is only when people get to the point of seeing that the price of the contradictions is yet more intolerable than the price of ending them that they acquire the nerve to go all the way through to a consistent socialist politics.

—Raymond Williams[1]

I

The theme of revolution has hardly been absent from political discourse in recent years in the countries of advanced capitalism. But it has been a theme far more confidently sounded on the right, where it has taken on the coloration of a revolution *from above*, than it has been on the left. "We were all revolutionaries," Ronald Reagan told his White House staff on his last day in office, "and the revolution has been a success."[2] It was tempting, of course, simply to characterize such verbiage as the ad-man's cover for counterrevolution, equivalent to Reagan's designation of the Nicaraguan *contras* as "freedom fighters." And a healthy degree of disdain is also more than justified regarding this kind of "revolutionary" rhetoric, coming as it does from those who even defined "reform" in terms of undoing the limited achievements of Social Democratic and liberal welfare states.

Yet there is a sense in which the self-characterization of contemporary capitalists and politicians as "revolutionaries" and "reformers" might well have deserved to be taken more seriously. Merely to dismiss such rhetoric as mendacious nonsense misses an important dimension of what they have been about. For they have sought to reinfuse their societies with the very kind of bourgeois norms and values that were identified in *The Communist Manifesto,* where Karl Marx and Friedrich Engels affirmed that the "bourgeoisie, historically, has played a most revolutionary part."[3] Could we not in fact say that they have sought to immerse their societies "in the icy water of egotistical calculation" and to leave remaining "no other nexus between man and man than naked self-interest, than callous 'cash payment'"? Have they not endeavored to resolve "personal worth into exchange value and, in place of the numberless indefeasible chartered freedoms ... set up that single, unconscionable freedom—free trade"? And, "for exploitation, veiled by ... political illusions" did they not try to substitute "naked, shameless, direct, brutal exploitation"? Whether or not their drive to prosecute the bourgeoisie's long revolution into the world of the twenty-first century will ultimately prove nearly as successful as they would like to think, surely we must nevertheless admit that the bourgeoisie at the end of the twentieth century seemed to have "conquered for itself, in the modern representative state, exclusive political sway."

The bourgeois revolution from above at the end of the twentieth century was not the same kind of thing as the heroic historic moment that 1789 represented two hundred years earlier. But setting aside what capitalist political leaders themselves say or do, there is a deeper sense in which it is still appropriate to see the contemporary bourgeoisie as continuing to play "a most revolutionary part." In the world of the microchip, of computer technology, of numerical control of production, of instant global communication and capital transfers; in an era of global restructuring of industry, occupation, finance, and control, of workplace relations as well as the relations between gender and work, culture and household, we are perforce reminded of the essential meaning of the *Manifesto*'s designation of the bourgeoisie as revolutionary. "The bourgeoisie cannot exist without constantly revolutionizing the instruments of production, and thereby relations of production, and with them the whole relations of society." Consider, moreover, the very contemporary ring that our present-day experience of the globalization of capitalism lends to a description penned a century and half ago:

> The need of a constantly expanding market for its products chases the bourgeoisie over the whole surface of the globe. It must nestle everywhere, settle

everywhere, establish connections everywhere. . . . [It] has drawn from under the feet of industry the national ground on which it stood. All old-established national industries have been destroyed or are daily being destroyed. They are dislodged by new industries, whose introduction becomes a life and death question for all civilized nations. . . . [We] have intercourse in every direction, universal interdependence of nations. And as in material, so also in intellectual production. . . . [The bourgeoisie] compels all nations, on pain of extinction, to adopt the bourgeois mode of production; it compels them to introduce what it calls civilization into their midst, i.e. to become bourgeois themselves. In one word, it creates a world after its own image.[4]

To be sure, such developments in our own time also accompany and, to some significant extent, emerge out of the renewal of capitalist crises. We live under the mark of a kind of global financial speculation that makes what Marx described in 1850 in France seem like small change. This rampant speculation stands astride the revolutionary era of the microchip in production and communication. The return to the heart-lands of the bourgeois order of mass unemployment in the course of the crisis of the mid-1970s and the recessions of the early 1980s and 1990s has remained all too visible in the rearview mirror even as the American economy has sped ahead in the last few years. The economic future appears precarious indeed not only to Marxist economists but to the *Wall Street Journal*. They watch, whether with bated breath or wringing hands, for another "great crash," even as they marvel at the stock exchanges and bond markets' resilience. And all this invites us to ask of the bourgeoisie's "revolutionary part" in our own time whether it is not still, again in the words of the *Manifesto*, "paving the way for more extensive and more exhaustive crises," all the while "diminishing the means whereby crises are prevented" (p. 73). Is it not now more than ever possible that the bourgeoisie "is like the sorcerer who is no longer able to control the pow-ers of the nether world whom he has called up by his spells"?

Perhaps. To say the bourgeoisie continues to play a revolutionary part, in the sense we have drawn from the *Manifesto*, is at the same time to say that the renewed dynamism of the bourgeoisie in every epoch emerges out of the contradictions that spawn capitalist crises. "Constant revolu-tionizing of production, uninterrupted disturbances of all social condi-tions, everlasting uncertainty and agitation distinguish the bourgeois epoch from all earlier ones" (p. 71). All these are present together, and to say the bourgeoisie remains revolutionary is really just to say that we continue to live in the bourgeois epoch. The reemergence of capitalist crises, the demise of Keynesianism, the class war from above prosecuted in the name of market freedom—all this has undermined the postwar Social Democratic notions of an eternally stable, harmonious, "mixed-economy" or "organized" capitalism. But must we not also cast aside such notions as "capitalism in its death throes" or even "late capitalism"? For even as the bourgeoisie increasingly merges and conglomerates, concentrates capital and socializes production and communication on a global scale, and even as this very concentration and socialization seems to lay the bases for new capitalist crises, so it remains the case that capitalism is still driven by competition even among global giants. It is this competition that is the source of the contemporary evidence that to exist the bourgeoisie must be revolutionary in production and in the changes it brings to relations in society more generally. It is one thing to say that capitalist development is inherently rent by its own contradictions: That remains the great insight of Marxism. But what is wrong about fatalistic expectations of breakdown is not just that capitalism has consistently outlived them, but that they ignore the fact that the bourgeoisie is distinctive among ruling classes historically precisely because it cannot exist without "constantly revolutionizing."

The bourgeoisie's continuing "revolutionary part" should certainly not be associated with unadulterated notions of "progress." The ecological damage being visited on the globe demonstrates how market competition pushes us against the limits of nature in a manner that is more horrific than it is "progressive." Barbaric social conditions, moreover, exist not only in the Third World's all-too-common combination of degrading poverty and brutal dictatorship. They also exist in the heartlands of capitalism in the form of massive inequality, racism, police repression, and bulging prisons. The point to be drawn from this, however, is not that capitalism is closer to "barbarism" than it was in the 1840s when Marx and Engels celebrated the wonders accomplished by the bourgeoisie even as the conditions of inhumane life in Manchester were fresh in their minds. Both the wonders and the degradation existed simultaneously as evidence of the bourgeoisie being the first class "to show what man's activity can bring about." The point is that both characteristics still simultaneously exist. In the capitalist epoch, the bourgeoisie is always both revolutionary and barbaric. The market freedom that has unleashed the wonders of the microchip and the "new economy" on Wall Street, and much more generally on production and communication, is the same market freedom that devastated the Bronx. And the rich and the poor remain equally free to sleep under the exit ramps of the expressway.

II

In relation to this, what can we say about the socialist "spirit of revolution" as we enter the twenty-first century? As the Raymond Williams quotation at the beginning of this essay suggests, the longing to achieve a humane society in a way that would avoid the upheavals of revolution predominantly defined the practice of the Left in capitalist democracies for most of this century. But the politics of reformist compromise, however understandable, agreed to leave in place a society in which the bourgeoisie continued to play the main part in production and communication, a society therefore subject to the competitive and contradiction-laden dynamic of capitalism. Even the Social Democratic state, or the state of the New Deal, was condemned to riding that tiger, and as that state expanded, in its bureaucratic fashion, to meet the minimal requirements of what was taken to define a humane capitalism, it became, for capital, a source of contradiction itself.

The discourse that defined the politics of compromise went as follows: why insist on the old revolutionary means, when the ends of socialism can be secured without them? Yet the politics of compromise could have no other effect than leaving the commanding heights of the economy in capitalist hands, and leaving the state itself far too insulated from popular pressures and controls beyond the electoral and lobbying devices of liberal democracy to be able to resist the bourgeoisie's assertion of its primacy. After decades of searching for the kinds of cross-class consensus that would meet the requirements of a humane capitalism, that discourse now is threadbare: The bourgeoisie's continuing revolutionary part demonstrates that the ends cannot be achieved without the means. The case for trying to define and practice a consistent socialist politics, and for marshaling the nerve to go all the way through with it—that is, of taking capital away from the bourgeoisie and democratizing control over the instruments and processes of production and communication to the end of transforming their content and function—is reinforced by the bourgeois revolution from above in our time. As Raymond Williams suggested, this is not because it can now be shown to be quicker or more exciting, and certainly not because capitalism is about to succumb to its own contradictions so that all socialists need to do is proclaim the fact, but because no other way is possible.

But to say that no other way is possible is not to say that socialism itself is possible. We are often given to think today of socialism's failures in terms of the record of postrevolutionary regimes, their disappointment of original aspirations and promises, if not much worse; or in terms of the less heroic, indeed often abject, entrapment of Social Democracy within the capitalist framework. But from another perspective, socialism's failure stands out in the sense of the absence, especially in the advanced capitalist countries, of that conscious, organized, and creative movement for a democratic, cooperative, and classless society which, in so far as it is an expression of massive popular support, is the *sine qua non* of realizing socialist aspirations. To recognize this is to come face to face with one of the most sobering facts that must confront socialists today.

To put this problem in perspective, two things must immediately be said. First, that a distinction between two meanings of revolutionary socialism, of which many socialists in the West have long been cognizant, must still be borne in mind. On the one hand, it may be taken to mean a fundamental transformation in the social order, however that transformation is brought about. On the other hand, it may also mean the overthrow of a system of government, the word *overthrow* being intended to convey the notion of a sudden and violent political convulsion outside the existing constitutional channels. The two notions may be related, insofar as fundamental transformation may be impossible without such a political convulsion. But however this may be, the two meanings need to be differentiated; and it is undoubtedly true that the overwhelming majority of the population of advanced capitalist countries, including the overwhelming majority of the working classes, has shunned revolutionary change in the second meaning of the term. There have very occasionally been circumstances when something approximating a revolutionary situation has occurred in one or another such country. But, even then, an essential ingredient to the overthrow of the system of government has usually been missing, namely the presence of a revolutionary party capable of developing extensive popular sympathy and support and determined to use the situation to take power. That Social Democratic parties in this century have not had such an intention has been unambiguously clear since World War I at least. And the Western Communist parties, certainly from the 1930s onward, also rejected out of hand what they denounced as ultra-left adventurism or petty bourgeois romanticism.

Moreover, the attempts that were made to build such revolutionary parties by groups of a Trotskyist or Maoist persuasion in more recent decades have proved largely barren.

In other words, revolutionary agencies with popular support have not existed in any significant sense for revolution-by-overthrow in these countries; and there is little reason to think that this will change in any relevant time frame. The fact may be deplored, viewed as the most blatant example of false consciousness in the people and of parliamentary cretinism and rank opportunism in the leadership of Socialist and Communist parties. Or it may be applauded as a demonstration of maturity and wisdom, a recognition of the fact that, given the relation between state and civil society in the West, given the very nature of hegemony, the notion of revolution by "seizing" and "overthrowing" the "state" is meaningless, absurd. But deplored or applauded, so it nevertheless is.

The second point that needs to be made, however, is that the absence of significant popular support for revolution-by-overthrow cannot be taken to mean absence of popular support for socialist aspirations altogether. And this was true even in the last decades of the twentieth century. It is worthwhile recalling that the 1980s opened with new programs for socialist change figuring centrally on the political agenda in a good number of Western countries: François Mitterand's and the Common Progamme's 1981 victory in France; the Wage Earners' Fund proposals in Sweden; the short "march to power" of PASOK in Greece; the strength of the socialist Left in the Labour Party in Britain, with that Left occupying governmental office in Europe's largest city. These developments did not appear out of thin air. They were the indirect products of the spirit of 1968, of the post–Cold War generation that spawned the New Left and the student and worker militancy of the late 1960s and early 1970s. Such developments, connected as they were in the bourgeois mind with the apparent "ungovernability" of this generation and with a rekindling of their old fears that they might lose any control over the state, were another factor in inducing the bourgeoisie's renewed determination to create the world in their own image.

Yet what is now all too evident is that there was a severe underestimation, on the one hand, of the hegemonic capacity of capitalist forces; and, on the other hand, an overestimation of the enthusiasm of the masses and the solidarity and/or commitment of the leadership. The disappointments regarding an electoral road to socialism in the West in the 1980s and the growing disaffection from classical revolutionary approaches combined, in the face of the bourgeois neo-liberal revolution from above, to produce great confusion and hesitancy among socialists for the remainder of the century.

Less weight may be given to the claims that there has taken place a great and irreversible ideological shift among the bulk of the population of a kind that betokens massive and deep popular support for the bourgeois revolution from above. It is probably the case that the socialist electoral options put forward in a number of European countries in the early 1980s were unable to garner positive support from more than a quarter of the electorate at the very most (with the rest of their support coming in the form of a negative vote against the bourgeois options). But it is worthwhile setting against this the fact that even the most ardent and successful of the bourgeois "revolutionaries" could hardly claim anything like absolute majorities. The victories of Ronald Reagan in 1980 and 1984, of George Bush in 1988, of Margaret Thatcher in 1979, 1983, and 1987, were all won with the support of something on the order of one-third of the population entitled to vote. And they took place against the backdrop of the failures and retreats of earlier Liberal or Social Democratic parties in government in the 1970s.

Still, there is small comfort to be drawn from this as matters now stand. In many countries of Europe, there occurred a distinct loss of support for, and commitment to, traditional parties of the Left in the eighties: and even where such parties were able to stage an electoral recovery in the 1990s, this has certainly not occurred on the basis of their seeking popular endorsement for socialist aspirations and programs. At best, they have presented themselves as offering a moderate defense of the welfare state against the radical excesses of the renewed bourgeois spirit of revolution. For the most part, as epitomized by the leadership of Tony Blair and Gerhard Schröder, such parties really did seem determined in government to prove above all how committed they were to the capitalist market economy.

Where does this then leave the socialist aspiration for fundamental change in the West? It is hardly surprising that one of the most notable characteristics of much of the Left in recent years has been the deep pessimism which the question evokes. Again and again, the same theme in different variations is heard, namely that even the advocacy of socialism is politically damaging and doomed to relegate its advocates to a marginal and ineffectual ghetto. The tactical and strategic accent, in this view, has to fall on a moderate pragmatism and on the defense and possible extension of old reforms in a manner that does not offend the sensibilities of those seduced by the appeal of the bourgeois revolution from above of the 1980s. Where Reagan and Thatcher proclaimed "we are all revolutionaries" in the bourgeois meaning of the term, large sections of the Left have thought it best to disclaim emphatically any association at all with revolutionary aspirations, even if these are conceived as being realized within existing constitutional channels. Are we to be stranded, then, with nothing other than the kind of alternative offered by Blair and Schröder who emulate Bill Clinton and Albert Gore and promise to run the market economy better than the right-wing parties? Better, to be fair, is intended to mean in a less barbaric and more just manner. But the debate remains conducted on the terms set by the "revolutionaries" of the right.

III

Here, then, lies a great paradox of our time. The continuing revolutionary part played by the bourgeoisie has undermined the politics of compromise that sustained Social Democratic and liberal reformism in their search for a humane capitalism. This ought to make the ethical and logical basis for socialist aspirations and commitment stronger than ever. But at the same time, even the advocacy of socialism is more than ever marginalized within the political systems of advanced capitalism. Moreover, the global competitive thrust of the bourgeoisie and the restructuring of industry that goes with it has exposed anew the trade union constituencies of these parties to that competition, weakening the institutional base that provided support to the old politics of compromise. For a period, the leaders of these parties, and the intellectuals associated with them, desperately clung to the example of the Scandinavian societies, especially Sweden, as evidence that their project was still feasible. But to do this they had to ignore the pull that the new era of bourgeois revolution, ideologically as well as materially, was having on the Swedish bourgeoisie itself. They had to pretend, moreover, that all that was needed to replicate Sweden's Social Democratic state elsewhere in the West was to adopt this or that Swedish "policy," technocratically conceived. They forgot that the dense institutional organization of the working class and cooperative movements which nurtured and sustained such policies emerged out of a cultural and political matrix, and a half-century of struggle and confrontation, which now could only be replicated elsewhere in the West with something very like a revolution. Many activists in these parties understood very well that a remobilization of support could not be achieved on the basis of dry explanations of the detailed structure of the Swedish Labour Market Board. Even if that is where they too hoped eventually to arrive, many of them understood that the first step in this direction entailed, as it did originally in Sweden, promoting the capacity for self-organization and activism at the base, a process that requires some renewal of the "spirit" of socialist revolution. But they were thwarted at every turn by the narrow-gauge logic of short-term electoral pragmatism that dictated the actions of those—and there were many at the base as well at the leadership levels—who still clung to the politics of compromise.[5]

In the absence of any alternative, however, the weakening of the old political and industrial institutions that practiced the politics of compromise only further exposes people to the vagaries of the ethos and reality of competition. To be sure, it provides an opening for remobilization and reorganization, but the immensity of the task—do we need to start all over again from scratch?—is daunting. Moreover, the failure of the Communist parties of the West, as well as of the Trotskyist and Maoist groups, promotes further ground for pessimism. Have not only the politics of liberal reform and Social Democracy proved a failure, but all possible variants of a consistent socialist politics?

To affirm this would be to retreat from the creative political role that socialist intellectuals can play. We are not confined, in recognizing the inability of Social Democracy or liberal reformism to tame the capitalist tiger, to jumping backward toward the practice of the Communists or Trotskyists or Maoists in the West, just because they too discerned the limits of the politics of compromise. There is no reason why socialists in the West today cannot reconsider the strategic possibilities of a consistent socialist politics free of the old preoccupations with sectarian debates over the lessons to be drawn from "classical" revolutions in very different times and places; free of the stultifying organizational structures of democratic centralism; free of the rigid teleological theories that posited an inevitable and imminent capitalist breakdown matched by an equally inevitable proletarian "seizure" of the state; and indeed, free of the simple positing of "workers' council–style direct democracy" in stark opposition to representative democracy.

In early 1919 (at what appeared to many then and, looking back, also to many today to be the high-water mark of socialist revolutionary possibilities in this century), the founder of modern Social Democracy in Canada, J. S. Woodsworth, entered into the debate then raging among Canadian socialists—the same debate that was raging elsewhere in the West—over Bolshevik versus Social Democratic strategy. Inspired by the British Labour Party's explicit adoption of socialist objectives in 1918, Woodsworth took the latter side in the debate, but he nevertheless averred:

> Our ultimate aim must be a complete turnaround of the present economic and social system. In this we recognize our solidarity with the workers of the world over. . . . Such a change, we hope, will be accomplished by means of education, organization, and the securing by workers of the machinery of government. . . . Revolution may appear to come more slowly [in Britain than in Russia] but there will be no counter-revolution. . . . It may take a few years to work out, but when it's done it's done for good.[6]

In light of what the neo-liberal counterrevolution has undone in respect to the reforms that Labour governments had introduced, some will now find it tempting to mock Woodsworth's words. Yet to see these words as nothing but a cover for the merest reformist ambitions would be a mistake. While some would point to the explicitly antirevolutionary behavior of the German Social Democratic leaders in the very year the above words were written, there are no good grounds for tainting thereby the sincere intentions of a great many of those who set out on the path of fundamental social change within the existing constitutional framework of liberal democracy. Indeed, in one crucial respect, and for the reasons we have already indicated, the premise that underlay the Social Democratic position, that an insurrectionary strategy was impossible in the West, must be recognized as having been fundamentally correct.

We must surely, finally, escape from the simplistic dualisms that bedeviled the Left throughout the twentieth century. The Left used to beat itself up, sometimes quite literally, with debates over parliamentarism versus extra-parliamentarism, reform versus revolution, and most notoriously even today, party versus movement, as if one ruled out the other, black and white, or, rather, gray and red. Such dualisms are terribly misleading. Posing the issues this way gets us nowhere. The question is not parliamentarism versus extra-parliamentarism, but what kind of parliamentarism will not give rise to the illusion that all people need to do—all they ought to do—is vote for representatives who will then put everything right. The real problem regarding parliamentarism occurs when the point of seeking election becomes only to offer a "team" of leaders who refuse to use their platform to engage in socialist mobilization and education. The question is not, by the same token, reform versus revolution, but what kinds of reforms, including reform in "the machinery of government" itself, produce the structural changes that can be said to be revolutionary, that is, that cannot be so readily undone as to tempt one to mock the aspiration that "when it's done it's done for good." And most important, the question is not party versus movement, but what kind of party—in what relationship to the state on the one hand and in what relationship to party members and supporters on the other—can sustain an organized thrust for education, organization, and participation over the broadest possible range of popular struggles for social justice; so that the intellectual and organizational capacities that are nurtured thereby yield the popular resources and support which are, in the end, the essential condition for revolutionary change—even when elections are won.

IV

All this, of course, is more easily said than done. If the very meaning of socialist change is more open today in terms of objectives, social forces, and agencies than ever before, this is less a cause for alarm or pessimism than it is an opportunity for creative socialist thinking and action. Although most recent reflections on and polemics over the crisis of socialism in the West have focused on the question of what is wrong about traditional socialist conceptions in terms of objectives and social forces, it may be more pertinent to focus on the problem of agency, in particular of party. This is because agency is the mediating variable between social forces and objectives, the nodal point through which the two intersect. It is also because the crisis of socialism, posed in terms of whether there is any longer a significant constituency for socialist change, is bound up with the crisis of agency, which is to say the role parties and movements play not just in the representation of preordained identities with "objective" interests, but in the very formation of identities and in the articulation of interests of social groups.

It is appropriate in this context to turn back, for a moment, to *The Communist Manifesto*. There is clearly much irony in the fact that the claims it made regarding the revolutionary vocation of the working class look quite shopworn alongside the insights that text still affords on the revolutionary part played by the contemporary bourgeoisie. Marx and Engels, while predicting ever greater and more insoluble capitalist crises, and incapable of imagining in 1848 that the bourgeoisie would still play "a most revolutionary part" at the end of the twentieth century, did not, of course, expect that socialism would emerge like a phoenix from the ashes of capitalist breakdown. On the contrary, the key to a socialist future lay in the organization of the working classes that developed on the basis of the wage labor called into existence by the bourgeoisie as the essential condition for the augmentation of its capital. The argument that in calling into existence these modern proletarians the bourgeoisie had produced "its own gravediggers" did not rest on any notion (as it became quite fashionable to argue in the confused intellectual climate on the left in the past two decades) that these modern proletarians carried revolutionary consciousness in their genes. What gave the bourgeoisie its historically revolutionary part was competition; what gave the proletarians their revolutionary part was organization. The conditions for such organization were in part established by the bourgeoisie itself, as it brought many workers together under one roof, and subjected them to similar conditions of life. It also provided means of communication that laid the basis for contact among workers of different localities, whereby they connected together their numerous local struggles against low or fluctuating wages, against appalling working conditions and despotism in production, against restraints on workers' freedom of association, and against the exclusion of the propertyless from the new structures of representative government that the bourgeoisie had fashioned for itself in relation to the state.

The *Manifesto*'s prediction on the revolutionary implications of working-class organization long appeared to be remarkably prescient. Imagine what bells it rang for people at the start of the last century to come across the *Manifesto* and to read: "Now and then the workers are victorious, but only for a time. The real fruit of their battle lies not in the immediate result, but in the ever expanding union of the workers. . . . And that union, to attain which the burghers of the Middle Ages, with their miserable highways, required centuries, the modern proletarians, thanks to railways, achieve in a few years" (p. 76). Even if "a few years" had to be taken metaphorically, can we not understand why it appeared to socialists that "every class struggle is a political struggle" just when the earlier local and craft organization of workers seemed indeed to be giving way to the "organization of the proletarians into a class, and consequently into a political party"?

To someone watching the rise of the independent and militant trade union movements in Brazil, South Africa, or South Korea in recent decades, such a conception might have seemed rather fresh and contemporary. Why did it sound so stale, then, in the advanced capitalist countries? The clear passage, through the postwar years, of the overwhelming majority of the population in all the Western capitalist countries to the status of people who had to sell their labor to gain a livelihood within capitalism is incontrovertible. The feminization of the labor force is a most notable contemporary dimension of this, as is the growing absolute and relative number of women in the membership of trade unions. Yet none of this any longer conjures up the image that "what the bourgeoisie produces, above all, is its own gravediggers," at least in the advanced capitalist countries. It is not just that the metaphor of "a few years" has been so badly stretched out of shape. Nor is it just that vast and growing sections of the "white-collar sector" remain unorganized, while the old industrial unionized sector is itself declining. The point is rather that it was wrong ever to claim that "the advance of industry . . . replaces the isolation of the labourers, due to competition, by their revolutionary combination, due to association" and that it, "therefore, cuts from under its feet the very foundation on which the bourgeoisie produces and appropriates products" (p. 79). The isolation overcome via collective bargaining simply does not do this, in and of itself. Trade unions are not by themselves "schools for socialism." Association for the purpose of collective bargaining is just that, that is, it is about bargaining over the price and conditions of wage labor, not over its abolition. And if this is what makes it compatible with the continuation of the bourgeois epoch, it also is what makes it subject to assault in a new era of capitalist competition and restructuring, the kind of era we are living through today.

This would not have been news to Marx and Engels, of course: their revolutionary aspirations often carried them away in their rhetoric, especially in 1848. Indeed, even in the face of such rhetoric, the *Manifesto*'s deep insight into what continuing capitalist competition and restructuring means for working-class organization still jumps out at us: "This organization of the proletarians into a class, and consequently into a political party, is continually being upset again by the competition between the workers themselves." Our confidence must be shaken in the notion, however, that "it constantly ever rises up again, stronger, firmer, mightier" (p. 76). Our confidence in this must be shaken not only because of the bourgeoisie's continually revolutionary part, but because of what else has been disconfirmed alongside the confirmation of what the *Manifesto* had to say about the development of the working class. The identity of workers, even organized workers, even politically conscious workers, has not been something that has erased other identities, sometimes, indeed often, more immediately compelling identities in social and political terms. The *Manifesto's* notion that "differences of age and sex have no longer any distinctive social validity for the working class" (p. 74) is plainly wrong, if it was meant to be taken as an empirical statement. The same must be said, *a fortiori*, about race and about national identity, and, to some extent as well, about ethnicity and religion.

The point is not only, moreover, that significant differences have always persisted in terms of wages and working conditions along many of these dimensions even in common places of work as well as across job ghettos; nor is it just that significantly different conditions of life separate workers along these dimensions in the context of patriarchy, residential segregation, relations to the agencies of social and state control, marginality on the labor market, and so on. Nor even is it that the bourgeoisie has played on these differences to ensure that the competition among workers essential to capitalism's existence persists. Nor even again that working-class organizations, industrial, political, and cultural, have institutionalized these differences. It is rather that the identities that exist and are reproduced along each of these dimensions cannot be, *and should not be*, effaced insofar as they also require organization and autonomy if the groups in question (even if the majority of them are also workers) are to be able to prosecute struggles against discrimination and oppression.

All this pertains directly to the view that the root of the inability to develop a sustained and creative socialist practice lies in false assumptions about the revolutionary potential of the working class. Having been for so long seen as the fount of the realization of socialism, a political practice that grounds itself centrally in the working class came to be seen by many people on the left over the last two decades as the obstacle to fundamental social transformation. There are really two versions of this by now quite common theme. The first focused on the sociological decomposition of the old industrial working class in occupational, residential, and cultural terms, and discerned in this the roots of "the forward march of labour halted." Out of this analysis came a renewed call, in the face of bourgeois revolution from above in the 1980s, to revive something akin to the popular front strategy of the 1930s, targeting an electoral alliance between the elite of the weakened traditional political and industrial institutions of the working class with whatever bourgeois elite could be weaned away from the barbarism of Thatcherism or Reaganism toward a renewal of the politics of compromise. The second version went beyond the first by challenging the notion of a distinct working-class "interest" in socialism, or indeed in anything else. Strategically, it was less concerned with alliances among various elites, but, taking its cue from the relative vitality of new social movements, it looked to an "articulation" of diverse social groups, with the emphasis placed less on traditionally socialist solutions and more on completing the unfinished business of the liberal democratic revolution begun in 1789. Although the two consistently intertwined, the first version inflected back toward Social Democratic state interventionism and tripartite corporatism; the second version inflected toward strengthening a rather loosely defined "civil society" against the state and capital.

Yet there is another way of looking at the problem. What becomes clear from a rereading of the *Manifesto* is not just how wrong Marx and Engels were to let their revolutionary aspirations carry them away to the point that they allowed their great insights on the historical development of capital and labor to lead them to the conclusion that the bourgeoisie's "fall and the victory of the proletariat are equally inevitable." What also becomes clear is that such a claim *only* makes sense in light of the very next dimension of revolution that the *Manifesto* addresses. That dimension is the critical role played by political parties in *"the formation of the proletariat into a class."* Only once this dimension is introduced can Marx and Engels's understanding of the bourgeoisie's continuing revolutionary role as a condition of that class's continued existence, and their sharp awareness of the vagaries that attend workers' struggles within the bounds of competition, be squared with their confidence in the revolutionary potential of the working class.

Little actual analysis of this followed in the *Manifesto*, however. Rather, what followed was a brilliant polemic directed against the bourgeoisie. But once we accept the idea that capitalism does not of itself self-destruct, and that a homogeneous working-class identity is neither possible, nor even desirable, then the work that parties do in the formation of the identity of the working class becomes the critical variable in the realization of socialism. The question becomes whether such parties, as they emerge out of the limited degree and form of working-class identity and solidarity that develops spontaneously and through trade union organization within capitalism, can transform that identity and solidarity into a force that can realize the possibility of socialist revolution. To say this is certainly not to say they actually or inevitably do it, of course. On the contrary, what we need to analyze, as we reflect on what lessons to draw from the twentieth century, is what they did and why, and what else they might have done or could do to realize socialist possibilities.

The failure to address the question of the party's role in class formation and identity at all seriously has been the most surprising aspect of that vast literature that has been produced in the past few decades on the strategic lessons that must be gleaned from how and why the working class has failed to be the fount of socialist change. The classic texts of Marxist politics from the beginning of the last century, in particular, have been pilloried for assuming that the working class was innately revolutionary; but the actual work that socialist parties did (or did not do) in forming the political and ideological identities of the working class has hardly been examined. One might think that those who put an emphasis on the importance of "discursive practices" in the formation of social and political subjects would want to undertake such inquiry, but their work has usually been highly theoretically abstract rather than what Antonio Gramsci called "empirico-historical." The result, of course, is that despite their disdain for "impressionist and sociologistic descriptivism,"[7] the writings of the "discourse" school has been particularly laden with exactly such impressionistic descriptivism in their discussion of the actual practice of working-class parties (as opposed to the "texts" of socialist intellectuals). This is also true of their discussion of the new social movements. For all their emphasis on the importance of "articulation" among a plurality of social forces themselves formed through discursive practice, the actual relation between leaders and led in social movements has been substantially ignored. So has been the way in which bourgeois hegemony operates to reinfuse with bourgeois norms and values even those people who happen to construct their identities in terms of "struggles against oppression," so that these movements often limit their struggle to securing for their supporters the mode and extent of opportunity, independence, and consumption afforded to the bourgeoisie itself.

If our objective is a socialist strategy that pertains to the overcoming of capitalism and the building of a new house in which freedom and equality might dwell, then we cannot leave substantially undiscussed the role that "the articulators of the articulation" would have to play—nor can we ignore what organizational forms this would have to take—in order to develop out of the experiences of black and white, female and male, young and old, people *who also have their labor for sale* a modicum of common understanding of the way capitalism works as a system; and a modicum of a common sense of class identity and of common fundamental divergence of interests from the bourgeoisie. For in addition to the need for respect and tolerance for the experiences that make people's identities so rich in their differences, there is also needed a sense of their common exploitation when they are able to sell their labor or their common marginalization when they cannot. The link between socialism, class consciousness, and class struggle lies not in the reductionist mind of the Marxist, as so many would have it today: It lies in the nature of capitalism, the system that socialists are committed to trying to transcend. For two central conditions of the bourgeoisie's existence—and continuing revolutionary part—are competition, including competition among workers, on the one hand; and, on the other, the exploitation of people who must sell their capacity to labor. The role parties or movements play in forming common class identities and perceptions of interest is an important (although not sufficient) determinant of realizing socialist possibilities precisely because it pertains to undermining these conditions of the bourgeoisie's continued existence.

It is, of course, possible to read the revolutionary classic texts of the turn of the century, given the idiom they were wont to use, in a manner that sees them as portraying political practice in terms of parties playing out nothing but pure Jacobin-style vanguardism; or, at the other extreme, as being nothing but the bearers of innate revolutionary aspirations of working-class people. But such readings miss that dimension of socialist thought and practice which understood political organization neither in terms of the formation of a self-contained crack troop of revolutionaries, nor in terms of the merely passive representation of preformed class consciousness, but rather as the very arena in which hegemonically oriented class identity and consciousness were formed. In any case, precisely because they were traversing such virgin terrain, those who were the embattled leaders of the mass working-class parties, which were, after all, an entirely new phenomenon in history, should hardly have been taken—on the basis of pamphlets and speeches wherein polemic and analysis were inevitably very much admixed—as providing the last word on the subject. Much less should they so be taken today either by those who pillory them for their faults or by those who treasure them for their insights.

Writing in 1922, Georg Lukacs appropriately began his essay, "Towards a Methodology of the Problem of Organisation," with the following words:

Although there have been times when problems of organisation stood at the forefront of debate (e.g. when conditions of amalgamation were under discussion), it nevertheless remains true that theorists have paid less attention to such questions than to any others. The idea of the Communist Party . . . has yet often been seen purely in technical terms rather than one of the most important intellectual questions of the revolution. . . . [N]o really vital theoretical energy seemed to be left over for the task of anchoring the problem of organisation in communist theory. If much activity in this sphere is correct, this is due more to correct revolutionary instincts than to any clear theoretical insight. On the other hand, there are many false tactical attitudes, e.g. in the debates on a united front, which derive from a mistaken view of the problems of organisation.[8]

This essay by Lukacs, now much ignored, still bears careful reading today. In many ways what he says here is not very much different from another great revolutionary theorist of the 1920s who carried much further still the analysis of the role of party in revolutionary change, Antonio Gramsci. Attention has been properly paid to the "war of position" versus "war of maneuver" in the West, to the problem of ideology, to the concept of hegemony, and to the question of "alliances." But the issue that concerned him most, the issue that pervaded his whole work—the determining role (and proper organizational form) of the mass party, of the "Modern Prince," not only in the formation of appropriate strategy for socialist change, but in the creation of the collective will for fundamental change, above all in the working class itself—has gotten much less attention in the past few decades of socialist confusion and hesitation. If we paid more attention to the stress he laid on "the importance and significance which, in the modern world, political parties have in the elaboration and diffusion of conceptions of the world"; and if we addressed the limits and failures of the predominant working-class parties in this respect; then we would probably learn far more about "what is to be done" than from dwelling on the sociological decline of the industrial working class or the proliferation of "identities."

In Gramsci's conception, the main role of the mass party, was not that of putting forward a team of political leaders, as broadly representative as possible of public opinion in an electoral contest. Nor was it that of forging a small band of revolutionaries. Nor was it that of coordinating a "network" of alliances. Its main role—and its organizational form and political philosophy had to be forged in relation to this role—was that of elaborating its own component parts—those elements of a social group that have been born and developed as an "economic" group—and turning them into qualified political intellectuals, leaders and organizers of all the activities and functions inherent in the organic development of an integral society, both civil and political. . . . That all members of a political party should be regarded as intellectuals is an affirmation that can easily lend itself to mockery and caricature. But if one thinks about it nothing could be more exact. There are of course distinctions to be made. A party might have a greater or lesser proportion of its members in the higher grades or in the lower, but this is not the point. What matters is the function, which is directive and organisational, i.e. educative, i.e. intellectual.[9]

Only with such a conception of what it means for parties to aim at "the formation of the proletariat into a class" can we conceive of realizing socialist aspirations. It may, of course, not be possible. But we need to ask, as a priority, whether socialist parties have been oriented this way and, if not, whether it is now possible to create parties and movements that are. It has been symptomatic of the crisis of the Left in recent decades, of the retreat from the creative role that socialist intellectuals can play, not only that this question has been so little addressed, but that on the few occasions it has been addressed, the tendency has been to substitute a mechanistic and pessimistic "inevitability of failure" for the earlier mechanistically optimistic "inevitability of revolution." For instance, Adam Przeworski and John Sprague's comparative historical study of the interrelationship between party and class formation, *Paper Stones*,[10] set out to prove that there is an insurmountable barrier to realizing socialist aspirations in the West. They appropriately stressed the role of socialist parties in organizing workers into the political and ideological force called the working class; and they recognized that this in turn generates the possibility of structuring social and political conflict along lines that go to the core of a challenge to capitalist hegemony, since this hegemony is founded on the denial of the relevance of class. But they identified a "catch," a trick of capitalist social structure which, when combined with political democracy, determines that the work that socialist parties do in relation to the formation of class identity and organization is inevitably frustrated. And this determines a miserable outcome for the aspiration to achieve socialism in the West.

What is this "catch"? As for choosing democratic means, there was, in the West, no real choice for socialist parties. They had to participate in elections, since votes offered a welcome and viable substitute ("paper stones") for the fraught and bloody confrontations of the barricades. But since elections are decided by numbers, the fate of socialism was sealed, because workers, according to the narrow definition adopted by Przeworski and Sprague, have always been a numerical minority. (Workers allegedly are only "manual" employees in "productive" industries; nonmanual employees in these industries and all employees in "nonproductive" industries, as well as the small farmers, are all defined as "middle class.") Consequently, to win elections Socialist parties had to broaden their appeal to potential allies in the "middle class" to achieve electoral success. They were therefore forced to cast their appeal in such a way that it undermined their ability to define politics, even for the workers they organized, in consistent class terms.

It is probably correct that the political practice of electoral socialist parties increasingly tended toward diminishing the salience of class identity among workers. But the question that needs to be asked is whether this occurred because of socialist parties' electoral appeal to the broadly defined "middle class." Despite the transformation of white-collar work amidst the passage of the vast majority of the population to the status of those who had to sell their labor to gain a livelihood, Przeworski and Sprague were able to cite attitudal surveys to show that even lower-level and unionized salaried workers tended not to think of themselves as working class and that manual workers did not recognize them as such. But is it in fact objectively impossible for these perceptions to be otherwise? Przeworski and Sprague undertook no detailed analysis of the nature of the appeal made by Socialist parties to salaried or "nonproductive" workers, or how it coincided with or differed from the appeal they made to allegedly "real" workers. In fact, they did not undertake any systematic examination of the actual ideological and organizational transformations of the parties in question. The strategies they ascribed to parties were largely intuited from the distribution of votes, as embellished only by the odd reference to this or that phrase in a party program. Other factors that might account for the attenuation of the parties' role in the formation of class identity, apart from the alleged minority status of ("productive") workers, were not systematically treated. Perhaps the parties diluted their class appeal (with appeals to nationalism, to local particularism, to deference to "expertise," to moderation and consensus) because they sought to gain (the easy way, i.e., on the terrain of a hegemonic bourgeois discourse) the votes of those many manual industrial workers who resisted or were at least unmoved by earlier "pure" class appeals? Perhaps they diluted their class appeal because the leaders themselves came to adopt some of these values? Perhaps their decision not only to engage in electoral competition, but to accept the very structure of parliamentary decision making, embodying the Burkean notions of a sharp separation between decision makers within the state and the class "without," itself had the effect of disorganizing the class they organized electorally in terms of a class appeal? Perhaps these parties diluted their class appeal because they sought to strike a compromise with capitalists, or to rationalize such a compromise entered into pragmatically by their leaders while in state office?

In other words, among the constraints socialist parties faced in respect to the formation of the proletariat into a class, not only the limited votes of industrial manual workers need to be counted; or at least such electoral constraints can only be counted in the context of other and ultimately more daunting ones, above all the power of capital and its ability to disorganize workers through competition as well as through its material and ideological reach among workers and among Socialist party leaders. In the face of this constraint, such class identity as these parties continued to develop even among manual industrial workers was based on a notion of class interest increasingly conceived within the framework of capitalism, elitist parliamentarism, and trade union identity. Some parties could for a considerable time retain electoral loyalties from many workers on this basis, especially where a strong trade union movement itself fostered continued working-class identity. But it became disconnected from any attempt to identify class interest with socialism, or at the very least it involved a redefinition of socialism so that it effectively meant corporatist-style state planning for capitalist economic growth.

The last paragraph of Przeworski and Sprague's book was cast in broad enough terms to fit this interpretation: "Leaders became representatives and the struggle for socialism was delegated to representatives. . . . They succeeded in making the very possibility of socialist transformation seem so distant from our daily lives." Nevertheless, they still gave the impression that it would all have been different if industrial workers were a numerical majority; that it might yet be different if socialist parties could only drop their ties to the working class; or that elections should now be simply ignored by socialists. Such either/or options are not the stuff of effective strategy. The first requirement for such must surely be that the parties become once again committed to socialism as a goal, and that they recognize clearly the salience of class for effecting a challenge to capitalist hegemony. This means actively engaging once again in fostering working-class identity (among "productive" and "non-productive" workers) in the face of a capitalism which constantly deconstructs and reconstructs industry, occupation, and locale. But it means above all (here we must learn well what Gramsci taught) developing the capacity among their members and supporters to offer socialist leadership in their communities in relation to multifarious forms of subordination, deprivation, and struggle. This is not a matter of imposing a rigid set of socialist maxims on every struggle; it is a matter of developing the capacity to organize in a manner that relates socialist understanding and commitment to the problems and struggles of everyday life; and to engage in political discourse in a manner that is educative and that recasts and challenges the terms of capitalist hegemony.

V

Let us turn, finally, from questions pertaining to whether constituencies for socialism can be fashioned by appropriate socialist agencies, to the question of socialist goals today. Here too, as we observed at the outset, hesitation and even pessimism are usually the order of the day. A recognition that Social Democratic reforms were inadequate to stay the "revolutionary part" played by the bourgeoisie forms some grounds, even among those who cling to the politics of compromise, for this hesitation and pessimism. If the answer to this offered by socialists is that these reforms had to be structured in a manner that led to popular support for taking capital away from the bourgeoisie, however, this answer then confronts another problem. For there is a widespread sense, in the context of the internationalization and globalization of production and finance which has advanced with extreme speed in recent years, that nationalization—the word itself is significant—is no longer capable of laying hold of such integrated means of production as would lay the basis for coherent production or socialist planning. In other words, insofar as the locus of political power and democratic participation remains at the level of the nation-state, the question is whether, even if a Socialist party were strongly legitimated at the polls, a socialist government could proceed very far to install a socialist program in a world of international capitalism, where production itself, let alone finance and commerce, is increasingly and ever more tightly intermeshed. On top of all this, the turn to capitalist markets in the former countries of "actually existing socialism" seems to many in the West to proclaim once and for all that socialism, as a viable alternative economic system to capitalism, is a nonstarter. We argued above that today's bourgeois revolution ought to reinforce on both ethical and logical grounds the basis for a commitment to socialism. Many would grant the ethical grounds; far fewer would grant the logical ones.

There are no easy answers to these problems, any more than there are to the problems of constituency and agency. What must first of all be said, however, is that insofar as these problems lead socialists straight back to the politics of compromise, then this is obviously no answer at all. It is not that reforms were not worthy. Who could say this about social citizenship reforms, which established rights in civil society such as education, health care, freedom of association? Or redistributive reforms such as old-age pensions, social security, progressive taxation? Or regulatory reforms such as occupational health and safety standards, pollution controls, hours of work, and minimum wage regulations? And who could say this about public ownership reforms, whether of utilities or transportation, or coal mines or steel mills, or indeed of housing and land? The only problem with these reforms was that they did not go far enough. They could not go far enough without fomenting a political break with capital, which, for all the reasons we already identified, the politics of compromise could not sustain.

It could not sustain this increasingly by the inclination of Social Democratic leaders themselves, but also by the fact, which was of course related to the question of leaders' inclinations, that the parties that conceived and introduced such reforms failed to prepare their constituencies for such a break. They therefore could not count on their support, much less on their "intellectual" capacities (in Gramsci's sense) to take over the organizational and administrative functions which seeing through such a confrontation would have demanded. In saying that these reforms did not go far enough, this does not just mean in a quantitative sense: more universal rights; more progressive taxation and social benefits; more regulation of capital, of its products, of the labor process and of labor markets; more public ownership. It means that the reforms that were introduced always qualitatively fell short of their promise. The rights to education were always compromised by a hierarchy in education, by restricted access to quality education, and by the content of education that reflected the class society in which education was embedded. The laws which granted and sustained freedom of association for workers also always policed trade union behavior and limited the range and scope of industrial struggle. What was given in the form of progressive taxation was taken away in income policies, sales taxes, and the absence of price controls even on basic necessities. The social benefits were administered in such a bureaucratic fashion that even those most dependent on them could hardly feel that the "welfare state" was theirs to influence, let alone control. Unemployment insurance was usually just that: insurance which reproduced the labor market even as it regulated and subsidized its vagaries. (That is, to get it, in most cases, you needed to have been employed; you then needed to be fired or laid off; you then needed to be actively looking for work; and you then lasted on it only as long as your previous payment of "stamps" allowed.) The regulation of capital and of production and of products was always compromised by the close inter-meshing of the regulators and the regulated when it came to the bour-geoisie—and by the distance from the regulators when it came to work-ers or consumers. The public ownership was state ownership, with eco-nomic democracy being outlawed (or, in a few instances, trivialized) to such an extent that few workers or consumers could feel they were losing something that belonged to them even when privatization threatened their livelihood or quality of service. There were many variations in the reforms introduced in the advanced capitalist states. Yes, Sweden was (and remains, mercifully) very different from the United States. That said, the picture is more or less recognizable in all of them.

The reason for this was inscribed in the politics of compromise. Partly this was because the reforms had to be structured and to operate in a manner that sustained capital accumulation and business confidence. But partly it was also because a dimension of reform, which would have rad-ically transformed every one of the others mentioned, the democratic reform of "the machinery of government" itself, was absent. A reform in the state's own *modus operandi*, which would have meant the integration of popular representation and administration, and the control of the rep-resentative through recall and regular turnover, was very rarely con-ceived within the Social Democratic project. Whether this was because of a lack of imagination or a sincere belief that parliamentary democracy was the endpoint of democracy or the oligarchy that developed in Social Democratic parties, remains an old but still interesting question. Or did it, perhaps, above all reflect an anticipation, conceived subconsciously in the politics of Social Democratic gradualism and compromise, that capi-tal would at all costs insist on the separation between decision makers and the people (short of the election of a political "board of directors" every four or five years) lest the state set an example for the "private sector" of a new form of decision making and administration which, if also struggled for and adopted in the "private sector," would divest the bourgeoisie of its control over capital? After all, at least under "nationalization," it got compensated and could employ this liquid capital for accumulation elsewhere.

Was it then surprising that capitalist competition continued to underpin the whole structure of the society? And as the bourgeoisie adopted new directions and patterns of competition in, through, and around the "interventionist" state, and as it entered new crises in the course of this competition, the "interventionist" state found itself condemned to managing these crises in a manner that usually quantitatively as well as qualitatively retrenched on the earlier reforms. Was it then surprising that some of those who still nevertheless really benefited from the reforms could recognize in the bourgeoisie's new "revolutionary" assault on the state some symbols that appeared to speak to their own alienation from it, although that alienation was very differently situated from that of the bourgeoisie? What is actually surprising is that so many people kept their heads and saw through that aspect of the revolutionary rhetoric of neoliberalism that was indeed mendacious nonsense. This not only kept their vote at the absolute (if not relative) low level mentioned above, but it also restrained the inroads neo-liberals could make against the old reforms.

Yet from the perspective of socialist goals, no matter how necessary it still is to defend the old reforms for what was always positive and humane about them, the project of restarting the motor of the old politics of compromise, even if the bourgeoisie could again find it in its interest to cooperate, is no answer at all to the problems we identified. We must admit, however, that to those other problems, we can offer no definitive answers. This is because any attempt at socialist transition, once we conceive it as something other than the inevitable outcome of implacable historical laws, is inherently risk-laden. It is beset, as Rosa Luxemburg once put it in a famous passage, by "a thousand problems." And that is why, as she insisted, the democratic freedoms of expression, assembly, and association are so necessary to finding "the thousand solutions" she hoped would also emerge. The main grounds for her optimism were not different from Gramsci's (or, indeed, Marx's): they lay in the reliance on the creativity of human beings (the same creativity that distinguishes the architect from the bee) and in the knowledge and experience that people might acquire from organizing sufficiently well (not only technically but intellectually) to make a revolution possible in the first place. To quote that famous passage:

> we know more or less what we must eliminate at the outset in order to free the road for a socialist economy. But when it comes to the nature of the thousand concrete, practical measures, large and small, necessary to introduce socialist principles into economy, law and all social relationships, there is no key in any textbook. That is not a shortcoming but rather the thing that makes scientific socialism superior to the utopian variants. The socialist system of society should only be, and can only be, an historical product, born out of the school of its own experiences, born in the course of its redefinition, as a result of the developments of living history. . . . The negative, the tearing down can be decreed; the building up, the positive cannot. New territory. A thousand problems. Only experience is capable of correcting and opening new ways. Only unobstructed, effervescent life falls into a thousand new forms and improvisations, brings to light creative force, itself corrects all mistaken attempts. The public life of all countries with diluted freedom is so poverty-stricken, so miserable, so rigid, so unfruitful, precisely because, through the exclusion of democracy, it cuts off the living sources of all spiritual riches and progress. . . . The whole mass of the people must take part in it. Otherwise it will be decreed from behind a few official desks by a dozen intellectuals.[11]

Luxemburg was, of course, speaking about the Russian Revolution as she wrote these words. And these words are still germane in relation to the pessimism on socialist possibilities induced by the turn to capitalist markets in the former Communist countries. If this is to be understood by socialists in the West as the paradoxical proof that the bourgeoisie's almost century-long aspiration to reverse the Russian Revolution has finally been realized, we also need at least to ask whether this was really because the horrendous problems experienced by socialism in the USSR over seventy years were due to the absence of market freedoms—or whether, as Luxemburg warned, it was due to the absence of democratic freedoms. The answer to this question could not but bear directly on the issue of whether the salvation of that society, if there might have been one at all, lay in the "icy calculations" of cost-accounting introduced through an economic *perestroika* from above or in the democratic creativity induced by a political and intellectual *glasnost* taking root from below.

Is logic then really on the side of a commitment to socialism, after all? We should probably not go so far as to claim this. We said earlier that socialists cannot achieve their ends without the means, that is, without taking capital away from the bourgeoisie. The experience with the politics of compromise has indeed proved this to be more and more logical, in the sense we have described. But the experience of "actually existing socialism" as well as the limited range of even a democratic state to plan in today's international capitalist order suggests that taking capital away from the domestic bourgeoisie is no answer in itself. This end can, in fact, really only be a means, as Luxemburg understood, to the realization of socialism, the "tearing down" that but opens up the possibility of the "building up." Robin Murray, who addressed very clearly the limits of "nationalization" in the face of capitalism's global integration of production, finance, and commerce, nevertheless also explained why "the case for public ownership is as strong as it ever was."[12] The restructuring of the past few decades reveals the limits of the new bourgeois revolution: "In the economy as a whole there are great barriers between sectors, which the market only makes worse. I am thinking of the relations between finance and industry, of military technology and civilian diffusion, or of branch plants and the wider economy. These are arguments for industrial restructuring and macro-economic planning which formed the core of the case for nationalization fifty years ago."[13] But there is even "an even stronger argument," as Murray affirmed, in so far as socialists have come to recognize, out of the experience with state ownership in this century, the priority that needs to be given not just to changes in ownership but to changing the social relations of production.

One has only to read a few pages by socialist economists in the 1930s—Marxist or Fabian—to sense the extent of change that has taken place in socialist thinking today. The experience of the guerrilla movements, of a variety of post-revolutionary experiments, of the women's movement, the black movement, and a multitude of progressive community campaigns, all have contributed to a shift of focus towards the social relations of socialism. . . . [T]his has meant a concern with the nature of work, with the division between mental and manual labour, with the question of working time and conflict between capital's time and labour's time (to have children, to collect them from school, to have time for meetings and classes, to control one's own working time rather than being paced on the line, and so on). It means a concern for different segments of the working class, unskilled as well as skilled, women and black people as well as the white male and white-collared workers. It also involves a concern for the use values of production and the diversity of need—with the saving of energy rather than nuclear production, for example, or with cultural variety and self-production rather than standardized mass consumption. . . . [I]t is now realized that the forces of production are not neutral but that technology has been developed in such a way as to increase capital's control over labour. Nor are commodities neutral. They reflect in their content, and even their design, the particular production relations of capital. (102)

This catalog of contemporary socialist "common sense," as Murray calls it, would not have sounded as foreign to the ears of the authors of *The Communist Manifesto* as many presume today. If much of this was ignored by socialists fifty years ago it reflected both the limits of the politics of compromise and the limits of a revolutionary socialism "decreed behind a few officials desks." Even then, such "socialisms" were not accomplished without considerable repression or marginalization of those socialists who did not forget that, above all, capital, as the *Manifesto* put it, "is a social power"; and that whereas in "bourgeois society living labour is but a means to increase accumulated labour," the point of the whole socialist project was to build a "society in which accumulated labour is but a means to widen, to enrich, to promote the existence of the labourer" (p. 81). But if it is now more widely accepted amongst socialists that this cannot be achieved if we just try to revive the old, now unpopular, state ownership, so it must nevertheless also be made clear again, not least to the confused and dispirited socialist intellectuals of our time, that, as Murray put it:

If the aim of socialist economics goes beyond re-structuring industry and improving productivity, if its aim is to change the social relations of production in production, then expanding social ownership becomes a necessity. For in spite of the fact that social enterprises are hedged round by monopolies and the market, in spite of the fact that they have to rely on capitalist managers to run them, these difficulties are only compounded if private property gets in the way. The reason why nationalization and social ownership should still be at the centre of any socialist strategy is that only in this way can we make progress in . . . "the politics of production." . . . It must match capital in productive performance, yet change the social character of production in such a way that it regains popular support. It must show that

it can work in practice, since nothing is as strong as the propaganda of practice. That alone will put nationalisation back on the political agenda, not as
a socialist solution but as midwife to the socialist problem. (102–3)

We must be clear, as well, that social ownership today, if it can be
revived as an aspiration among socialists, and if political agencies can
win the popular support to try to effect fundamental change through its
introduction, can itself only lead at present to a new politics of compromise. Socialism will still not happen at one go. Certain sectors—whether
they will be commanding heights or more modest fortresses of capital
will depend on the locus and extent of popular support—may be taken
away from capital and transformed in their social purpose and administration. But they would still have to negotiate between the rocky shoals
of powerful bourgeois hostility and market competition. Less metaphorically speaking, they would have to negotiate a degree of autonomy
amidst their dependence on domestic and international bourgeois forces
sufficient to allow them to act in a manner that liberates the human creativity that is in the end the sole basis of solving the socialist problem. But
to look at public ownership as a necessary means to socialist ends is to see
things in a very different way from the old politics of compromise. It
would, indeed, be more akin to the politics of compromise that postrevolutionary regimes have always had to follow to survive in a world still in
the bourgeois epoch. Our hope must be that we can gradually build out
of a new "spirit of revolution"—and on the basis of the limited autonomy that spheres liberated from bourgeois control could furnish—the
grounds upon which that epoch would really be, gradually but fundamentally, challenged. This would then be a very different politics of compromise, a very different gradualism, precisely because it would be based
on developing the intellectual capacities in the mass of the people to organize and administer, to plan and create, wherein lies the true meaning of
socialist revolution.

But this must take us back once more to the question of agency. The
first goal of all Socialist parties and movements, on the basis of whatever
organizational resources they can muster today, and eventually with the
resources they can liberate from capital and the capitalist state, must be
to help form such new working-class identities and intellectual capacities
as would permit the members and supporters of these parties and movements actually to become, as Gramsci put it, "leaders and organisers of
all the activities and functions inherent in the organic development of an

integral society, both civil and political."[14] They would need to be able to replace the capitalist managers on which even public ownership is now dependent. But they would need, first of all, to be able to learn and explain clearly how capitalism works as a system in the process of the organizational work they do, and to try to prefigure the kind of practice that will contribute to learning how to "build up" even while people become committed to "tearing down." Programs will be needed, but socialist intellectuals—partly because they are still too oriented to trying to educate the ruling class to socialism—are mistaken to give the priority they do to this today. The reforms they advance must rather be oriented to reviving, indeed building anew, the "spirit of revolution" against the existing structures of power and privilege. The socialist purpose even today does involve "building up," but this must mean building up whatever prefigurative changes can be achieved within the framework of actually existing capitalism, whether the sphere is health, education, housing, transport, the environment, or day care, or whether it is trade unions, parties, or social movements themselves, since their organizational structures and political and ideological practices are far from conducive to the task.

Popular support, in the form of votes for parties committed to socialist change, is essential; but such expression of support at the polls can never be enough. What is required is the penetration of socialist ideas and creative organizational and intellectual capacities throughout society. Revolutionary socialist change, in other words, requires the implantation and development throughout society of a socialist presence, at the moral, ideological, political, and economic levels in the broadest possible range of institutions in society: in the parties, unions, and movements long identified as composing the Left, but also in factories, offices, schools, universities, churches, community centers, and even in that contemporary center of working-class life—the shopping mall. This implantation forms part of what Gramsci called the "war of position." But there is today no single "Modern Prince." The task cannot only devolve today on socialist parties—although such parties must be built, or transformed into something very different from what they have been. But the task must also be undertaken by other organizations and agencies—labor, feminist and ecological movements, antiracist and peace movements, the movements of the disabled and the movements of those handicapped by poverty. In the new anti-globalization movements as well, and in alliances among them, those committed to fundamental social change must also pay careful attention to ensuring that the relationship between leaders and led is productive of popular capacities for organizational and intellectual development. Only in this way—and obviously, after all we have said, nothing is inevitable—will socialists be able to find once more "the spirit of revolution." And only in this way will that socialist spirit of revolution really make itself felt against capitalist classes that will certainly continue to struggle with working classes over who will play, historically, the most revolutionary part.

Notes

1. Raymond Williams, *Politics and Letters* (London: Verso, 1979), pp. 383, 411.

2. For the capitalists' own more recent version of this, see Gary Hamel, *Leading the Revolution* (Cambridge, Mass.: Harvard Business School Press, 2000).

3. Karl Marx, *Political Writings*, vol. 1, *The Revolutions of 1848*, David Fernbach, ed. (New York: Vintage, 1974), pp. 69–70. All ensuing quotations from the *Manifesto* are drawn from this edition, pp. 69–81.

4. Ibid., p. 71.

5. See Leo Panitch and Colin Leys, *The End of Parliamentary Socialism*, 2d ed. (London: Verso, 2001).

6. Quoted in Kenneth McNaught, *A Prophet in Politics: A Biography of J. S. Woodsworth* (Toronto: University of Toronto Press, 1959), pp. 134, 96.

7. Ernesto Laclau and Chantal Mouffe, *Hegemony and Socialist Strategy* (London: Verso, 1985), p. 2.

8. Georg Lukacs, *History and Class Consciousness: Studies in Marxist Dialectics*, trans. by Rodney Livingstone (London: Merlin, 1971), p. 295.

9. *Selections from the Prison Notebooks of Antonio Gramsci*, Q. Hoare and G. Nowell Smith, eds. (London: Lawrence and Wishart, 1971), pp. 15–16. See p. 335 for the quotation in the previous paragraph.

10. Adam Przeworski and John Sprague, *Paper Stones: A History of Electoral Socialism* (Chicago: University of Chicago Press, 1986).

11. Rosa Luxemburg, *Selected Political Writings*, R. Looker, ed. (London: Jonathan Cape, 1972), p. 246.

12. Robin Murray, "Ownership, Control and Markets," *New Left Review* 164 (July–August 1987): 101.

13. Ibid., pp. 101–2.

14. *Prison Notebooks of Antonio Gramsci*, p. 16.

2

Observations on Communism's Demise

I

In 1918 Lenin wrote a comment to Anatoli Lunacharski, the minister of culture in the new revolutionary regime, expressing the opinion that statues were "even more important" for the regime's propaganda than slogans. His advice was that, instead of making statues, as in the past, "of marble, granite and gold-incised lettering," statues appropriate to the building of socialism should be "modest"; and he added: "*let everything be temporary.*"[1] This was a statement worth recalling as the world watched scenes of the enormous statues of the old leaders being smashed and removed amidst the collapse of the regimes of authoritarian Communism. We were perforce reminded of just how many things prove to be temporary even if you seek to immortalize them in concrete or marble, let alone embalming fluid. Among those many things may be counted socialist party institutions: These also prove to be temporary even if, indeed especially if, they become encased in the state.

Revolutionary socialist movements stepped onto the world stage near the beginning of the last century promising alternatives to capitalism and, indeed, presenting themselves as the historic successors to capitalism. Yet, at least from the vantage point of the proponents of the *fin de siècle* "new world order," socialist ideas, movements, regimes seemed to have been mere temporary barriers to the realization of global capitalism. Certainly, the notion of a "new world order" intoned at the beginning of the 1990s was intended to mean the establishment, finally, of capitalism's complete and definitive global sway as the twentieth century drew to a close. The explicit reconfirmation through the 1980s that even the ambitions (let alone the deeds) of Social Democratic parties in the West did not extend beyond the management of capitalism seemed of little moment beside the dramatic collapse of the Communist regimes in the East, given their origins, history, and character as the only rival mode of economic organization that the enemies of capitalism ever were able to bring into being. "The world," *The Economist* said in September 1991, "used to have two seriously different ways of trying to run an economy. Today it has only one."[2]

This liquidation of the Communist economic model was an event of historic importance. It had in recent decades produced stagnation as well as shortage, although the system of centralized planning overseeing extensive economic development had in earlier decades appeared impressive to a multitude of economists and others who were by no means exclusively of the left. Indeed, urgent warnings used to be issued by many such people that the Soviet Union was launched on a course of development which would before too long bring it level with the West. Such estimates were clearly wrong, having paid insufficient attention to the qualitative differences between extensive and intensive phases of development. Still, some achievements under the extensive growth model of central planning were real enough in certain social as well as economic terms, even though it must always be stressed that the human and environmental cost they demanded was horrendous, sustainable only by repressive political regimes.

Such regimes were destructive of the creativity necessary to sustain socialist innovation and motivation. During the decades of stagnation, attempts at economic reform were repeatedly made in country after country, but these reforms required a degree of cooperation from workers which these regimes could not hope to achieve: either because the reforms were cast within, or ran aground against, the encrusted interests of the bureaucracy; or because they depended on price increases and increasing the level of inequality and worker insecurity. So Communist regimes entered upon a period of permanent crisis; and, in the Soviet Union, this led to Mikhail Gorbachev and *perestroika*. But *perestroika* itself turned into a gigantic failure: The actual attempt to shift toward market socialism in practice threw up even more contradictions than the notion already raised in economic theory. In this context, the political opening of *glasnost* led to pro-capitalist revolution.

In most ways, the Communist model was an appalling deformation of socialism; and there is a good argument to be made that it was not socialism at all, if one takes socialism to have at its core constituent elements not only the socialization of the predominant part of the means of economic activity, but also democracy and egalitarianism. On this ground, its disappearance in the Soviet Union and elsewhere is hardly a matter for regret. What is a matter for bitter regret, on the other hand, is something else altogether: the disappearance of the hope that existed at the beginning of *perestroika* in the Soviet Union that this might in due course produce something that would begin to resemble socialist democracy, on the basis of a loosened but predominant public sector. That hope turned out to be an illusion.

The fact that Communist regimes were unable to realize democratic reform and economic restructuring, and left their successors with a catastrophic legacy as well, has also been of great help to the broader anti-socialist cause, in so far as it has lent further plausibility to the notion that the only alternative to Communism was indeed capitalism. It will take time for this to be effectively countered. Although the limitations of market freedom will also not be lost on people, as they observe the suffering that accompanies a transition to capitalism, the notion that there is no alternative will not be effectively countered without a great effort by many people to construct a new strategy for socialism that appears attractive and viable. An important part of the process will involve making sense of the demise of Communism.

II

It is important to recall that some quite specific factors were at play in the birth of this particular political expression of socialism. Not least among these was the factor so often pointed to by these parties themselves: the need for discipline in the face of capitalist encirclement. Although this was clearly used as apologetics, the formative effects on new revolutionary regimes of "powerful foreign countries, fearing the spread of revolution or the march of red armies, [doing] what they could to weaken or destroy the socialist countries," as Franz Schurmann once put it,[3] cannot be lightly dismissed. The coercive military and police apparatus in this context acquired enormous weight inside the postrevolutionary state.[4]

This was also reflected in a broader cultural discipline which came to pervade the whole of society. For instance, in 1923 the Regional May Day Commission of the Moscow Committee of the Russian Communist Party had a long and acerbic debate on what form the celebration of the international workers' holiday should take. Four of the eight people on the committee took the position that workers were fed up with having to come into the center of Moscow and go to Red Square and watch a military parade. They proposed that the celebration should be decentralized, enshrining local freedom of action and initiative, which might take the form of picnics or street theater or fairs in various residential areas of the city. The other four took the position that, because the capitalist powers were looking to see whether the Bolshevik government had let down its guard, it was necessary to continue with massive military parades, which symbolized Soviet state strength in a world of hostile states.[5]

Another specific historical factor in producing authoritarian Communism had to do with the fact that the revolution was made against an authoritarian regime, in a political culture where liberal democracy had sunk few roots. Anthony Giddens has argued that "the revolutionary potential of the working class depends upon its initial encounter with capitalism," suggesting that a socialist revolution at the beginning of the twentieth century was most likely to occur in those political systems in which the working classes had been least recognized and institutionalized.[6] But if the lack of a preexisting liberal democracy abetted the staging of a viable revolution, it hindered the emergence of the kind of political organization capable of carrying the revolution forward. Organizations suited to underground activities (the lines of communication are more vertical than horizontal: people at the base have few links with one another to minimize the number of people who can reveal too much if and when captured) are not well suited to developing democratic skills and capacities in the vast majority of their members.

This is not to say that the prerevolutionary Bolshevik party was already, in embryo, the Communist party-state. Up to 1921, as Moshe Lewin has shown, opposing factions and internal debates "were not only tolerated but were actually used as a widely accepted *modus-operandi*." In the chaotic decade after the revolution, the party itself was transformed by the "international situation, the test of power—which always has a conservatising effect—and finally the structure of society." Still, it would not be incorrect to suggest, as Lewin does himself, that the prerevolutionary Leninist party nevertheless at least provided "a certain foretaste of things to come."[7]

The extent to which the struggle against the old regimes colored the form taken by the new revolutionary ones was chillingly captured in Milovan Djilas's memoir, *Rise and Fall*. It opens by describing a meeting

of senior members of the new Communist regime in Yugoslavia in 1946
called to discuss building a new jail in Belgrade:

> When we convened and took a look around, it was apparent that to the last
> man we were all former convicts. . . . That we had to have a new jail was
> obvious, and no one argued the point. There were appeals to hygiene and
> humanity, but if the meeting had one keynote, it was this: . . . it should have
> none of the imperfections or "conveniences" that Communists had turned to
> advantage in their illegal prison communication back in the days of the
> Yugoslav monarchy. We would exclude any exchange of tapped messages by
> doubling the walls, and prevent notes or food from being pushed through
> the sewage pipes by building them with twists and bends. . . . The jail was to
> be spacious, with many autonomous units. Otherwise total isolation could
> not be secured. . . . Ironic remarks were heard in this connection, to the effect
> that real masters of prison building had at last been found, instead of
> Austrian bureaucrats and brutally primitive royal police.[8]

From a historical materialist perspective, we may certainly agree with
Rudolf Bahro that the fact that Communist revolutions occurred in "predominantly pre-capitalist countries," embarking on a process of industrialization which imperialism had barely begun, was probably the key factor in determining the authoritarian shape which this institutional
expression of socialism actually took.[9] The other factors mentioned above
played an "over-determining" role in relation to this more fundamental
one. The statist mode of development characteristic of the Communist
regimes both reflected and reinforced the limited resources of
autonomous social forces outside the state.

It is not fashionable to quote Lenin these days, nor should it be, except
insofar as he can offer us insight into the mistakes that were made in the
past and that might be avoided in the future. It was exactly in this respect,
in fact, that C.L.R. James, in a remarkable article written for a political
journal in Ghana in 1964, once urged a careful consideration of Lenin's
last three articles, written at the beginning of 1923.[10] Lenin insisted in
these articles that the state apparatus still remained entirely unsuited to
allowing the subordinate classes to learn how to govern themselves. In
his debate with Leon Trotsky in 1921 over the trade unions, Lenin had
stressed that the main criterion for judging their new role was whether
they were suited, from all aspects of their structure and practice, to be a
school for the development of working people's capacities: "a school of

unity, a school of solidarity, a school for learning how to protect one's interests, a school of management, a school of administration."[11] Now, in his final articles, he developed the same ideas of the state in its relation to the peasantry, which constituted the main bulk of the population.

In the most famous of these articles, "Better Fewer, but Better," Lenin soberly addressed the need "to reconstruct our [state] apparatus, which is utterly useless, and which we took over in its entirety from the preceding epoch; during the five years of struggle we did not, and could not, make any serious alterations in it. . . . It has only been slightly repainted on the surface, but in all other things it is a typical relic of our old state apparatus."[12] Accordingly, Lenin proposed to reorganize the Workers' and Peasants' Inspection, not as a separate government department, but as a section in all departments, enlisting, via local authorities, all workers and peasants, "particularly women" and "unfailingly . . . non-party peasants," on a rotation basis to exercise wide control over "the accounting of products, goods, stores, materials, fuels, etc."[13] Lenin's purpose in this was clear. It was popular education in the art of governing: "we must set ourselves the first task of learning, the second of learning, and the third of learning. . . . We have been bustling for five years trying to improve the state apparatus, but it was mere bustle. . . . It is better to get good human material in two years, or even in three years, than to work in haste without hope of getting any at all."[14] What remained particularly important about these final reflections, James insisted, was that "Lenin's thesis all through . . . [was that] the backwardness of Russia imposed on the party the necessity of teaching and above all teaching themselves. We have to administer but the main business is to teach."[15] James concluded: "If his ideas were utopian then it is clear that after six years in power, he turned to them as the sole solution to the mess into which the Soviet government was sinking, had already sunk."[16]

It appears that Marx was correct to insist that a mature capitalism, one that had at least come close to establishing the material basis for overcoming scarcity, was an essential condition for realizing the kind of self-directed human development that socialism aspires to. By the same token, however, Marx was clearly wrong to expect that the more mature capitalist countries, the home base to bourgeoisies with the kind of remarkable dynamism and hegemonic power portrayed in the *Communist Manifesto*, would themselves be in short order ripe for revolution. The international effect of the Russian Revolution—the premise of the "weakest link" thesis—was realized in large part only to the extent that Communist parties in the West themselves became dependent on the Soviet party-state. The resources provided to those parties that associated themselves with the ideals of the Russian Revolution became in time the ties that eventually bound such parties to the ruthless statecraft of a renewed, if much changed, Russian empire, as well as with the attempt to create a parallel form of industrial development to that of capitalist development. An appalling degree of state coercion and repression was entailed in both facets of this transmutation of the socialist project.

Whatever the initial high rates of growth during the extensive phase of development, the political alienation generated by authoritarian Communism barred the creativity necessary to make a transition to a more intensively productive economy. The Gorbachev generation of reformers, the political offspring of the Khrushchev era, recognized this. Reflecting the ideology of convergence that was so popular during their coming to maturity in the late 1950s, they became resolute admirers of European Social Democracy. Paradoxically, they came to power just when the Social Democratic model was itself in a state of critical decline. What lay in wait for the Communist reformers as they turned to the West was not a convergence between the old Social Democratic "mixed economy" ideal and the Communist reformer's "market socialist" one, but rather an abrasive privatized capitalism.

III

The severe limits of *perestroika* had already become very clear by the spring of 1990 when I accompanied Sam Gindin, assistant to the president of the Canadian Automobile Workers union, on a visit to Russia. In addition to the perspective afforded by meeting some of the intellectuals, journalists, academicians, political leaders, and activists who composed Moscow's political class, we especially wanted to see what impact the process of political and economic change was having on workers. To this end, the Institute of the USA and Canada, our hosts in Moscow, cooperated with the international department of the Automobile and Farm Machinery Industries Workers Union in arranging visits to Yaroslavl (about 400 km east of Moscow), where a major strike had taken place at a large diesel engine plant in 1987, and to Togliatti (Tolyatti) (800 km east-southeast of Moscow), where the Lada is produced in what was, at least at the time, the largest automobile plant in the world. It was a year before the "August Coup," soon to be followed by the end of Communism and indeed of the USSR. Boris Yeltsin had just been elected president of the Supreme Soviet of the Russian Federation, but Gorbachev still occupied the Kremlin, and the Communist party, in every formal sense still in power, was readying itself for its 28th Congress in July—which turned out to be its last as the ruling party.

Like most of the Western New Leftists of the 1960s, we became socialists despite the Soviet example of authoritarian Communism. We had little patience with an earlier generation given to be more apologetic for many of the practices that amounted to a tragic and terrible aberration of socialist ideals. But while we celebrated the turn to political freedom in the USSR after Gorbachev and the revolutions in Eastern Europe in 1989, we were at the same time disturbed that the trajectory of change appeared to be directed toward capitalism. We wanted to see for ourselves whether a transition to democratic socialism was on anyone's agenda, if not in Eastern Europe, then at least in the USSR. The answer mattered for the scope of socialist politics in the West. Having been hamstrung in our politics (among many other reasons) by the negative example afforded by authoritarian Communism in the East ("See what socialist revolution leads to!"), were we now to be hamstrung again by the collapse of authoritarian Communism ("Even they have opted for capitalism!")?

There was a broad consensus among virtually everyone we talked to that the whole country was in the throes of a severe economic crisis. Its immediate symptoms were a massive hidden inflation in the context of consumer shortages existing alongside a vast pool of savings (estimates varied on the size of this, from 300 to 600 billion rubles) which could neither be spent on the limited goods available nor tapped for investment purposes. The structural roots of this crisis were generally located in the following factors: the "extensive" nature of Soviet economic development wherein something akin to what has come to be called "Fordism" in the West (that is a virtuous circle of mass production and mass consumption) never developed; the hypercentralization of production which inhibited modernization and technological innovation; the rigidities of the bureaucratically administered system of distribution, made worse by the effects of underinvestment in infrastructure; the historic suppression of the agricultural classes in the 1930s that entailed forced collectivization, and the consequent low agricultural productivity due to superexploitation in the form of extremely poor wages and conditions; the increase in real wages in industry and services since the 1960s, which neither domestic production nor imports (especially after the fall in oil prices ended hopes of a hard currency windfall) were capable of soaking up and recycling.

The effects of all these longstanding problems were now rendered more severe by the disruption to the old political-administrative system introduced by Gorbachev's revolution from above, and at the same time rendered more visible with *glasnost*. It was generally agreed that no structure in the political-administrative system was functioning smoothly. Even the security system, which had been the most efficient, was incapable of coping with the wave of crime that accompanied the process of change. As for the success of the new market economy, as we arrived, the USSR Supreme Soviet was debating Prime Minister Nikolai Ryzhkov's newly announced package of forthcoming price increases, the key element in Gorbachev's explicit turn to markets. But the contradictions that accompanied this were seen in the fact that the Moscow city council had just imposed residential restrictions on access to the shops in reaction to the run on goods induced by the anticipation of the price increases.

In this context, Gorbachev was little revered (to put it mildly). The things for which we gave him credit, for inaugurating *glasnost* itself or for a foreign policy explicitly designed to undo Cold War attitudes and structures, did not impress people at home. Instead there was the lament (more often the complaint) that after five years he had "done nothing." What was meant by this was, first of all, that he had accomplished nothing to improve the domestic economic situation, above all the economy of consumer shortages; and, second, that the system of privileges for the bureaucratic-administrative elite, the old Communist "nomenklatura," still remained in place. Yeltsin's popularity rested largely on his insistent speaking on this latter theme.

The main test almost everyone wanted to apply for any measure of success was how quickly life would become "normal." This was a word much used to describe what people wanted ("a normal society," "a normal economy," "a normal life") and by this was mainly meant achieving what they perceived "normal" to be in the United States. There was a strong sense of inferiority to all things American, and this was felt especially strongly in comparison with the humiliation that Muscovites, especially, felt as consumers. But the American way of life is a composite of many things. And one already could see that what they were heading for could well look like the Chicago gangsterland of the 1920s that Bertolt Brecht so brilliantly used as a backdrop to satirize the roots of Fascism in his play *Arturo Ui*. The culture of *glasnost* had opened vast new spaces for corruption, even as it led to the exposure (and some prosecution) of some of the more venal practices of high Communist officials. As a means of coping with consumer shortages, petty appropriation was always commonplace. The halfway house that cooperatives became between the market and statist modes of distribution under Gorbachev created new, vast forms of corruption. There was already much talk in Moscow of "the mafia" as a power in the land, thriving in this halfway house.

Yet no one we met thought it possible to go back to the old system as it had evolved under Leonid Brezhnev, even if there were many who blamed the incompleteness or, on the other hand, the rapidity of the changes since 1985 as the cause of the current crisis and its many discontents. Indeed, five years after Gorbachev's coming to power, the most visible and important change remained *glasnost* itself. Outside the offices of *Moscow News* a hundred people crowded the sidewalk debating politics, amidst a profusion of hawkers of crudely printed newspapers ("Read all about it: How much Raisa Gorbachev costs the people!"). Some of these papers were religious, some pornographic, yet all of them were politicized if only by virtue of the novelty of their relatively unhindered distribution. But what was especially important to register was that the street culture of *glasnost* was already as commercial as it was political. The profusion of craft and artist stalls on the Arbat or at Izmailovsky Park gave Moscow some of the vibrancy that was so notably absent in the past. Yet this directly blended with some of the most unsavory aspects of this kind of market freedom. There were, near the Arbat, many beggars pathetically attempting to scrounge a few kopeks by turning pity for their physical handicap or the visible impoverishment of their children into some sort of exchange value. Rather more pleasantly interspersed among the stalls were many street musicians, such as a jazz band playing with gusto Dixieland renditions of Glen Miller's greatest hits. Reflecting a far more traditional aspect of Russian culture, a much larger crowd gathered amidst the stalls to hear a poet declaim his verses in the richest of Russian tones. His poems were all political and all splenetically antiregime. One anti-Gorbachev poem in particular, in which he did a quite brilliant satirical portrayal of the man himself, produced rapture from the crowd, even from a clutch of young men in militia uniform who, far from taking notes or making arrests, displayed in their laughter and applause as much appreciation of the poet's sentiments as everyone else.

This remarkable discursive openness stood in sharp contrast to the strong sense of constraint a visitor could palpably feel disfiguring even private conversation in the earlier era. The confusing (and often just plain confused) profusion of new movements, parties, and workers' groups reflected a high degree of politicization amidst this absence of discursive constraint. Indeed, one sociologist told us that surveys had revealed that Soviet society was increasingly polarizing into two camps, defined in terms of their positive or negative orientations to the politicization itself. On one side were the "activists"; on the other the "active nonactivists," whose insistence on their right to be left alone to tend their own gardens had to be no less militantly asserted in the face of the overall trend to politicization.

IV

This politicization was also visible in the sphere of production. In 1987, when industrial democracy and self-management (along with cost accounting) were the watchwords of *perestroika*, the Supreme Soviet passed a law on state enterprises which established that all the employees of each enterprise were to be constituted as a labor collective, empowered to elect managerial personnel as well as a representative council which would participate in managerial decisions and monitor their implementation and administration. An excellent example of how laws alone do not transform power relations occurred in December 1987 at the Yaroslavl Autodiesel Associated Works, where 40,000 workers were employed, and where a seven-day strike took place over management's proposed work schedule for 1988.

At issue had been the "Communist subbotniks," the "voluntary" Saturday work which Lenin in *A Great Beginning* (1919) had described as follows:

Communist subbotniks are of such enormous historical significance precisely because they demonstrate the conscious and voluntary initiative of the workers in developing the productivity of labour, in adopting a new labour discipline, in creating socialist conditions of economy and life. . . . [S]tarving workers, surrounded by malicious counter-revolutionary agitation . . . are organising "communist subbotniks," working overtime *without any pay*, and achieving *an enormous increase in productivity of labour* in spite of the fact they are weary, tormented and exhausted by malnutrition. Is this not supreme

heroism? Is this not the beginning of a change of momentous significance? . . . Communism is the higher productivity of labour—compared
with that existing under capitalism—of voluntary, class conscious and united workers employing advanced techniques. Communist subbotniks are
extraordinarily valuable as the *actual* beginning of *communism.*[17]

It perhaps says more about the actual démarche of Soviet Communism
than anything else that these "Communist subbotniks," institutionalized
as they were by management and unions over the ensuing decades
throughout industry, soon came to be called "Black Saturdays" by the
workers themselves. Workers had a song in the 1930s, "We are just cogs
in the big machine," and it was alleged that they sang it enthusiastically
on their way to work. Be that as it may, the image such a song conjures
up, in the decade of Stalinism's greatest advances in terms of industrial
productivity at the greatest human cost, is certainly very different from
that of the free voluntarist working-class subject of history which Lenin
saw in embryo in the "Communist subbotniks." Gorbachev's own "new
beginning" sought to break definitively with Stalinism not only for its
inhumanity but because the "big machine" could not continue to meet
the definition of the Communist project as minimally set out by Lenin in
terms of the "higher productivity of labour . . . employing advanced techniques." But far from unleashing the missing agent of "the conscious and
voluntary initiative of the workers," which inspired Lenin's definition of
Communism, the opening provided by Gorbachev rather was taken up
by workers as an opportunity finally to rid themselves of the hated
"Black Saturdays."

The issue came to a head in Yaroslavl late in 1987 when the management of the diesel engine plant put forward the work schedule for 1988.
In the face of evident worker resentment over the subbotniks (management had always found them useful at the end of each month when they
were scrambling to meet planned production quotas—this was known as
"storming the plant") their number had been reduced from 21 in 1986 to
19 in 1987. For 1988, management proposed to reduce the number of
"Black Saturdays" to 15 and to compensate for them by reducing the
basic weekly shift by 10 minutes off the eight-hour day. The workers
hardly seemed surprised when the trade union committee endorsed
management's plan, but when the new collective council did so, this so
manifestly frustrated the expectations raised by the newly established
"participatory" structure (in a classic example of cooptation, the director

general of the plant had managed to get himself elected as chairman of the council) that it became the spark that started the strike. The strike, replete with mass meetings at the plant gates and marches to the director's office, was led by an informal group of rank-and-file workers. Notably, with the trade union committee effectively sidelined as a foil of management, the 1987 law also laid the basis for the resolution of the dispute. The law had provided that in extraordinary circumstances workers might call for a general assembly of the entire labor collective, and during one of the confrontations between the strikers and the general director it was agreed that the issue would be put to 700 delegates directly elected by workers from the various sections of the plant. It was at this meeting that a compromise was arranged—with the director guaranteeing that there would be only eight "Black Saturdays" in the 1989 work schedule. This strike received considerable attention in the Soviet press. An opinion poll by *Izvestia* found that 69 percent of the worker respondents approved of the Yaroslavl workers' stand against "Black Saturdays."[18]

One of our main interests in visiting Yaroslavl and Togliatti in 1990 was to try to see what had happened with the new structures of industrial democracy that had only just been established in the automobile industry when the 1987 strike took place. Little did we know, when we arranged the visit, that on the day after we arrived in the Soviet Union, a new law on enterprises would be passed which would renege considerably on the powers given to the labor collectives in the 1987 law. Managerial personnel (except for brigade leaders) were no longer to be elected by the collective, and ultimate authority in the enterprises was to pass to a new enterprise council based on parity representation between managers and workers. If the 1987 law was inspired by radical Yugoslav self-management notions, the 1990 law was clearly based on the more tepid example of West German codetermination. *Perestroika* had taken a clear turn, one which put less stress on the "voluntary, class-conscious, and united" participation of workers. The questions that immediately arose for us concerned why this shift had taken place and what the response of workers to it would be.

The move was endorsed by the official trade unions in the USSR, which always had been directly enmeshed in the ruling apparatus. Their leadership was a secondary, but by no means entirely powerless, element in the bureaucracy. They were conveyor belts downward to the workers of party, ministerial, and managerial decisions; recruiting stations for those who showed the inclination and aptitude to rise in the hierarchy; organizers of worker passivity amidst ersatz displays of mass support. Their control of resources in the form of the considerable "social wage" (health clinics, housing, pensions, vacation camps, cultural centers) at the enterprise level yielded them whatever social base they could genuinely claim (especially since wages were set centrally by the ministries) and furnished the backbone of their power over workers—leaving aside, of course, the coercive apparatus they could call on to suppress dissent.

By 1990 the central trade union apparatus, the AUCCTU, was widely regarded as an empty shell. The national leadership, for its part, was aware that it had to somehow evolve a new role: "We are first-year students in how to act as trade unionists," Alexander Kashirin, president of the Central Committee of the autoworkers union, told us. They were caught, as it were, in a pincer movement between their declining power in the party and influence with the government, on the one hand, and the local unions' assertion of their independence on the other. In the context of the changes taking place, their orientation was mainly reactive and defensive. Kashirin told us that the AUCCTU accepted the market economy "in principle." He used a chillingly familiar phrase that we were to hear time and again: "There is no alternative."

Kashirin claimed that in the previous year, the AUCCTU had "done everything to prevent limiting the rights of working people in the enterprises." But the examples he gave all pertained to resisting price increases. No mention was made about working conditions, or health and safety, or technological change. Most significantly, the AUCCTU leadership clearly put up no opposition whatever to the new law on the state enterprise despite the fact that it considerably retracted the democratic powers that workers had formally been accorded in the 1987 law. In terms very similar to what we were to hear later from the deputy director of the Autodiesel enterprise in Yaroslavl, Kashirin told us that the collective councils in the enterprise were "no longer needed." There was much conflict between the councils and the local unions. On the other hand, they tried to "take over" management of the enterprise and encouraged workers to ignore managerial commands. He personally would like even the new parity council of the enterprise to be dominated by "specialists" in finance, technology, etc. It was very clear that the official unions, at least at the national level, still defined their role in terms of an alliance with managers.

Although three other central labor organizations had formed at the national level (SOTSPROF, the United Front of Working People, and the

Russian Federation of Independent Labor Organizations, which held a founding conference in May 1990), none of these had significant organizational strength, nor did the latter two have very much independence from the old union leadership. Notably the local leaders and activists we met in two major industrial centers knew little or nothing about them. Insofar as there were any effective challenges to the old union practices, they primarily came from the informal unions, the "workers' clubs," at the local level.

In Yaroslavl, a local Popular Front of informal movements had formed in the city in 1988 and within it was a broad informal workers' group which had its roots in the 1987 strike at the Autodiesel plant. The popular front had been holding mass meetings in a local stadium of some 1,000 people every Saturday over the past year. Among 178 municipal soviet deputies, some 20 percent were elected on a Popular Front ticket, and they worked closely with the many Communist party deputies who were aligned with the Democratic Platform group in the party.

The Autodiesel enterprise, the largest in the city, had produced its 650 horsepower engines mainly for truck and tractor plants in Minsk, Byelorussia. This meant they had very little direct access to hard currency and thus little autonomy from the central planning apparatus. In a meeting with the deputy director, we were told that until 1990 only those enterprises integrated enough to produce a final product for export had secured much autonomy. Having finally secured more formal independence from the plan, they were looking to export engines directly themselves. This would mean cutting back delivery to the plants in Byelorussia, but they saw no advantages accruing to Autodiesel any longer from the monopoly position they had with these plants, which were likely to be forced to close down. Displaying very much a *sauve qui peut* attitude, the manager was coldly unconcerned about their fate. Autodiesel was now being allowed to keep 50 percent of its profit, but since their profitability level was only 4 percent, their main problem was where they would secure new capital. They had some slim hopes of obtaining this from one of several new banks that had been created (including an AutoBank formed by 200 enterprises in the industry) or from a partner to which they might be able to sell the engines in the West.

It was apparent that the temptation was very great to solve the problem of obtaining the new capital by increasing the extraction of surplus from the workers. The manager told us that the main reforms that were needed were those that would give enterprises flexibility in wage and employment levels, at the time still dictated by Gosplan. "Bonuses are important now, but workers feel they are underpaid in terms of the centrally set basic rates, and they therefore demand bonuses regardless of productivity. Work discipline and motivation are very low now. Only if workers feel their income is dependent on the enterprise rather than the center will they work better." When we suggested that workers seemed to be working harder than in North American plants, he explained this in terms of the plants there having been built according to Western standards, where "technology controls the workplace."

He considered the victory that the workers won over "Black Saturdays" to have been a disaster. Not only did it have the effect of a significant loss in the volume of production, it established the working collective council as a real power in the enterprise, something that he insisted did not happen elsewhere despite the provisions of the 1987 law.

> Nothing good came of that law. The workers' level of culture meant that not very conscious or educated workers were elected to the councils. The democracy came before the culture. The law is being changed now because many directors of enterprises refused to remain directors if they lost their decision-making power. Instead of taking quick professional decisions, there were long involved discussions that dragged out. These inevitably ended with redistribution questions coming first, since these are the problems closer to the people, while the main questions of production and modernization were ignored.

What this manager meant when he said workers would work better if their income were dependent on the enterprise rather than the center was that managers would have more control over workers. Yet there were many signs of class struggle over this strategy, and as we immediately saw when we left his office to meet the union representatives, their support of enterprise autonomy had primarily to do with a conception of workers' control. There were twenty-four people there, most of them elected leaders in various sections of the plant, and one of them also the vice president of the informal workers' club. Sixteen of them were women in their forties or fifties.

The representative of the informal workers group (which had emerged two years before) was particularly eloquent and direct:

> We felt that the traditional administrative power structure in the factory would talk much about change, but not do much in fact. Lots of talk but no

action. Not much was tried by the traditional union structure, so workers elected their own representatives to defend their rights and their wages and conditions. Up to now the trade unions are still too much engaged in social functions. For so many years people have been kept in a passive position, they may have become passive themselves and refused to believe the trade unions would be participating in the changes. And the opposition in the union to change is still strong, especially to democracy. Very few workers are satisfied with the pace of change in the trade unions. . . . If [work] discipline is low, it is because workers were so alienated from the means of production that they developed poor working habits. The main question now is how the independence of the enterprises will change this. The workers' clubs are fighting for collective ownership of the means of production along with the independence of enterprises. But this is being undermined. For example, the proposed price rise is a purely bureaucratic administrative decision by the center.

There was considerable dissent over whether workers were nearly as passive as he contended, and there was more sympathy with the managers' attempts to rid themselves of control by the "center." The general consensus was that, since the central control by the ministries in Moscow limited the labor collective's power as well as managers' power, once the enterprises became free of the ministries, the workers' representative council would really become strong. When we interjected to ask whether the new law on enterprises did not already negate what they expected in this respect, they appeared confused and said that they had heard that a new law was being considered but did not really know what was in it. When we told them the law had already been passed the previous week and that their own national union president had confirmed that it removed the power of the collective to elect managers and restricted the workers' representatives' control over decision making in the enterprise, there was uproar in the room. The main reaction was that this was proof of how the system at the center, despite the new parliamentary institutions, remained undemocratic, the same bureaucratic system that delivered decisions from on high without popular involvement.

The chair of the trade union committee spoke up at this point (for the only time during the meeting) and tried to cool things down by saying: "We are not yet owners of the means of production. When we are we will have more rights." A middle-aged woman, who had to this point been silent, followed this with a long and eloquent speech on the meaning of socialism. It ended with this bald statement: "When the state owns the means of production, then they appoint managers. But if socialism really means that workers own the means of production, then they should elect managers." Another woman disagreed: "Not everyone feels all managers should be elected. People who were not competent enough were elected." The informal representative interjected forcefully: "A good manager should have nothing to be afraid of." There seemed overwhelming assent to this, and when he went on to say that he was in favor of municipal soviets plus workers in each enterprise having joint control of the enterprises, they all agreed.

They were anxious to turn the discussion toward the situation in Canada. Significantly, the first question was whether managers were members of the unions as in the USSR. This was followed by a series of questions on the right to strike in Canada. And then, surprisingly, given the clearly syndicalist approach he had taken throughout the meeting, the informal workers' club vice president raised a naïve question, the kind we were later to hear put by Moscow liberal intellectuals who were keen to deny the contemporary relevance of any conceptual distinction between capitalism and socialism: "We hear that there is socialization of the means of production going on in the United States." When we asked him what he could possibly mean, it turned out that he had heard about profit-sharing schemes by corporations. It seemed to us that such naïveté might presage the workers' clubs' demands for industrial democracy being sooner or later bought off with the issuance of shares to individual workers which would leave them with no effective democratic control over their enterprises. This led us to offer a sketch of the reality of such schemes in the West, which ended with our expression of the need to democratize our economic system in order to displace our ruling class of capitalists, just as they needed to democratize their system to displace the ruling "nomenklatura" class. Our translator at this point thought it necessary to preface her translation by telling them that we were speaking as Western Marxists, but when she had finished translating what we had said about our respective ruling classes, there was a burst of spontaneous and enthusiastic applause throughout the room. The trade union chairman thought this an appropriate moment to end the meeting.

The union chairman, elected two years earlier, was a Communist party member in his early forties and seemingly very committed to the democratic changes taking place and to making the union an effective representative of its workers. One measure of this commitment was that he had recently been offered a senior management position and had responded to this in uncharacteristic fashion for a union official. He had gone to the union council, told them of the offer, and said he wanted to put the matter in their hands, since they had elected him and he was responsible to them rather than to management. They told him they wanted him to reject the offer, and he did so. When we pressed him on the degree of independence the union now had from the party, he stressed that a key to this was the fact that the industrial committees of the regional party apparatus had been abolished, and since they had been the locus of party control over both unions and enterprises, this was an important factor in understanding the transition that both local unions and enterprises were going through. But he was anxious to get on to another matter that he considered far more important. He demanded to know what "social justice" meant in our view. We clearly had not agreed with the deputy director's call for flexibility on wages and employment, but was it socially just that some workers do nothing at work, or don't even show up for work, and yet get paid the same as those who work hard? He proceeded to make a strong defense of income differentials in the workplace, and, if necessary, the right of managers to fire unproductive workers. We responded that it was hardly socially just to tie income to measures of productivity, since this reflected not only individual worker effort, but the way the labor process was organized in each plant and the nature of the technology. Workers who are in two different plants and are working just as hard would, on the measure he was proposing, be paid wildly different amounts. Moreover, what would be socially accomplished by firing someone who didn't work hard? Since he was in favor of full employment, he would just be passing the problem that worker's lack of effort represented to another enterprise. In the end, we appeared to come to an agreement that the essential problem was not an individual one to be solved by introducing the discipline of the labor market, but was related to alienation from the polity and from a labor process workers did not control.

As we went on to discuss the role that unions could play in relation to this, we noted that we were surprised that union leaders in Togliatti and Yaroslavl seemed not to know each other or even anything about each other, let alone actually discuss these matters together. He complimented us for having in such a short space of time "grasped the essential point" about the working class in the Soviet Union. There were virtually no linkages across the unions, even in the auto industry, at the base. Democratic centralism, which fostered this division as a matter of organizational principle, had produced its negation in terms of local hostility to the center, but it had left that hostility embedded in a series of unconnected localisms.

V

The VAZ empire of highly integrated assembly, parts, foundry, and machine plants in the city of Togliatti, where three parallel assembly lines stretched out for some three kilometers, looked rather like North American ones of twenty years earlier (when VAZ was built with the help of Fiat). VAZ produced 750,000 vehicles each year, about 40 percent of these were exported, and about half the exports went to the West. In good part due to its direct access to hard currency, there was no consumer crisis in Togliatti, and the integrated production of virtually all parts of the product had also made it highly independent of the central planning apparatus.

The massive assembly plant was dirtier and noisier than plants in North America. Apart from this, the most striking difference was that at least half the assembly-line workers were women. (In North America, the most gender-integrated assembly plant has, at most, 20 percent women workers.) Remarkably, many of the women were wearing sandals, while no one in a Western plant would be permitted to go without protective footwear. A group of women on the line told us that they put much more effort into their work than the men do—to which the men who heard this replied: "of course!" At breaks one generally saw men and women sitting separately, but it was also obvious that some romantic attachments were formed at work. One unforgettable scene on the line was of a young man and woman, having completed putting electrical wiring into the car frame that just passed their station, running around to each other for a passionate kiss before the next car made its way to them along the line. It appeared to us, however, that the workers were working harder than they do in North American assembly plants, worth noting in light of the conventional wisdom that job security made the Soviet worker lazy.

At a tiny shop steward's office near the cafeteria, a fifty-five-year-old male steward was meeting with three thirty-ish women who were discussing their maternity benefits. He was the head of a group of thirteen elected stewards representing a section of 900 assembly-line workers, and ten of the thirteen were women. Only the chief steward's position was full-time; he had been elected for a two-year term and was not a party member. As we discussed the degree of activism and democracy in the union, he told us that his section was having a meeting the following Saturday to discuss the impending price increases and what the union should do about them; 300 delegates had been elected—one for every three workers—and on the basis of precedent (such meetings were held about once a month) he expected that about 280 would attend. He mentioned all this casually, as if there was nothing remarkable about such a form of delegate democracy. Could it be that, long buried beneath the Stalinist structures and practices, the 1917 revolution had left some legacy of direct and delegate democracy which was now coming back to life?

In Togliatti, all union positions, from the chair, vice chair, and seven vice presidents to the chief stewards in every shop (in the auto industry every 700 workers were allotted a full-time representative) were elected in contested elections over the previous two or three years. The system of open elections appeared to have been sparked by the example of the elections for managerial personnel and workers' councils inaugurated under the auspices of the 1987 law on enterprises, but it was not clear that this was the cause of, rather than the moment of opportunity for, this change from the top-down system of appointments, nominations, and ersatz elections in the past. In fact, the Communist party secretary at VAZ told us that the idea for the 1987 law was born at a factory Communist party committee meeting in Togliatti in 1985. This emerged out of a "strong feeling that the old system limited participation and productivity insofar as sole responsibility fell on management and the trade union bureaucracy and most workers had no way to participate in decisions on the process of production." But the main change in labor-management relations in Togliatti pertained mostly to the behavior of the union. In contrast with what happened in Yaroslavl, the union leaders dated their experience with "fighting management" back to a similar attempt to knock twelve minutes off each working day in exchange for "Black Saturday" work. It was the union that resisted this in Togliatti and managed to get the management to retreat on this completely without a strike.

The new local party and union leadership were close allies. As with Gorbachev at the national level (although they were a generation younger), they did not stage a coup against the old leadership but rather developed within the local union and party organizations and waited for the retirement of the old guard. Most of them were skilled engineers and technicians (the traditional recruiting ground for industrial and political leadership) and had been Komsomol leaders when they were younger. Thus, as with Gorbachev, with whom they clearly shared a common trajectory and perspective (these kinds of local leaders were clearly his real political base in 1985), their rise was not a product of the new system of elections. Rather, they repeatedly insisted that the key thing about their being freely elected was that it gave them legitimacy among the workers, so that they could go to the workers with this or that initiative and say: "You elected me—now you have to support me."

The strongest material grounds for their support continued to rest on the considerable facilities run by the union in Togliatti: the massive cultural center with its cinema, concert halls, and library; the preventative health care and herb medicine clinic; the network of pioneer camps for the children. Moreover, these facilities were now run in the spirit of *glasnost*. The staff at the pioneer camp told us that they had been completely liberated from the previous "narrow-minded" party control over their curriculum. A particular blessing was that they no longer had to waste the children's time and energy practicing the songs that the party used to want them to perform for visiting dignitaries. Among the two million volumes loaned from the library in the previous year, Nabokov—long associated in the Soviet Union with "decadent" literature and support for the Whites in the civil war—was the most popular of the authors. The cultural center regularly sponsored rock concerts—although we were told that there was a serious problem in Togliatti with teenage gang violence.

Of course, the union leadership enjoyed perks that went with holding office, not least the excellent meals we enjoyed with them, the union-owned yacht on which we spent a pleasant few hours, and the union minivans with their drivers who were at the beck and call of our hosts. But these perks were probably not any greater, relative to their members, than most union leaders have in the West. When we told one of the vice presidents that we were going to ask workers on the assembly line whether they saw these new leaders as "apparatchiks," he said if they did they would be partly right, as they were the "new apparat" now. When we put this question to about a dozen men and women taking a break from the line, this immediately sparked an argument among them pro and con, but there was a general consensus that the leaders were more responsive for being elected. Another smaller group clearly didn't want to discuss the question, or any other, but rather preferred to be left alone to get on with their lunch. But this would have been a typical attitude we would have confronted had we bothered a group of workers with our questions during their break in a North American plant.

Below the top leadership level, there were some thirty elected committees representing different groups of workers in the vast VAZ enterprise, within which there was also a large network of elected shop stewards. When we met with a group of thirty workers who were the chairs or vice chairs of these committees, only four were women. The chairman of the Trade Union Committee had asked us to start the proceedings by talking about unions and autoworkers in Canada. Hoping to steer the subsequent discussion toward these issues, we put particular emphasis on unemployment, restrictions on the right to strike, and problematic aspects in the relation between leaders and rank-and-file workers (including a brief, but deliberately pointed, primer on Robert Michels's "iron law of oligarchy" in working-class organizations). A heavyset man in his sixties then opened the discussion with a question on how extensive the sports facilities were for workers in our car plants (clearly making a point thereby on how comparatively blessed their own workers were). He followed with a claim that the turn to markets in the USSR would not necessarily lead to unemployment due to the retraining schemes being planned. (While he was speaking the chair of the trade union committee whispered to us: "Not a problem in theory—but in practice?") The same man then followed with a statement which offered a defense of democratic centralism. He had not gotten very far in this before he was forcefully interrupted by the vice chair of the union committee in the foundry, a vivacious woman in her early thirties (most of the foundry's 9,000 workers were men), who insisted that we needed to know who was speaking. "That is the deputy director of the enterprise," she loudly proclaimed to much laughter and assent all around, and went on to suggest that Michels's thesis on oligarchy very much applied to the practice of democratic centralism in the Communist party. At this point we asked what difference the union elections had made, and a fifty-seven-year-old manual worker responded pointedly that over twenty-seven years of working he had never held a union position because he wasn't a member of the party, but now he had been elected. The chair of the trade union committee in one of the parts plants then turned the discussion to the market, arguing that it would force the unions to take up the issues of protecting workers from the rise in prices, and looking at the deputy director, said they would be taking this up with the enterprise management. Notably, a number of questions were then put to us on how strike funds worked in Canadian unions.

For all we were told about how the union had become more independent and far more active over the previous two years, it was nevertheless significant that there was an informal workers' club in Togliatti which operated outside the union. (Perhaps this was why the chair of the trade union committee refused to take any credit for the union's activism, ascribing it rather to the fact that "people were really active now, especially workers.") The workers' club had recently distributed leaflets putting forth a set of demands on improving the "work environment" and had challenged the union leadership to take these up with management. On the Friday before we had arrived, the union had taken these demands to management and apparently had them resolved, including a promise to install equipment to control the level of emissions in the plant. But on the following Monday morning, management had announced—without telling the union—that they might at the same time reduce wages by taking away the compensation given for working in poor conditions. On the following day, the union organized a "collective headache," with large groups of workers leaving their station to go to the medical staff. The union leaders were convinced that management had intended to sabotage the union, to teach them a lesson about not cooperating with the workers' club. But they were equally convinced that this was a strategic blunder by management, since the union was strong enough to win on this issue. Indeed, the amount of time the union leadership spent with us on the very day this work action was going on provided some measure of their degree of confidence about the strength of their organization on the shop floor.

In general, the union leadership admitted the workers' club were playing "a very useful role." One described them as a "barometer," another as a "catalyst." Since so much of the leadership's time and energy was involved with the extensive network of clinics, shops, vacation camps, and cultural centers run by the union, they saw the workers' clubs as "crucial for raising discontents" and helping the union "pinpoint what the priorities ought to be." The leaders in the clubs were mostly people who had left the Communist party. One of the union vice presidents described them as "extremist" in the sense that they put forward "impractical" demands, but the vice chair of the union saw them in different terms: "They are active workers, not passive like most. In some ways they are personalities like the union leaders themselves, and are engaged in a power struggle for leadership of the workers. Ideologically they range from greens to Social Democrats, but they are, in a positive way, searching."

An important area of disagreement between the workers' club and the union leadership was over whether skilled engineering and technical staff ought to be members of the union. In fact this was the main topic at a meeting between the chairman of the trade union committee in the foundry and leaders of the workers' club the day after the "collective headache" work action. Insofar as managerial personnel, who were drawn from this stratum, were union members, and insofar as there had been traditionally a high degree of career interchange between union leadership and managerial positions, this clearly was an important element in the "power struggle" taking place at the time. The chair of the union in the foundry, speaking with us immediately after this meeting, expressed both puzzlement and dismay at the position being taken by the workers' club on this. A thirty-five-year-old engineer, highly committed to working with the workers' club and to making the union more independent of management, he insisted that engineers and technicians were not a class apart despite their education but "still workers like the rest." He pressed us closely on whether unions in the West reflect such divisions and how Marxist theory should comprehend them. There was much interest in the Lucas Aerospace example we told them about where, in England in the 1970s, technicians had set out a plan that involved sharing their skills with manual workers to the end of developing alternate production schemes to prevent layoffs or plant closures.

This new union leadership was itself searching for precisely how to define their role in an independent manner from management. There was in Togliatti, as everywhere else in the world auto industry at the time, interest in Japanese styles of management. The union leaders we talked to about this were not overtly hostile to this but were aware of the passivity of Japanese unions. One of them recounted to us his amazement when he had discovered on a visit to Japan that collective agreements prohibited the posting of union bulletins on the shop floor. "We would never allow this here," he insisted. We were questioned closely on how strike funds worked in Canada and the extent to which they effectively sustained workers and their families during strikes. At the same time, they were concerned lest strike action would have the effect of making an enterprise uncompetitive, thereby leading to a loss of jobs. As we used the instance of the Canadian autoworkers' successful strike against General Motors to emphasize the importance of unions having the capacity to make independent judgments regarding the financial position of corporations, they expressed their concern about their dependence on management for information and the need, at the local union level, for the economic expertise that would enable an independent assessment of that information.

Although Togliatti provided the prototype for the 1987 law on state enterprises, the head of the workers' representative council at VAZ (a manual worker in his late fifties) told us that the council "had made little difference." The Communist party secretary took the position that the structures established in the 1987 law had not worked in most enterprises, partly due to the fact that managers had coopted the labor collective councils, but also partly due to the fact that the higher the level of the managerial position, the more difficult it was for workers to decide whom to vote for. He welcomed the new law which "took into account the mistakes which had been made and which we felt in our practice here. It ought to be the manager who made the final decisions. The limit of the workers' council's power is the power of the manager. Theoretically the workers' council had been the collective master of the enterprise, but practically it had not been." The local union leaders, while they did not appear very exercised about the new law, did not entirely share these views. Indeed, they told us that not only the union committee but the Communist party secretary himself had sent a document with their deputy to the Supreme Soviet opposing the new law. But it was clear that even the local union had not done much to consult with the rank and file on this. Shortly after the new law was passed, the workers' club on the main assembly line issued a strong condemnation of the failure to have submitted it to the labor collectives for discussion.

How then did the local leaders in Togliatti see the future? It was easier for them to formulate their views on the mistakes of the past. We were told by the vice chairman of the trade union committee: "Insofar as workers are backward and underdeveloped, this is because there has in fact been no real political education since 1924." And he added, emphatically: *"The workers were made fools of by the party."* They were also unanimously of the view that the command economy had failed. They were proud of the autonomy that VAZ had from the central plan and did not appear terribly troubled that Togliatti was "an island of economic stability" while other cities were experiencing severe shortages. Yet at the same time many of them asserted repeatedly that Communist values should never be given up. In the CP secretary's view the problem with the Soviet Union was that it had tried "to set those values up apart from life—now it was necessary to let life take its course." The central material condition he was referring to was that "the free market is dynamic around the world"—and life taking its course meant that a stage of integration with international capitalism was necessary before the material conditions for communist values could be established. (He admitted this sounded naïve about the benefits of the "free market," but this was because "we have had no experience with markets.") In Togliatti this would entail the establishment of joint ventures with Western capital which they believed would still remain under the control of VAZ.

The local union leadership, while certainly not opposing joint ventures, expressed considerable concern that the integration with Western capitalism would lead to a "Latin-Americanization" of the Soviet economy. They were cognizant of and concerned by the rush to embrace capitalism in Eastern Europe (while at the same time highly supportive of the democratic revolutions there, including independence from the USSR; indeed, one them spoke movingly about the trauma of having been one of the young soldiers sent to Czechoslovakia in 1968). But they doubted that the conditions for the reestablishment of capitalism existed in the USSR, and were certain that the workers would not accept a radical market reform unless it were forced upon them by a return to authoritarian government.

At the same time, however, they were concerned that price increases and the inevitable pressure to compensate for them by wage increases would lead both the "center" and local enterprise managers to cut back on the resources needed to maintain the collective services the unions ran. They claimed that signs of this were already visible, and they worried that such a turn away from collective consumption might be sustained by a widespread narrow individualism they detected among workers. As the deputy chair of the trade union committee put it: "Egoism is everywhere. People's apartments are neat and well maintained, but the hallways are a shambles. People respect what is 'mine,' but have no respect for what is 'ours.'" If our experience in Togliatti confirmed that the localism we had already detected in Yaroslavl was one of the main legacies of Soviet Communism, this last insight further suggested that, even at the level of local identity, there was no genuine community.

VI

As we returned to Moscow, it was clear that the consequences of the Communist party's time-honored strategy of divide and rule were now coming home to roost. Moscow was losing control over the vast geographic space, with its great diversity of peoples, gradually assembled under the old czarist empire. Indeed, it is arguable that only the Bolshevik revolution, with its unique blend of internationalism and coercion prevailing through the civil war, preserved most of that immense space as a distinct territorial-political entity after World War I. It is in this light that not only the Baltics', but also Poland's, undoing of Stalin's reclamation of those bits of the old empire that were lost after 1917 could already be understood by 1990. And an even larger drama of detachment from the territorial reach of the old empire was now being played out in many areas that were retained under a new regime after 1917. But while projects to break with, or at least secure or extend autonomy from, the center were ubiquitous in the Soviet Union in 1990, all eyes still turned to Moscow in order to discern whether the projects of the political class there would complement or frustrate, promote or prevent, the decentering process that so markedly motivated politics everywhere else. Moreover, Moscow remained the communications hub of the Soviet Union: it is a political class's business, after all, to collect, control, and dispense information. And while the information received in Moscow was by no means complete (indeed what the political class does not know about a society in transition probably always exceeds what it does know), such "facts" as became generally "known" in the Soviet Union still primarily made their way through Moscow in 1990. Indeed, it is arguable that the rest of the country now relied *more* on Moscow for credible information than in the days when everything was filtered through, or concealed behind, the party line. Despite all the centrifugal localisms that had asserted themselves so insistently, Moscow remained the summit that afforded the broadest perspective.

Notably, everyone we talked with in Moscow took the view that the package of market reforms which the Ryzhkov government had announced, and especially the price increases on basic necessities scheduled to come into effect on July 1, was unacceptable to the population. And, indeed, as we watched on our last day in Moscow the Supreme Soviet decide to postpone the introduction of this package, an aura of foregone conclusion pervaded the rather desultory debate. There could be no doubt that the overwhelming concern among the political class, inside and outside the Communist party, was about finding both short-term and long-term solutions to the economic crisis through the more or less gradual turn to "free markets." Although this phrase set the terms of all debate and discussion (far more than "democracy"), it concealed as much as it revealed.

Gorbachev's leadership team, having taken in 1985 the driver's seat of the old locomotive at the head of the stalled Soviet train, had already experienced many assaults. The railway metaphor, however strained, is an apt one, and not only because the frustrations of *perestroika* called to mind the freight trains that were reputedly loaded with goods but stuck at sidings all over the country. It is also apt because this leadership still understood what it was doing in terms of the "locomotive of history" following the tracks laid by the development of the forces of production. But it now wanted to find a way to get back on the track laid by capitalism's development of these forces of production, having accepted that the Bolshevik attempt to construct a parallel track was not only unorthodox in terms of the classics of historical materialism, but, much more important, actually futile. Their view was that it was necessary to integrate with a stage of dynamic world capitalism: This alone would lay the basis for the eventual emergence of socialism on solid foundations. The people who led the Bolshevik party in 1990, insofar as one wanted to understand them in terms relevant to the political history of Marxism in Russia, were Mensheviks.

These were precisely the terms in which their philosophy and strategy was presented to us by Andrei Grachev, the deputy head of the international committee of the Central Committee. Responsible for theoretical issues, this very handsome, expensively dressed fifty-two-year-old (Paul Newman could play him in *Reds: The Aftermath*) was influential with Gorbachev, with whom he had just returned from the United States, having handled the media side of the visit. The goal of the Gorbachev leadership, he told us, was "normalcy," by which he meant a stage of parliamentary democracy and market relations. "But this is *only* a stage. For this is not where we should have landed in the end. But we should have made use of the universal aspects of parliamentary democracy and markets, which we ignored before. The goal is to arrive to the point that socialism grows out of normal capitalist society." When we taxed him with the likely costs in human misery of a transition to such a stage, he responded: "We are not too afraid of going too far towards capitalism, as there is great resistance to it here. There is a strong spiritual basis in this society which does not accept the excesses of capitalism. This is the traditional collectivism which goes back before 1917." This, in conjunction with the "cultural" success of the Communist regime's mass public education system, had yielded in his view a widespread political consciousness which would at least ensure that some version of Social Democracy would be the outcome of *perestroika*. That was why he believed "we have a good chance of reaching a Scandinavian, more cooperative version" of the stage they needed to go through. He did not dissent when we said this sounded classically Menshevik.

Unlike so many other enthusiasts for the market and multiparty elections we met in Moscow, Grachev displayed a sophisticated appreciation of the limits and contradictions of liberal democratic capitalism. Nor was he apologetic about the limits of the Gorbachev reforms. For instance, when we told him about the anger we had witnessed among workers in Yaroslavl that they had only heard about the passage of the new law on enterprises by the Supreme Soviet from us, he saw this as an instance of the negative aspect of parliamentarism, its elitism, and the separation, apart from the act of voting for representatives, between decision making and the people. "Many of the new structures which were a year ago seen as incredible developments for this society are now questioned because they see the negative aspect of bourgeois parliamentarism, while not yet having any evidence of the positive benefits."

This was aggravated in Russia, however, by the "filter between the party at the top in the center and the lower levels." When in response to the emergence of the Democratic Platform group inside the party, the Central Committee had issued a statement on the impermissibility of factions amidst a strong defense of democratic centralism, the text had in fact been drafted by the Politburo without even consultations with the Central Committee. All this reflected "old-fashioned" compromises at the top forced on Gorbachev, who never had more than minority support on the Politburo. On the other hand, especially in the run-up to the July congress, Grachev told us it was fascinating to observe how the old "apparatchiks," who had gotten where they were by never stirring from their desks, keeping their noses down, pushing paper, and following orders were discovering how to be creative politicians, making speeches, organizing opinion to the end of holding on to their political careers. A very sizable section of the political class were strongly in favor of a rapprochement between Yeltsin and Gorbachev and were actively pushing for it, as the sole immediate means of laying the political grounds for a market reform. Even those who recognized that Yeltsin's politics was defined by sheer opportunism and demagoguery conceded that the population believed in him.

To survive, in Grachev's view, the party would have to confront four fundamental but absolutely necessary changes:

First, to convince people that it means what it says; that is, that it will not remain a party-state and that it is sincere in looking for a role separated from the state, as an organization and movement. Second, to redefine its relation to other movements and parties. Having accepted the principle of a multi-party system, it must renounce its monopoly of power and respect fair play with other forces. And it must do so because it believes in socialism and social justice and because it believes it can get support politically from people, rather than just rule administratively. Third, self-renewal: the internal remaking of the party. It must stop being vertical and monolithic from the top. It must become a lively party which would be open for internal debate and with horizontal connections across the base. Finally, we have to look at the role of parties in general, which is declining everywhere in the face of the social movements. We need to allow for movements here. And it is possible that the party may not be able to survive their attacks.

It was clear that the reformers in the Communist party were looking for a market solution less drastic than Poland's not only because of their antipathy to "the excesses of capitalism," but because the party lacked the legitimacy to survive such a drastic imposition of hardship on the population. Perhaps the most remarkable illusion widely shared among Russia's political class in the dying days of Communism was that the capitalism they would become integrated with would look like Swedish Social Democracy. This was wishful thinking, a hope that a transition to market relations would be something less brutal and more democratic than it could have possibly been. On the other hand, the leaders of what was still in 1990 called the "cooperators' movement" (representing private businesses which were already capitalist enterprises in all but name), were rather more hard-hearted and less naïve. Andrei Fadin, the political editor of *Commersant*, the newspaper of the movement (which was a joint venture with a group in Chicago, and which billed itself as "Russia's *Business Weekly*") knew exactly what "the capitalist road" meant in terms of hardship for millions of people and the uneven development it would spawn. This is not to say that his newspaper was honest about this, by any means. Indeed it painted capitalism only in glorious colors. But the morning we spent with Fadin over the kitchen table in the tiny and shabby apartment out of which the newspaper was produced provided a very sharp counterpoint, in substance as well as in surroundings, to our meeting with Grachev.

Fadin had been one of the Marxist dissidents in Moscow imprisoned, along with Roy Medvedev and Boris Kagarlitsky, a decade earlier, and moved through the "informals movement" that had arisen in the 1980s to being a militant in the Social Democratic party and then to a political position of an explicit endorsement of capitalism. Yet his account of the effects of a transition to capitalism was informed by a much surer materialist analysis than the softer analyses of those who hoped for an easy transition to a Swedish type of "mixed economy." There was no possibility of establishing a consumer market without a fully free capital market as well as labor market, he insisted. Capitalist modernization through the market depended on the large pool of savings being mobilized through the sale of shares in state enterprises. This would lay the basis for a capital market, which would inevitably be quite concentrated in terms of ownership. The legalization of foreign currency ownership and the legalization of foreign enterprises, not just joint ventures, would come quickly, and he had no illusions about the kind of development this would lead to. The outcome for Russia was either a South Korean or Brazilian path to modernization, and he preferred the former, since the Brazilian route would leave a hundred million people destitute. "Moscow, Leningrad, the far east, and the northern region—and unfortunately even most of the western region—will be the 'vegetative sector of the economy,' as the Brazilians say. The role of government will be to soften the effects of this uneven development."

Although it seemed bizarre to Western leftists, such advocates of capitalism were designated as being "the Left" among the political class. There was a rather more genuine Left which, while also opposed to those who seek to preserve the undemocratic party-state structures, was searching for a socialist route out of the crisis, but they were very thin on the ground. The initial tendency among the political class at the outset of *perestroika* to look back to New Economic Policy (NEP) as a model for reform was already a thing of the past by 1990. "They have now been able to read Bukharin and have discovered that he really was a communist, so he is no longer their hero," Vadim Rogovin, a Marxist sociologist, told us. "Increasingly among the intellectuals here the heroes are the Whites, [Aleksandr] Solzhenitsyn, and [Vladimir] Nabokov. If you can show you had an ancestor who was a merchant or a kulak, it is now a badge of honor." The only organized political forces in 1990 that articulated a clear democratic socialist vision (untainted, at least, by a preliminary stage of integration with capitalism) were the Democratic Platform inside the Communist party led by Alexander Buzgalin, and the newly formed Socialist party led by Boris Kagarlitsky. Both were highly committed and creative Marxist intellectuals, although Buzgalin's group tended more toward worker self-management as the road forward, while Kagarlitsky's party placed greater stress on local soviets as the building blocks of a democratic socialist alternative. But both were weak, if not entirely marginal, political forces in 1990 and had little chance of influencing the pattern of events that were all too soon to mark the end of the USSR and the demise of Communism.

This left only the Gorbachev reformers as representing any alternative to the full embrace of capitalism, at least apart from those who clung to the old authoritarian system. We had put three objections to Grachev, from the perspective of the Western Left, concerning his Menshevik strategy. First, as regards his confidence that their capitalist stage would be relatively benign, did he take into account the fact that even the Swedish model was in danger of collapsing under the weight of the new mobility and globalization of financial capital? Second, what were socialists in the Third World to make of a strategy, emanating from the Soviet Union, that seemed to condemn them to living with the status of dependent capitalism? And finally, was he not at all bothered that the Western Left, having had to endure the charge earlier that socialist ideals lead to the gulag, were now to be subjected to the charge that even Soviet Communists had come to accept the virtues of the capitalist market? Grachev responded:

> all this could be answered if the Left in the West and the Third World can make sense of *perestroika*. We really believe that democracy is not synonymous with bourgeois democracy; that the market is not synonymous with capitalist markets; that socialism is not a system of shock absorbers but a whole car. We know we won't, because we can't, go too far to become a capitalist country. Socialism is a living creature which can live without coercion and distortion, which has power in people's consciousness and willingness to work for it and arrange social life so that the freedom of one does not become a barrier on the freedom of others. It is just that the next stage in the advance of socialism now falls on the western left.

Was he trying to pass the torch—or the buck? Either way, the more important question, for the Left in the West, was: Were we up to it?

Notes

1. Lenin's comment on "monumental propaganda" to his minister of culture is quoted in Vladimir Tolstoy, Irina Bibikova, and Catherine Cooke, eds., *Street Art of the Revolution* (London: Thames and Hudson, 1990), p. 13.

2. *The Economist*, 28 September 1991, p. 25.

3. Franz Schurmann, "Back to the Cold War . . . Or Worse," in Schurmann, *The Role of Ideas in American Foreign Policy* (Dartmouth, N.H.: University Press of New England, 1971), p. 11.

4. The long-term effects of this on the whole state apparatus and the economy was analyzed particularly well by Robert Cox, "Real Socialism in Historical Perspective," in Ralph Miliband and Leo Panitch, eds., *Communist Regimes, The Aftermath: The Socialist Register 1991* (London: Merlin, 1991), pp. 169–93.

5. A fascinating excerpt of the minutes of this meeting may be found in Tolstoy, Bibikova, and Cooke, *Street Art*, p. 144.

6. Anthony Giddens, *The Class Structure of the Advanced Societies* (London: Hutchinson, 1973), pp. 280–87.

7. See Moshe Lewin's brilliant essay, "Leninism and Bolshevism: The Test of History and Power," in his *Making of the Soviet System* (New York: Pantheon, 1985), pp. 191–208.

8. Milovan Djilas, *Rise and Fall* (London: Macmillan, 1985), pp. 3–4.

9. Rudolf Bahro, *The Alternative in Eastern Europe* (London: New Left Books, 1977).

10. C.L.R. James, *Nkrumah and the Ghana Revolution* (London: Allison and Busby, 1977), pp. 189–213.

11. Ibid., p. 196. Cf. V. I. Lenin, *Selected Works*, vol. 3 (Moscow: Progress, 1971), p. 545.

12. James, *Nkrumah*, p. 204. Cf. Lenin, *Selected Works*, vol. 3, p. 776.

13. James, *Nkrumah*, p. 206.

14. Ibid., p. 209.

15. Ibid., p. 197.

16. Ibid., p. 206.

17. Lenin, *Selected Works*, vol. 3, pp. 233, 236.

18. See David Mandel, "Revolutionary Reform in Soviet Factories," in Ralph Miliband and Leo Panitch, eds., *Revolution Today: The Socialist Register 1989* (London: Merlin 1989); and Fred Weir, *The Soviet Revolution: Shaking the World Again* (Toronto: Progress, 1990). Also see Mandel's "Why Is There No Revolt? The Russian Working Class and Labour Movement," in Leo Panitch and Colin Leys, eds., *Working Classes, Global Realities: The Socialist Register 2001* (London: Merlin, 2000).

3

Liberal Democracy and Socialist Democracy

What I have been trying to do all along (and am still trying to do) . . . is to work out a revision of liberal-democratic theory, a revision which clearly owes a good deal to Marx, in the hope of making that theory more democratic while rescuing that valuable part of the liberal tradition which is submerged when liberalism is identified with capitalist market relations.

C. B. Macpherson[1]

I

There have been two different ways in which radical intellectuals in the West have sought to make use of Marxism in their life's work. One way is for intellectuals to take their standpoint and measure their contribution to the maximizing of human potentialities as expressed in the revolutionary aspirations of socialist movements. The role of the intellectual, in this view, is to employ Marxism to help develop the theory and strategy of the socialist movements; *and* to help develop Marxism in response to the changing world and the changing needs of socialist movements as they confront this world. A second approach of radical intellectuals is to attempt to bring the insights of Marxism to a critique of the capitalist order without locating themselves theoretically and strategically in a Marxist framework or seeing themselves as part of the socialist movement. During the Cold War, for instance, this second approach characterized the work of such intellectuals in the United States as Reinhard Bendix, C. Wright Mills, and Barrington Moore, Jr.[2] In the antinomies of an intellectual like C. B. Macpherson, the most internationally prominent

Canadian political theorist of that generation, we can instructively discern the two approaches in tension with each other.

One should be careful not to caricature either approach. The first approach did not necessarily mean subordinating one's intellectual work to the momentary "political line" of a Communist party or any other party. It did not require refraining from passing critical judgment *on any part* of the revolutionary socialist movement or on the inadequacies and errors of Marxism itself. Precisely because this approach did not entail reducing science to ideology in the narrow sense of the "Party School," it did *not* mean cutting oneself off from, or merely attacking, other intellectuals who embraced an alternative, even an opposing, theory to Marxism. On the contrary, the task of the Marxist intellectual, in this view, is to maintain a scientific dialogue in order to *incorporate* the best of opposing and alternate theories *into* Marxism. As Antonio Gramsci put it:

> In the formulation of historico-critical problems it is wrong to conceive of scientific discussion as a process at law in which there is an accused and a public prosecutor whose professional duty it is to demonstrate that the accused is guilty and has to be put out of circulation. In scientific discussion, since it is assumed that the purpose of discussion is the pursuit of truth and the progress of science, the person who shows himself most "advanced" is the one who takes up the point of view that his adversary may well be expressing a need which should be incorporated, if only as a subordinate aspect, in his own construction. To understand and to evaluate realistically one's adversary's position and his reasons (and sometimes one's adversary is the whole of past thought) means precisely to be liberated from the prison of ideologies in the bad sense of the word . . . that of blind ideological fanaticism. It means taking up a point of view that is "critical," which for the purpose of scientific research is the only fertile one.[3]

There is no less danger that the second approach may be caricatured, however. Its difference from the first approach *cannot* be captured in a presumed rejection of Karl Marx's famous aphorism about the point of philosophy being to change the world, not just understand it. The work of Bendix or Mills or Moore was often explicitly directed toward contributing to progressive democratic social change and even justifying revolutionary change to the end of overcoming human degradation. Much more clearly still, Macpherson's life work was so directed. As we shall see, he used Marx as an ethical benchmark to measure how far change has to go to realize human potential.

It is perhaps one of the ironies of the second approach, however, that it may sometimes lead one to be much more *tolerant* of Marxism's weaknesses and failures than one ought to be, or than the best practitioners of the first approach are. At least in the case of Macpherson, because he was mainly addressing himself to liberal democratic theory's failure to accept the insights of Marxism, rather than to Marxism itself, he failed to address himself in any systematic way to those weaknesses in Marxism which have contributed, all too often in this century, to the perversion in practice of Marxism's ends. He recognized this perversion but, given whom he was talking to, he was content to show that Marxism is not *necessarily* totalitarian and that its perversion is the result

> direct and indirect, of the failure of liberal-individualist theorists and defenders of an established capitalist society to see what impediments to [individual self-direction] are inherent in that society, and hence their failure to recommend, or permit to be taken, those actions required to remove those impediments.[4]

Macpherson's argument often appeared to be that the dictatorships that have been produced in the name of socialism came about because of the tenacious opposition they faced from those opposed to changing capitalist social relations. On the question of what Marxism and the socialist movement can accomplish itself in terms of developing appropriate theory and strategy to usher in socialist democracy, Macpherson had relatively little to say. Through a critique of Macpherson's contribution as one of the leading political theorists on the left during the Cold War, I want to argue that, if it is to contribute to a genuine renewal of socialism, Marxism must be capable of evolving means appropriate to its ends without being able to count on the support or acquiescence of its opponents.

By locating oneself outside Marxism while seeking "to learn from it" so as to improve liberal democratic theory, the intellectual fails to take *responsibility* for Marxism, as one must do if one recognizes and seeks to correct Marxism's own serious deficiencies. Macpherson justified Marxism and the socialist movement in terms of its *ends* for liberal democratic theory, when what is needed, at least as much as justification to non-Marxists, is *improvement* of Marxism's and the revolutionary socialist movement's *means* (i.e., its theory and practice) to those ends. Insofar as this improvement may entail incorporating what is valuable in liberal democratic theory *into* Marxism, it is arguable that by concentrating on the liberal tradition, Macpherson implicitly was indicating the power and value of liberal freedoms to Marxists. But Marxist intellectuals of the first approach will want to be much more explicit in this regard. Paradoxically, they necessarily will have to be less tolerant of Marxism's weaknesses and errors than C. B. Macpherson was.

II

Macpherson's project was to demonstrate, on the basis of a sophisticated understanding of Marxian political economy and ethics, that liberal democratic theory must, to be true to its claim to the ethic of the full and equal development of individual human capacities, be prepared to accept that the impediments of capitalist society to this goal—the absence of free and equal access to the means of life and labor—must go by the board. That his critique of liberal democracy was rooted in his understanding via Marxism of the necessary operation of capitalist relations of production seems to me absolutely clear from all his major works. Because he addressed himself to, and located himself in, the liberal democratic tradition in the ethic he asked it to live up to, there developed a rather misdirected charge that he did not employ a Marxian mode of analysis in his work. In response to this, a student of Macpherson's, Victor Svacek, undertook a fulsome demonstration that Macpherson was in every sense employing a Marxian mode of analysis *only not to the point* of accepting the necessity of a violent proletarian revolution. This was a judgment which Macpherson himself readily accepted, although he questioned whether the necessity of violent change was in fact a view which Karl Marx and Friedrich Engels themselves held.[5] Not surprisingly, perhaps given the subsequent publication of *The Life and Times of Liberal Democracy*, where Macpherson still located his project in terms of fulfilling liberal democracy's promise, the issue of Macpherson's Marxism did not go away.

Ellen Wood, who has succeeded Macpherson as Canada's most internationally prominent political theorist on the left, and who very clearly situates herself within the first approach to Marxism outlined at the outset of this chapter, has tried to come to terms with Macpherson by arguing that what he brought to a critique of liberal democracy was actually poorly informed by the essential tenets of Marxian analysis, and was, moreover, virtually *incompatible with such an analysis*. In good part on the basis of a *The Life and Times*, Wood concluded that Macpherson, in the grand tradition of Anglo-Saxon radicalism and Social Democracy, has been "seduced" by liberalism's mystifications of capitalist society.[6] Were she to have rested her case simply on Macpherson accepting as genuine liberalism's claim, as expressed via John Stuart Mill and T. H. Green, to pursue "the highest and most harmonious development of [man's] powers to a complete and consistent whole,"[7] she would have been on safe ground, although Macpherson's own demonstration that this claim remained inconsistently combined, even in Mill and Green, with the acceptance of capitalist market society, would need to be stressed as well. But Wood went further, arguing that Macpherson's seduction by liberalism went as far as his "accepting capitalism on its own terms" (i.e., liberal theory) and that "his account of capitalism differs very little from conventional portraits by apologists for capitalism." This argument was based on the assertions that (1) Macpherson meant by "class inequality" and "capitalist market relations" nothing more than the Weberian definition of class in terms of unequal market competition to the exclusion of the understanding of class as a *relation of production* in which surplus extraction and domination are inscribed, and (2) by virtue of his characterization of the contemporary "pluralist-elitist" model of democracy as "substantially accurate" as "a description of the actual system now prevailing in Western liberal democratic nations." Macpherson thus "confirms that he shares its most fundamental premises and is unable—or unwilling—to confront in more than the most superficial ways the consequences of class power and the nature of the state in a class society."[8] Because I detect traces here of Gramsci's "public prosecutor," it may be difficult to avoid the posture of acting as Macpherson's unsolicited defense attorney in what immediately follows. My main concern, however, is to clear the way for my own critique of Macpherson, which is based on other, and less sweeping, grounds.

As against Macpherson, Wood contended that Marxian class analysis involves understanding that capitalism is "the most perfect form of class exploitation: the complete separation of the producers from the means of production and the concentration in private hands of the capacity for direct surplus-extraction."[9] But this was *always* the centerpiece of Macpherson's analysis, so much so that one faces an embarrassment of riches when searching for an appropriate quotation to make the point. (Indeed, one hesitates to quote any one passage at all, lest it be thought that the quote is unique rather simply indicative of the *basis* of all Macpherson's work.) In Macpherson's view, there are three assumptions that are basic to Marx and Marxism, all of which he accepted, but only the first two of which liberal theory accepts. These assumptions are

(a) that the human essence is to be realized fully only in free, conscious, creative activity; (b) that human beings have a greater capacity for this than has ever hitherto been allowed to develop; and (c) that a capitalist society denies this essential humanity to most of its inhabitants, in that it reduces human capacities to a commodity which, even when it fetches its exchange value in a free competitive market, receives less than it adds to the value of the product, thus increasing the mass of capital, and capital's ability to dominate those whose labour it buys.

This is the philosophic underpinning of Marx's whole enterprise. It is difficult for a liberal to fault (a) and (b), the assumptions about the nature and capacities of man: virtually the same position was taken by, for instance, Mill and Green. And it is shortsighted for the liberal not to give serious consideration to the validity of (c)—the postulate of the necessarily dehumanizing nature of capitalism—for that does not depend on the ability of Marx's labour theory of value to explain market prices (which has been the main complaint about his economic theory) but only on *his path-breaking argument that the value produced by human labour-power (i.e., by its capacity of working productively) exceeds the cost of producing that labour-power, the excess going to the increase of capital.* This position is more difficult to fault than is the adequacy of his price theory.[10]

Macpherson's concept of the "net transfer of powers" was entirely founded on the theory of surplus value, only *extending* it to point out that, in addition to the material value transferred by the laborer to the capitalist in the process of production in the form of value over and above what it takes to reproduce the wage of the exchange contract in material terms, there is an additional *loss* to the laborer. This takes the form of the non-material "value that cannot be transferred but is nevertheless lost by the man who, lacking access [to the means of production] has to sell his labor power, namely the value of the satisfaction he could have got from using it himself if he had been able to use it himself." And it takes the form also of a certain loss of his "extra-productive powers": "that is, his ability to engage in all sorts of activities beyond those devoted to the production of goods for consumption, to engage in activities which are simply a direct satisfaction to him as doer, as an exerter of (and enjoyer of the exertion of) his human capacities, and not a means to other (consumer) satisfactions."[11] It is through this concept, clearly derived from Marx's theory of value, that Macpherson was able to see "that there is no dichotomy between Marx the humanist and Marx the analyst of capitalism."[12]

Macpherson affirmed in 1976 that this concept "has been prominent in most of what I have written in the last fifteen years" and suggested that he personally "made it a test of my critics' understanding of my analysis whether they understand the concept of the net transfer of powers."[13] That as outstanding a Marxist political theorist as Wood should have missed it entirely was rather surprising. Could it result from the fact that she concentrated on *The Life and Times* and one earlier essay "Post-Liberal Democracy," where Macpherson adopted a use of class and of capitalist market relations which omitted the "net transfer of powers" inscribed in capitalist production relations as a result of the separation of the worker from the means of production? To be sure, Macpherson did not explicitly use the term in either text. Yet his understanding of surplus value remained, in my view, an unmistakable facet of in his analysis.

Wood quotes a passage from "Post-Liberal Democracy," where Macpherson defined capitalism "as the system in which production is carried on without authoritative allocation of work or rewards, but by contractual relations between free individuals (each possessing some resource be it only his own labour-power) who calculate their most profitable course of action and employ their resources as that calculation dictates."[14] To Wood, this descriptive definition proved that Macpherson shared the fundamental premises of bourgeois economics, including marginal utility theory. But one can find passages in Marx's own writings very similar to this one, as a descriptive statement of the contrast between a competitive, contractual market system of production and a coercive, noncompetitive system of production. Were Macpherson unaware of the fact that *surplus extraction* was taking place via economic relations in the first case and extra-economic relations in the other (with market relations disguising what before had been open, i.e., the appropriation of labor's productive efforts), Wood might have a case. But the whole first half of Macpherson's article entailed a critique of marginal utility theory, not just in terms of unequal distribution of resources and income, but in terms of the *necessity* (which Mill did not recognize) of the "degradation of wage-labor" under capitalist production, in terms of the "concentration of capital ownership," in terms of (not the quantitative but) the *"qualitative* differences in utilities" maximized, and in terms of the "massive inequality between owners and workers, an inequality which stood in the way of any extensive development and fulfillment of individual capacities," which, in his view, cannot be measured simply in terms of (manufactured) consumer wants. If Macpherson maintained the definition of capitalism he did, it was to show that the process of production in question remains capitalist, even in the context of monopolies and oligopolies operating under extensive state regulation. The development of capitalism may have further undermined the justificatory nature of classical and neoclassical economics, but it did not "alter the basic nature" of the system, in that the actors in the system still related to each other in terms of competition for commodities (including labor power) and access to the means of production; and "the driving force" of the system remains the competitive "maximization of profit" among corporate giants: "for it is only by accumulating profit that the corporation can continue to grow."[15] Without seeing capitalism as a competitive market system, in this way, one cannot usefully employ Marx's political economy in the contemporary era of globalization.

As for *The Life and Times*, Macpherson made himself even clearer and explicitly rejected a liberal definition of class. "Class," he wrote, "is understood here in terms of property: a class is taken to consist of those who stand in the same relations of ownership or non-ownership of productive land or capital. A somewhat looser concept of class, defined at its simplest in terms of rich and poor, or rich and middle and poor, has been prominent in political theory as far back as one likes to go." As for class inequalities under capitalism, what could be clearer than this: "Mill was able to think that the capitalist principle was not in any way responsible for the existing inequitable distributions of wealth, income and power, and even to think it was gradually reducing them. What he failed to see was that the capitalist market relation enhances or replaces any original inequitable distribution, in that it gives to capital part of the value added by current labour, thus steadily increasing the mass of capital."[16]

If Wood failed to see this, it was perhaps because Macpherson, like Marx (and Gramsci's "advanced" intellectual), also often pursued the logic of alternate theories in their own terms to show what is valuable in them and to show at the same time the serious inconsistencies in their own constructions, which he challenged them to correct by incorporating Marxian assumptions. *To demonstrate a theory's inconsistency one must confront it on its own terms. To transcend it, one must move to an alternate problematic.* Wood mistook the one procedure with the other to make her case against Macpherson, especially with regard to his acceptance of pluralist-elitist theory as an accurate description of existing liberal democratic societies. In saying this, Macpherson was saying no more than that in terms of democracy defined narrowly (as the "realist" school of Joseph Schumpeter and Robert Dahl did), as merely "a mechanism for choosing and authorising governments or in some other way getting laws and political decisions made," it was accurate; but he clearly recognized that this definition came at the expense of denying any explanatory and justificatory problematic which defines democracy more broadly "as a kind of society, a whole set of reciprocal relations between the people."[17] Wood upbraided Macpherson for adopting the use of the terms *elite* and *political system* rather than *class* and *state,* and for measuring the comparative effectiveness of demands between "socioeconomic" (i.e., income- and status-defined) classes in terms of unequal "purchasing power" in the political "market," rather than in terms of relations of domination and exploitation. What she did not see was that Macpherson adopted this terminology in order to be able to engage in a discussion with pluralist-democratic theory at all, to show that as an explanatory and justificatory theory (and to some extent, as he made clear, even as a descriptive model, since the elites between whom the voters choose can decide what are issues and what are nonissues), it failed *even on its own terms.*[18]

Macpherson's own preferred political mode of analysis, for descriptive, explanatory, and justificatory purposes, was already made clear in the text before he engaged with pluralist-elitism on its own terms: "I think it is not overstating the case to say that the chief function the party system has actually performed in Western democracies since the inception of a democratic franchise has been to blunt the edge of apprehended or possible class conflict, or if you like, to moderate and smooth over a conflict of class interests so as to save the existing property institutions and the market system from effective attack."[19] This description was not necessarily inconsistent with Schumpeter's famous definition of democracy as "that institutional arrangement for arriving at political decisions in which individuals acquire the power to decide by means of a competitive struggle for the people's vote."[20] But Macpherson's is better, as a description, because of its explanatory and justificatory connections, and it can be shown to be better by revealing the weaknesses of the pluralist-elitist model in terms of its correlate connections. Having done this, Macpherson could then return to his own model later in the text and say "underlying class division and opposition . . . requires that the political system, in order to hold the society together, be able to perform the function of continual compromise between class interests, and that function makes it impossible to have clear and strong lines of responsibility from the upper elected levels downwards."[21]

We may safely conclude that it was unjustified for Wood to claim that Macpherson had "no conception of the state as an institution whose function it is to sustain a particular social order, that is a particular set of production relations and a particular system of class dominance"[22] in light of Macpherson's own critique of mainstream liberal political science: "What is lost sight of is that political power, being power over others, is used in any unequal society to extract benefit from the ruled for the rulers. Focus on the *source* of political power puts out of the field of vision any perception of the necessary *purpose* of political power in any unequal society, which is to maintain the extractive power of the class or classes which have extractive power."[23]

III

This now leaves us where we began: with the question of why Macpherson, despite his critique of liberal democracy as a theory and a system in terms of a Marxian mode of analysis, chose to continue to locate himself within the liberal democratic rather than the Marxist project, and the implications thereof. Wood herself began with this puzzle:

> Macpherson's account of the foundation of liberal democracy as a class ideology makes the rest of the argument rather puzzling. If the doctrine is based on class-division one must question Macpherson's characterization of its ethical position as a commitment to the free and equal development of all individuals. For that matter, one might wonder why he chooses to single out liberal democracy as the embodiment of this cherished principle when a doctrine opposed to the class nature of liberal democracy—that is, Marxism—is more centrally and genuinely concerned with this ethical commitment than is liberalism in any of its forms. . . . It is typical of Macpherson's approach that he is often able to treat capitalism as if it were merely the (temporary) instrument of liberal democracy, or even of liberal democratic thinkers and their ethical goal.[24]

As we have seen, Wood's answer to the puzzle was incorrect: it was not because Macpherson rejected the essential tenets of the Marxian analysis of capitalism that he located himself within liberal democracy.

Macpherson explicitly accepted these tenets and used them in his *critique* of liberal democracy. This not only included the theory of value but also the acceptance of the claim that it was *Marx, more than Mill or Green*, who provided the most genuine formulation of the ethic of the full and equal development of all individuals. It was Macpherson's position that the measure of a society's approximation to this goal is not some existing or previously existing standard of achievement in this regard, but the extent to which it approximates the *socially possible* attainment of this goal. "A democratic theory must measure men's present powers down from the maximum rather than up from a previous amount because it asserts that the criterion of a democratic society is that it maximizes men's present powers."[25] And what was that maximum for Macpherson? To him, it was obviously that provided by Marx. "The Marxian vision of the ultimately free classless society offers, *of course*, the greatest conceivable opportunity for each individual to use and develop his human attributes."[26]

What then was going on? Why did Macpherson not locate himself within the Marxian rather than the liberal democratic project? Macpherson himself gave two reasons, one related to liberal democratic, the other to Marxian, theory. First, he did not accept "the proposition that liberal democracy must always embrace the capitalist market society with its class-division."[27] It has done so historically, he argued, because capitalism appeared to theorists like Mill and Green the only way to establish the necessary material basis (to overcome the economy of scarcity) for the fully democratic society. Second, he rejected that "one-sixth" (as Svacek called it) of Marxian theory which propounds a necessary revolutionary transition to socialism. As he put it:[28]

My reason for not accepting the revolutionary theory as necessary is fairly simple. It is not . . . that I consider the possible cost in terms of denial of individual freedom to be always too high. That is a judgement that must be made for each time and place. I do not think it can be made in advance. But to assert the necessity of forcible revolution is to do just that. It is no doubt true that the creation of a good society requires the conscious and active participation of those who are to live in it, but it does not follow that in all circumstances that must be forcible revolutionary participation.

It does not seem to me that either of these reasons can be taken too seriously. In the first place, it is notable that the "overcoming of scarcity through capitalism" argument is one much more made by Marx, rather than Mill or Green, and one that Macpherson derived from Marx. As he himself showed, neither Mill nor Green ever adequately resolved the tension (I would say contradiction) in their works between their developmental theory and their acceptance of capitalist society. Indeed, Macpherson suggested that they did not *understand* the political economy of capitalism.[29] Were they to have understood it, would they have rejected it? We cannot know this. But was Macpherson really suggesting that those in power in capitalist society would reject the foundation of their power even if their greatest political theorists did so? The democratic element in liberal democracy, he was under little illusion, derives less from the necessary requirements of capitalism as a system, and less from the progressive theorists of liberal democracy, than from the *organization of the working class.* "It cannot be too often recalled that liberal-democracy is strictly a capitalist phenomenon. Liberal-democratic institutions appeared only in capitalist countries, and only after the free market and the liberal state have produced a working class conscious of its strength and insistent on a voice."[30] On these grounds alone one would have had to expect Macpherson to locate himself, not with Mill and the contemporary successors to William Gladstone, but with Marx and the contemporary working-class successors to the Chartists (i.e., the working-class socialist movement).

As for the second reason, it will not stand up to serious scrutiny, and Macpherson knew it couldn't. He said himself that "there is some doubt how essential a part of Marx's theory was the theory of revolutionary transition."[31] Although he believed that the reasons Marx gave for the possibility of a peaceful transition in Holland, England, and the United States (i.e., the lack of standing armies and the decentralization of state power) no longer held, he contended that once the possibility is recognized, it is entirely arguable that different conditions will establish the possibility anew. In any case, Macpherson not only admitted that a forcible revolution does not *necessarily* entail too great a cost in terms of individual freedom, he explicitly argued that in a great many circumstances the balance of cost and advantages favors forcible revolution, precisely because his concept of the net transfer of powers indicates that more is gained from the revolution than the reclamation of the surplus previously appropriated by the capitalists (because the previous absolute loss of nonmaterial powers due to the treatment of labor as a commodity no longer obtains). Where a Stalinist dictatorship emerged to negate these advantages, Macpherson explained this development in terms of either

(1) the necessity of forced industrialization in an economy of scarcity, or (2) the intransigence of those in power in liberal democratic society toward a peaceful revolution.[32] As we shall see, I don't think Macpherson's explanation of Stalinism will do in these terms. But the very fact that it is offered suggests that his self-location within the liberal democratic tradition did not rest primarily on the question of violent versus peaceful change.

So again, what was going on? Two more possibilities have been suggested to explain Macpherson's position, one by Macpherson himself, one by Wood. Macpherson claimed that to provide an alternative theory of transition to that of classical Marxism would involve a great deal of empirical study of the "actual and possible forces making for and against change." And he added: "I do not regard this as my métier. . . . I have thought myself better occupied with seeking to improve the theoretical understanding."[33] This was a much more plausible explanation of his position than the one he offered on the other two grounds, but it still didn't resolve the question. One still can ask why he didn't address himself then to Marxist *political theory*, to improve *its theoretical understanding*, of which it was much in need. Indeed, *after* offering this explanation in 1976, Macpherson explicitly advised neo-Marxist theorists of the state to turn their attention from political economy to political philosophy (albeit in terms of probing "the limits of the possible relation of the capitalist society and state to essential human needs and capacities"). He still resolutely placed himself, however, with the theorists of the liberal democratic, rather than Marxist, tradition.[34]

Another plausible explanation was offered by Wood herself:

> It could conceivably be argued that the contradictions in his position result merely from *tactical considerations.* He does often write as if his primary object were to persuade liberals that some kind of socialism follows naturally from their convictions, by representing his own brand of socialism as an extension of liberalism. He often appears to be self-consciously addressing an audience that needs to be persuaded that socialism—a doctrine which, apparently, must parade in sheep's clothing as something called "participatory democracy"—is the last and best form of liberal democracy, preserving what is essential and valuable in the liberal tradition and devoid of its evils. Such a conspiratorial interpretation of Macpherson's argument would suggest that he *intentionally obscures* as much as he reveals about the nature of both capitalism and liberalism.[35]

Without accepting Wood's judgment that Macpherson *did*, in fact, obscure as much as he revealed, I think there is a great deal in this explanation. Wood rejected it, however, in favor of her conclusion that his very analysis of capitalism was fundamentally liberal and thus is merely an unusually critical variant of pluralist democratic apologetics. We have seen that this view is insupportable. But, if we accept the alternative explanation, as I believe we should, we still have to ask why Macpherson thought it best to adopt the tactic that he did. The reason I think lies in a whole complex of factors related to what Macpherson accepted and rejected in Marxist political theory.

IV

Macpherson's main approach to Marxist political theory can be characterized in one word: defensive. That is, his main interest appeared to be to demonstrate, against theorists like Isaiah Berlin and Milton Friedman, or against popular conceptions of the effects of a social transformation, that tyranny is not *necessarily* the result of Marxist theory. He argued against Friedman that the absence of a capitalist market does not mean that a socialist state must be incapable of providing the conditions for "effective political advocacy." And he argued against Berlin that a commitment to "positive liberty" in the sense of individual self-mastery does not mean that people must be forced into a single, monist pattern which denies human diversity. He asserted that it is possible, and that Marx and Lenin thought it was, that once people were allowed equal freedom "there would emerge not a pattern but a proliferation of many ways and styles of life which would not be prescribed and which would not necessarily conflict"; "a society where diverse, genuinely human (not artificially contrived) desires can be simultaneously fulfilled." As against this, he characterized Berlin's "negative liberty" as one where "chains, enslavement, direct physical domination are counted in. But domination by withholding the means of life and labour is not: it is put outside the province of liberty altogether."[36]

These arguments are powerful and uplifting, but they scarcely put to the test the more detailed and daunting problems of what Marxist political theory has to say about the transition to socialism. For insofar as Macpherson (and Marx) admitted that the exploited may "hug their chains" by internalizing domination,[37] and insofar as he admitted that socialist revolutions have commonly led to dictatorship in the twentieth century, the question remains of how Marxist political theory stands up not just in terms of the *possibility*, but in terms of suggesting the likely basis for the *reality* of a transition that will usher in a democratic socialist order.

The central concept of the classical Marxist political theory of the transition to socialism is the "dictatorship of the proletariat." It expresses not one, but two ideas, indissolubly linked together in Marx, Engels, and Lenin, which are, nevertheless, in a state of severe *tension* (if not contradiction) with one another. In one respect, the concept means the coming to power of the working class in the same sense that the bourgeoisie is in power in capitalist society. Insofar as this includes the vast majority of the people, it is referred to in the classics as "mass democracy," "democracy taken to its limits," etc., and conceived in conjunction with the democratic forms (election to administrative posts, a popular militia, workers' cooperatives, communally elected deputies, recall, etc.), described by Marx in *The Civil War in France* and, with the addition of the Soviets, by Lenin in *State and Revolution*. To Macpherson, it made perfect sense to accept the concept on democratic terms. Insofar as (preliberal) democracy originally "meant rule by or in the interests of a hitherto oppressed class," and insofar as this new class state was to abolish capitalism and lay the basis for a classless society, to call this dictatorship "democracy was not outrageous at all: it was simply to use the word in its original and then normal sense."[38]

But there is another side to the concept which expresses the idea of dictatorship in a way other than direct rule by the working class. It is unclear that Marx would have accepted that the notion of such rule "in the interests of" rather than "by" the hitherto oppressed class was "democracy." At certain times Lenin apparently did, as Macpherson immediately made clear. But even for Marx the concept expressed the notion of coercion in the transition. In the class struggle of the transition period the proletarian state was to play the role against the bourgeoisie which the bourgeois state hitherto played in its repressive function against the proletariat. Even if the point was to lay the groundwork for a classless society, it was necessary "to appeal for a time to force" (Marx) against the counterrevolutionary class. The tension in the concept arises not so much in the question of whether the taking of power is to be peaceful or violent, as in the question of how this coercive aspect of the state was to be married with the forms of democratic participation of soviets, communes, recalls, etc.; and if it could not be, how one could move to establish such participation once power—and the institutions of state control and repression—were consolidated.

Insofar as one treated, as Lenin did in *State and Revolution*, the liberal democratic state simply as the "dictatorship of the bourgeoisie," whereby it is alleged that the previous state excluded the exploited from participation, and the proletarian state is simply excluding the exploiters from participation, the tension seems to go away. But this device, if good rhetoric, is poor theory. For the question is: How can one evolve principles of political (not social) exclusion which allow working-class participation and deny the same to the exploiters and their many supporters (without which they would not constitute a serious political force)? As Rosa Luxemburg pointed out to Lenin at the time, his "simplified view" of the capitalist state "misses the most essential thing: bourgeois class rule has no need for the political training and education of the entire mass of the people, at least not beyond certain narrow limits. But for the proletarian dictatorship that is the life element, the very air without it is not able to exist." And she continued: "Without general elections, without unrestricted freedom of press and assembly, without a free struggle of opinion . . . bureaucracy becomes the active element—a dictatorship to be sure, not the dictatorship of the proletariat, however, but only the dictatorship of a handful of politicians."[39]

Nor does the matter end here. For it is not just a matter of political theory, but of *political economy* at the same time. In a capitalist society the short-term demands of the working class are not inconsistent with the long-term interests of the working class in socialism even if they are not themselves revolutionary. For to engage in struggle over distribution of the surplus, over conditions of work, over control of the labor process not only weakens capital, but also develops the organization and consciousness of the proletariat. In a transitional socialist state, however, long-term and short-term interests are dissociated. The realization of short-term material interests undermines the ability of the socialist state to consolidate its power, to cope with economic sabotage by the reactionary forces at home and abroad, to lay the basis for socialist economic growth. Precisely because of this phenomenon, there is a tension between the need to restrict the self-organization of the working class (lest it compromise the revolution) and the need to allow it to flourish in order to develop the political capacities and participatory satisfactions which will compensate for the economic sacrifice.[40] To be sure, the tension is lessened considerably in a society which is industrially advanced at the moment of transition. But it does not go away. This is not only because scarcity is inevitably a relative concept, and not only because the question of *global* scarcity must impinge on the meaning of socialism in a highly economically developed state; it is also more, because we are talking of a *transitional* period, in which, unless the transition takes place simultaneously throughout the advanced capitalist world, the new society will find itself cut off from that global capitalist system which provides so much of the basis of its material sustenance. Some economic hardship, in a relative sense, is virtually inevitable for the majority of the population of a transitional society for a certain period.

What this means is that the tension in Marxist political theory between discipline and consent is not there by chance. The *weakness* of Marxist political theory is that it has not dwelt on it enough. If it decides that the balance must be tilted toward discipline, it must make damn clear how it thinks the organizations of control, superimposed from above, whether party or state, can eventually be democratized, or specify the foundations for their democratization that can be laid in the period of discipline.

Macpherson was certainly cognizant of all this. But he shared with Marxist political theory many of those elements that *get in the way* of posing this problem centrally. All too often Macpherson adopted a rigid economic determinism when considering this tension in the revolutionary project. This was seen most clearly in *The Real World of Democracy* (1965), where the political evolution of the Soviet Union since 1917 was entirely accounted for in terms of "material scarcity," without even so much as a bow to the distinctions between Stalinism and Leninism, let alone any possible defects in Leninism. He granted that the "vanguard route" is "exceedingly dangerous," but "in the circumstances we are talking about, there seems no less dangerous way." The "vanguard state," moreover, should have no great difficulty in transforming itself into a democratic state once material scarcity, the old class system, and "the desires and value judgements of the people have so changed . . . that the people will freely support the kind of society that the vanguard state has brought into being."[41] Macpherson gave some indication, moreover, that he thought the Soviet Union was tending toward achieving this and democratizing itself. In any case, he contended that in principle the one-party state could be democratic provided: "(1) that there is full intra-party democracy, (2) that party membership is open, and (3) that the price of participation in the party is not a greater degree of activity than the average person can reasonably be expected to contribute." The case is plausible, but his assertion that "the first two conditions can scarcely be met until the old class society has been replaced,"[42] leaves one gaping. Excluding the exploiters from participation gives way all too quickly to the virtual exclusion of democratic participation in the transitional political process, even through intraparty democracy.

In subsequent, less popular writings in the 1960s, Macpherson's position became clearer. He granted that Stalin's Russia was the classic case where the vanguard went "the whole way to the perverted doctrine, the doctrine that only they can know and that it is sufficient for them to know."[43] (He still seemed to entertain the notion that the USSR was democratizing itself, citing repeatedly Nikita Khrushchev's famous Twentieth Congress speech in 1956 which Macpherson apparently took as an abandonment of "the doctrine of the class war and proletarian dictatorship."[44]) But what is most important, he attributed Stalinism simply to "the long-continued and intensive refusal of the beneficiaries of unequal institutions on a world-wide scale to permit any moves to alter the institutions in the direction of more nearly equal powers." Thus he added to the material scarcity explanation of Stalinism the intransigence of the bourgeoisie as a factor, seeing this either in terms of capitalist "encirclement or cold-war" or in terms of the origins of the regime in revolution or civil war. (The only other possible cause he mentioned was that a country with a high level of development might be subject to "external domination," e.g., Czechoslovakia.[45] But he did not raise the question, on which Marxist political theory had no handles, of what one socialist state was doing dominating another.)

Macpherson's argument was (1) that scarcity (and the stunting of individuals by an exploitative society) often *necessitates* "coercion not only of those who upheld the old order but also, in some measure and for some time, of those whose support and effort are needed to install the new order"; (2) that this is not a sufficient condition for any advance to full liberty but is a necessary one; and (3) that such an illiberal regime (he offered the examples of new African states) can still make it its business "to develop grass roots participation." But for the purpose of explaining why the latter does not happen, and why resort to the "perverted doctrine" (epitomized by Stalinism) occured in the twentieth century, he argued that the problem was not due to revolutionary theory but "it is due rather to a specific failure of liberal theory, and of those who hold power in the societies which justify themselves by liberal theory, to take account of the concrete circumstances which the growing demand for fuller human realisation has encountered and will encounter." He meant, as we have seen, the bourgeoisie's refusal to "recommend or permit to be taken, the action required to remove [capitalist] impediments."[46]

The question is whether Marxist political theory can be let off the hook in this way. Were he to have taken some *responsibility* for Marxist theory, Macpherson would surely have had to go further to ask, at least, whether the theory of the Leninist vanguard party did not display some internal deficiencies unexplainable by material scarcity and the intransigence of the bourgeoisie. In response to Friedman's complaint that Western social-ists have not "made even a respectable start at developing the institu-tional arrangements that would permit freedom under socialism," Macpherson replied that their time is better spent seeking ways to mini-mize the likelihood of civil war and preventing international antago-nisms during the Cold War. But he agreed that institutional arrangements should not be neglected and immediately went to the heart of the matter: the question of the party. He argued that there should be "no ubiquitous party or that, if there is, such a party should consistently put a very high value on political freedom (which stipulation can scarcely be set out as an institutional arrangement)." In other words, as he baldly put it: "Where there's a will there's a way." So we move from the extreme of economic determinism to the extreme of sheer voluntarism (only conditioned by the "circumstantial forces that are going to shape that will").[47] Only an intellectual who does not see Marxism and its revolutionary project as his personal business can afford such theoretical luxury. (Even then it is hardly likely to be convincing to liberals and thus reduce the likelihood of civil war or the hostility of capitalist states.) To take this stand is to negate the need for Marxist political theory, to reduce it entirely to polit-ical economy on the one hand and ethics on the other.[48]

In a sense, however, all this was beside the point, since Macpherson, for all his explanation of the trajectory of "actually existing socialism" in terms of material scarcity and capitalist resistance, came to reject a Marxist theory of transition at some point in the mid-1960s. He did so not for the faults in it we have been suggesting, but because he came to reject its central ingredient: the theory of class struggle as the agency of change, and of the proletariat as the revolutionary class. Taking at their word the leaders of some new African states in the 1960s, he accepted their claim that their societies were classless and that their one-party systems were appropriate to democracy. He found entirely plausible and worthy their apparent adoption of a Marxian humanist morality combined with their rejection "as applicable to their countries or the contemporary world the Marxian theory of class struggle as the motor of history, nor the theory of the state as essentially an instrument of class domination, both before the proletarian revolution and in the post-revolutionary dictatorship of the proletariat."[49] As for the advanced capitalist societies, one position he took in *The Life and Times* seemed pretty well to sum up his view over the previous decade: that Marx's political theory rests on the premise of the development of capitalism sharpening the class consciousness of the working class and that since there is "little evidence of this in prosperous Western societies today, where it has generally declined since Marx's day," Marx no longer provides "a way out of our vicious circle."[50]

This uncritical attitude toward the rhetoric of African populist leaders, and this despair of the Western working class, certainly entailed a sharp break with Macpherson's earlier writings in the 1950s, where he had analyzed the shortcomings of petit bourgeois radicalism. He argued that a radicalism that emanated only from a perception of unequal exchange at the level of the price system could not penetrate to an understanding of the necessary workings of capitalism as a system of production and could only produce a political thought of oscillation and confusion. He held the view at this time that only those that experienced the fundamental relations of exploitation in capitalist production, i.e., the working class, could evolve a "positive class consciousness," and had in fact done so at crucial historical periods. Moreover, however socially homogeneous a quasi-colonial society appeared in relation to an advanced capitalist society, it could not be described as "classless" so long as it remained "a subordinate part of a mature capitalist economy." And he concluded: "In such a society a one-party state does not even theoretically meet the requirements of democracy."[51]

The outcome of Macpherson's break with this view was that while continuing to employ Marxian political economy in his critique of liberal democracy, he dissociated himself from Marxism when addressing the question of transition to socialism. The result was that he lost the precision that he had credited Marx with introducing to the age-old (pre-liberal) notion of democracy. "The old notion had been rather vague about how the liberation of a class was to be the liberation of humanity. Marx gave it a new precision by relating it to the historical development of systems of production, and particularly of the capitalist system of production. The working class created by capitalism could liberate itself by taking political power."[52] Losing that precision, Macpherson became almost as vague as the age-old tradition. Moreover, he was no longer able to provide a link between the capital–labor relation of exploitation as being at the heart of the "net transfer of powers" and the specification of social forces making for revolutionary change. All this produced a vague conception of the "whole people" of poor nations being exploited by foreign domination (and with the underlying problem apparently being removed "once the imperial power has been driven out"). As for the West, the precise location of the internal contradictions of the system generated by exploitation in the capital–labor relationship was displaced, and Macpherson saw the challenge to the system being mainly *external*, coming specifically from the "moral advantage" of the Soviet Union and the Third World *vis-à-vis* the capitalist liberal democracies.[53]

In *The Life and Times of Liberal Democracy*, Macpherson dropped this "moral advantage" claim. One can only presume that the costs of his idealism became apparent as the "moral advantage" of both the Third World and the USSR did not materialize. Perhaps he took account of some Marxist political economy of Africa.[54] As for the Soviet Union, his judgment became unequivocal: "If a revolution bites off more than it can chew democratically, it will chew it undemocratically."[55] In any case, he put more stress on internal developments in capitalist countries: a growing consciousness of the costs of economic growth; the development of neighborhood and community associations, and movements for democratic participation in the workplace; and a popular doubt about the ability of corporate capitalism to meet consumer expectations, which he explained in terms of traditional "underconsumptionist" crisis theory. There surfaced a strange tension in his argument as it pertained to the Western working class: for on the one hand he argued that established trade union practice did nothing to increase workers' consciousness; on the other hand, he argued (in classical Marxist terms—just having rejected it a few pages before) that the economic crisis of the 1970s was leading to an erosion in earnings and increased trade union militancy and participation in Communist or Socialist parties. "It is to be expected that working class participation in political and industrial action will increase and will be increasingly class conscious."[56]

It is difficult to know what to make of such contradictions, especially in light of the fact that in this book Macpherson finally did turn his attention, albeit very briefly, to the institutional arrangements of "participatory democracy," a democracy still stringently defined in socialist terms, a democracy only possible "in the measure that the capital/labour relation that prevails in our society has been fundamentally changed."[57] He proposed a pyramidal council system of direct democracy at the base and delegate democracy at every level above. And he thought it essential that this be combined with a competing party system which maintains the existing structure of government but relies on the parties themselves to operate by pyramidal participation. Significantly, however, this was a model in which the revolutionary party played no role at all. He envisaged, apparently, that such a system might be introduced by an electoral coalition similar to that which brought Salvador Allende to the presidency of Chile (albeit with clear control of the legislature as well as of the executive). But he made no statement about the necessary internal organization of the parties in the prerevolutionary period and their links with the working class; and he did not specify what role they will have to play in terms of meeting his stipulation that there must be a strong and widespread popular commitment to the "liberal democratic ethic."

Wood was correct to say that Macpherson's political program was "far too sketchy to sustain close analysis."[58] I believe she was also correct, however, when she said that the contradictions in his position resulted from tactical considerations. But the tactical considerations pertained to more than trying to convince the liberals that socialism is their true goal. They also pertained to Macpherson's overly defensive attitude to Marxist political theory, despite the weaknesses of that theory. Let me explain and conclude.

V

Let's face it. The lot of a Marxist political philosopher who attempts to raise seriously the question of the relationship between state and individual in general terms is not a happy one. Whatever one may think about the failings in the Marxist political theory of transition, there can be little doubt that the weakest part of Marxist political theory is its conception of the state in terms that go beyond class-divided society. Marxism simply does not have, as Wood and I have both argued, a very credible theory of the relation between state and individual in socialist and Communist society.[59] The "withering away of the state" appears to excuse Marxism from the necessity of such a theory at all. But it does so only apparently, since the concept of the state employed here is a very special one. It means the state in the sense of an organ of class domination. But amidst inconsistent and loose usages in Marx and Engels, it is clear that they did not see the state only in this way. As Marx once put it (in a passing comment), even in "despotic states, supervision and all-round interference by government involves both the performance of common activities arising from the nature of all communities, and the specific functions arising from the antithesis between the government and the mass of the people."[60] References to the "legitimate functions of the old government power," to "social functions" in Communist society "analogous to present state functions" are not uncommon, but they are not systematically examined in light of the predominant concern with demonstrating that these activities were contained within the primary social function of a class state. The fact that Marx and Engels generally refused to call the public authority they envisaged under full Communism a state, and failed systematically to analyze the possible tensions between individual and state in a classless society, has been unfortunately replicated in most subsequent Marxist literature. It has contributed to the general failure of Marxism to pay more attention to how the political institutions of the transition will develop appropriately for the exercise of public authority in classless society. But the point pertains not just to socialism and Communism. It pertains to the weakness of Marxism in its examination of the relationship between individual and state in those dimensions of class society which nevertheless carry a degree of autonomy from class repression.

All indications—for example, the scattered comments Marx had to make on the question, the writings of two of the genuinely great political theorists of the early twentieth century, Rosa Luxemburg and Antonio Gramsci, the work of both Ralph Miliband and Nicos Poulantzas later in the century—are that to construct such a theory, Marxism will have to incorporate within its problematic those elements of the liberal democratic theory of the state that can be found to be consistent with a non-market, classless society. This is not as impossible as it sounds, since arguably the best of liberal theory assumes a harmonious society to discuss the relationship between individual and state, while merely neglecting, rather than explicitly assuming, "market man." Indeed it is arguable that liberal democratic theory can only truly address the question of the individual and the state in a classless society. This is, after all, what Macpherson was telling us all along.

But the vision of a classless, nonmarket-determined society, and the political strategy to achieve that vision, does not emanate in our era from liberalism; it emanates, "of course," as Macpherson admitted, from

Marxism. And what needs to be done is to incorporate the valuable and non-historically limited insights of liberalism into the Marxist theory of the state under socialism. These elements may be suggested to be (1) aspects of representative and responsible government; (2) an understanding of the state that includes its "performance of common activities arising from the nature of all communities"; and (3) the preservation of the civil liberties so central to liberal theory—freedom of speech, freedom of association, freedom from arbitrary arrest—in order to guarantee for the individual what Macpherson called "Protection Against Invasion by Others" (including the state). All these elements are necessary to construct a viable Marxist theory of the state in general terms as well, a theory which is only hinted at in Marx's statement (which Wood also quotes) that "Freedom consists in converting the state from an organ superimposed upon society into one completely subordinate to it, and today, too, the forms of state are more free or less free to the extent that they restrict the 'freedom of the state.'"[61]

Would it be going too far to suggest that Macpherson was preparing liberal theory for this "raid" by Marxism? One might have wished that, in addition, he had explicitly undertaken the raid himself, concentrating on demonstrating liberalism's strengths to Marxism, as well as Marxism's strengths to liberal democratic theory. But the necessary first step in this would entail subjecting Marxist political theory to a rigorous critique. And one can understand the reluctance of a radical intellectual in the midst of the Cold War, and without the supports of a vibrant Marxist intellectual community or a large-scale socialist movement in his own country, to risk contributing further to the denigration Marxism has generally received in the West by opening up even a comradely critique of Marxist political theory. From the other side, and as was the case for so many others of his generation, the heavy "official" interpretation of Marxism among most Communist parties in the West certainly ensured that any critique of Marxist political theory would be treated as "anti-Soviet," and hence reactionary. All this is entirely apart from any relatively modest individual recoiling at the enormity of the task involved in actually reconstructing Marxist political theory (not least because of the weakness of Marxist political economy of "actually existing socialism" on which he would need to draw).[62] It is scarcely surprising, in these conditions, that the political philosopher who works with Marxist tools might be tempted to shift his attention instead to a critique of that theory—liberalism—which centrally posed the question of the state and the individual, but which ignored or accepted what Marxism pointed to and rejected, that is, the class exploitation and domination inscribed in liberal capitalist society. One works from one's strengths. Unfortunately, this sometimes means that one limits oneself, in classical Fabian fashion, to trying to educate the ruling class, in this case its theorists, to socialism.

By all means, let us "soften up" the enemy when we can. But let us not mistake tactics for strategy, or defense for offense. Let us not forget that if one of Marxism's greatest weaknesses has been its tendency to underestimate the power and value of liberal democracy, one of its greatest strengths has been its ability to pierce the illusion that "those who hold power in the societies which justify themselves by liberal theory" might be persuaded to embrace socialism. To take responsibility for one's Marxism means being intolerant of Marxism's weakness to the end of improving theory and strategy so that those social forces upon which the socialist movement must rely in the struggle for socialist democracy may be better equipped and strengthened. There have been—and there will still be—occasions when proponents of liberal democracy and socialist democracy can coalesce against a common enemy. But this cannot obliterate the difference between them in terms of the goals and interests they represent. The choice between liberal democracy and socialist democracy remains, as it always has been, a choice of sides in a class struggle. We can enrich socialist theory and political practice by recognizing what is valuable in liberal democracy, but we must ensure that in doing so we do not relegate our socialism to the status of a critique of "actually existing liberal democracy," or to being a subordinate aspect in the struggle to preserve either liberal democracy or "actually existing socialism" against reaction. Rather we must incorporate what we can of liberal democracy as a necessary, but not sufficient, element in the politics of socialist renewal.

Notes

1. C. B. Macpherson, "Humanist Democracy and Elusive Marxism," *Canadian Journal of Political Science* (September 1976): 423.

2. For Bendix see especially "Socialism and the Theory of Bureaucracy," *Canadian Journal of Economics and Political Science* 9,3 (1950): 501–14; for Mills, see *The Sociological Imagination* (New York: Oxford University Press, 1959) and *The Marxists* (New York: Dell, 1962); and for Moore, see *Reflections on the Causes of Human Misery* (Boston: Beacon, 1970).

3. Antonio Gramsci, *Selections from the Prison Notebooks*, ed. and trans. by Q. Hoare and G. Nowell-Smith (London: Lawrence and Wishart, 1971), pp. 343–44.

4. C. B. Macpherson, *Democratic Theory: Essays in Retrieval* (Oxford: Clarendon Press, 1973), p. 116 (hereafter *DT*).

5. Victor Svacek, "The Elusive Marxism of C. B. Macpherson," and C. B. Macpherson, "Humanist Democracy and Elusive Marxism," *Canadian Journal of Political Science* 9,3 (September 1976): 394–422, 423–30.

6. Ellen Wood, "C. B. Macpherson: Liberalism and the Task of Socialist Political Theory," in Ralph Miliband and John Saville, eds., *The Socialist Register 1978* (London: Merlin, 1978), pp. 215–40.

7. John Stuart Mill, quoted in C. B. Macpherson, *The Life and Times of Liberal Democracy* (Oxford: Oxford University Press, 1977), p. 48 (hereafter *LT*).

8. Wood, op. cit., pp. 226, 216, 223–24.

9. Ibid., p. 224.

10. C. B. Macpherson, "Do We Need a Theory of the State?" in Macpherson, *The Rise and Fall of Economic Justice and Other Papers* (Oxford: Oxford University Press, 1985), p. 64.

11. *DT*, pp. 66–67. For an interesting critique of Macpherson's distinction between material and nonmaterial, see William Leiss, "Marx and Macpherson: Needs, Utilities, and Self-Development," in Alkis Kontos, ed., *Powers, Possessions and Freedom: Essays in Honour of C. B. Macpherson* (Toronto: University of Toronto Press, 1979), pp. 131ff.

12. "Do We Need a Theory of the State?" p. 61.

13. "Humanist Democracy," p. 424. Macpherson cites *The Political Theory of Possessive Individualism* (Oxford: Oxford University Press, 1962), p. 56; *The Real World of Democracy* (Toronto: Canadian Broadcasting Corporation, 1965), p. 43; *Democratic Theory* (Oxford: Clarendon Press, 1973), 10–14, 16ff., 40–41, 64–66. But see especially p. 67, where the concept of extra-productive powers is discussed.

14. "Post Liberal Democracy," in *DT*, p. 181. Wood (p. 224) cites the article from R. Blackburn, ed., *Ideology in Social Science* (London: Fontana/Collins, 1972), p. 29, where it earlier appeared and remarks (apparently critically) that it was selected as the first in this collection of essays by "radical scholars."

15. "Post Liberal Democracy," p. 182.

16. *LT*, pp. 11, 55. As an indication of Macpherson's consistency regarding this definition of class, see his *Democracy in Alberta*, 2d ed. (Toronto: University of Toronto Press, 1962), p. 225:

> The concept of class which finds the significant determinant of social and political behaviour in the ability or inability to dispose of labour—one's own and others'—demonstrated its value in nineteenth-century historical and sociological analysis, but has been rather scorned of late years. No doubt it is inadequate in its original form to explain the position of the new middle class of technicians, supervisors, managers, and salaried officials, whose importance in contemporary society is very great; yet their class positions can best be assessed by the same criteria: how much freedom they retain over the disposal of their own labour, and how much control they exercise over the disposal of others' labour. Nor is this concept of class as readily amenable as are newer concepts to those techniques of measurement and tabulation which, as credentials, have become so important to modern sociology. Yet it may be thought to remain the most penetrating basis of classification for the understanding of political behaviour. Common relationship to the disposal of labour still tends to give the members of

each class, so defined, an outlook and set of assumptions distinct from those of the other classes.

17. *LT*, pp. 5–6; cf. p. 83ff.
18. Wood (p. 222) counterposed this to Miliband's *State in Capitalist Society* (New York: Basic Books, 1969), although Miliband's approach in this respect was rather similar to Macpherson's (including some common terminology).
19. *LT*, pp. 65–66.
20. Quoted in *LT*, p. 78.
21. *LT*, p. 110.
22. Wood, p. 229.
23. *DT*, pp. 46–47.
24. Wood, p. 220.
25. *DT*, p. 58.
26. *DT*, p. 15 (emphasis added).
27. *LT*, p. 21.
28. "Humanist Democracy," p. 424.
29. See *DT*, pp. 98–99.
30. *DT*, p. 173.
31. "Humanist Democracy," pp. 424–45.
32. *DT*, pp. 72–76, 106–16.
33. "Humanist Democracy," p. 425.
34. "Do We Need a Theory of the State?" p. 62.
35. Wood, p. 217 (emphasis added).
36. *DT*, pp. 111, 113; cf. pp. 73–76, 150–53.
37. *DT*, p. 76.
38. *The Real World of Democracy* (hereafter *RWD*), pp. 12–15.
39. "The Problem of Dictatorship," in Rosa Luxemburg, *The Selected Political Writings* (London: Jonathan Cape, 1972), pp. 244–47.
40. See Jean-Paul Sartre's outstanding elucidation of this tension in *The Ghost of Stalin*, trans. by M. H. Fletcher (New York: George Braziller, 1968), pp. 66–68.
41. *RWD*, pp. 19–20.
42. Ibid., p. 21.
43. *DT*, p. 107.
44. *DT*, pp. 165, 168, 172.
45. *DT*, pp. 151–52.
46. *DT*, pp. 106–7, 115–16.
47. *DT*, pp. 151–53.
48. For my own suggestions, see "Workers Control and Revolutionary Change," *Monthly Review* 29,10 (March 1978), and "The State and the Future of Socialism," *Capital and Class* 11 (Summer 1980), both reprinted in my *Working Class Politics in Crisis* (London: Verso, 1986).
49. *DT*, p. 163.
50. *LT*, pp. 100–101.
51. *Democracy in Alberta*, pp. 225, 245.
52. *RWD*, p. 15.

53. See *RWD*, esp. p. 66, and *DT*, pp. 166–69.

54. Ranging, for instance, in the *Socialist Register* alone, from Giovanni Arrighi and John Saul, "Nationalism and Revolution in Sub-Saharan Africa," in 1969, to Colin Leys, "Capital Accumulation, Class Formation and Dependency—The Significance of the Kenyan Case," in 1978.

55. *LT*, p. 109.

56. *LT*, pp. 102–6.

57. *LT*, p. 111.

58. Wood, p. 218.

59. See Wood, pp. 231–40; and Panitch, "The State and the Future of Socialism," pp. 57ff.

60. *Capital*, vol. 3 (Moscow: Foreign Languages Publishing House, 1959), pp. 376–77.

61. "Critique of the Gotha Programme," in Marx and Engels, *Selected Works*, vol. 3 (Moscow: Progress, 1970), p. 25.

62. For Macpherson's view on how "our lack of knowledge about the inherent properties of the socialist model" presents an "insuperable" difficulty, see *DT*, p. 15. Cf. Stephen Lukes, in Alkis Kontos, ed., *Powers, Possessions and Freedom*, p. 149–52.

4

The Legacy of *The Communist Manifesto* in a Global Capitalism

I

We are living in interesting times. The tide of reactionary neo-liberal "revolution" is still flowing, but with diminishing confidence and force, while the counterflow of progressive feeling and ideas gathers strength but has yet to find effective political expression. As the contradictions of unbridled neo-liberalism become increasingly plain, fewer and fewer people any longer mistake its real character. What *The Communist Manifesto* a hundred and fifty years ago called "stubborn historical facts" are breaking through the illusions fostered by neo-liberal rhetoric—and equally through the pseudo-left illusions of "new times," "radicalism of the center," the "third way" and all similar dreams of a capitalist world miraculously freed from alienation, immiseration, and crises.[1]

At the peripheries of the global economy—in most of Africa, in Central America, in South Asia—historical facts have never permitted most people the luxury of such illusions, even if the elites of these countries embrace and foster them. Such recent experiences as the misery and barbarisms provoked by "structural adjustment" in dozens of countries in Africa, or the rape of the public sector in Mexico, have done nothing to make neo-liberalism more beguiling to ordinary people anywhere in the former Third World. Where the propagandists of the "Washington consensus" did achieve some ideological sway over working people was above all in the North. But there too, after nearly two decades of capitalist restoration, painful reality increasingly prevails over corporate newspeak. The great economic "success" story of the mid- to late 1990s, the United States, rested on an unprecedented reduction in American workers' real incomes over the past quarter century, and throughout the advanced capitalist countries weekly hours worked rose, and so did chronic sickness, and so did crime and the number of people in jail.

Some 40,000 multinational corporations—fifty of them now receiving more revenue than two-thirds of the world's states—frenetically merge, restructure, "re-engineer," "reconfigure," and relocate themselves, in an almost parodic speedup and transnationalization of Karl Marx's famous *Manifesto* script. "Whole populations"—from the women workers in the free trade zones of southern China and northern Mexico to the huge new immigrant workforces of Western Europe and North America—are now "conjured out of the ground" (in Marx's unforgettable phrase) in less than a generation; while others—like older manual workers, and the growing reserve army of young people—are as rapidly conjured back into it again.[2]

All this is becoming clear. Journalists can no longer speak, as they did in the 1980s, of "the business community," as if it were some benign college whose interests were more or less identical to those of the nation as a whole; simply to stay credible they must now talk about "the corporate agenda" and the threat that capitalism (no longer a taboo word) poses to the environment, and about the problems of poverty and homelessness it is creating, the erosion of Social Security and the negative impact on standards of health and education. As Boris Kagarlitsky has remarked: "Reaction is a natural historical phenomenon, but it becomes exhausted just as revolutions do. When this exhaustion sets in, a new phase of revolution can begin."[3] We are still far from witnessing the exhaustion of neo-liberalism, although the symptoms of its fatigue are accumulating (including the inability of parties too ostentatiously identified with it to continue to win elections).[4] Neo-liberalism is already overreaching itself, partly because, as Kagarlitsky also noted, the postwar settlement in the West was underpinned by fear of the Communist threat, and the lifting of this threat removed a significant constraint on capital's political ambitions. Since the collapse of the postwar settlement in the 1970s, capitalists had wanted to "lower expectations," and as neo-liberalism in the West began to emerge, led by Margaret Thatcher and Ronald Reagan, it aimed at breaking the power of organized labor, expanding the scope for capital accumulation through privatization, and replacing collective welfare by entrepreneurship and individualism as the legitimating values of liberal democracy. With the collapse of Communism, however, the project could be pursued even more ruthlessly. Unemployment could be raised to mass levels, public services and welfare programs could be cut more and more drastically, and inequality restored to nineteenth-century levels, without any anxiety about the need to maintain social cohesion in face of the red menace, or to prove to workers in the West that they were as secure as their Soviet bloc counterparts, as well as better paid.[5]

So the social contradictions of capitalist competition returned in force, with mass unemployment through much of the 1980s and early 1990s in the West, ruthless downward pressure on real incomes, and growing class inequalities giving new meaning to the *Manifesto*'s portrait of how "growing competition," "commercial crises," and the "unceasing improvement of machinery" make people's livelihoods "more and more precarious." All this could happen without capital any longer feeling even a lingering vestige of concern about the threat of Communism. But it could not continue without even the Western working class eventually starting to ask themselves again for whose benefit all these sacrifices were being made, and when they would end. There was, in this context, a sharp rise in class awareness, as even *The Economist* noted: "Many commentators think that class is dying, but ordinary people are not convinced. In fact class antagonisms may even be worsening—the proportion of voters believing there is a 'class struggle' in Britain rose from around 60 percent in the early 1960s to 81 percent in the mid-1990s, according to Gallup."[6] And in the United States, a *New York Times* poll in 1996 found that 55 percent of Americans now defined themselves as working class, while only 36 percent defined themselves as middle class, a major reversal of the traditional American pattern.[7] By the mid-1990s, general strikes in France, the USA, and Canada once more occupied the front pages, as did "IMF riots" throughout much of the former Third World from Zimbabwe to Mexico. And by 2000, while the image of American steelworkers joining young anarchists in anticapitalist protest on the streets of Seattle was still fresh in people's minds, there were more general strikes in Argentina, Nigeria, South Africa, India, and South Korea.

II

To see the outlines of a new period of class struggle taking shape, however, is not the same thing as seeing clearly how to engage in it; and it remains true that the left has been severely disempowered and disorganized by the scope and ruthlessness of the capitalist restoration and the effects of global deregulation. The independent Left, the militant activists in both the trade unions and the new social movements who have with-stood the pressures to capitulate to market hegemony, are a potentially far more significant force than the Right likes to pretend. But there is nonetheless an acute sense, within this left, of a political *absence*: the lack of a capacity to go beyond "networking," beyond pluralism (hard-won and rightly cherished as that is), to find new ways to give coherence and strategic direction to collective efforts to mobilize and make effective the developing reaction *against* the market, *against* capital.

It is this widespread sense of a political absence that continues to make the legacy of the *Communist Manifesto* especially relevant ten years after the demise of the "actually existing" Communist regimes and parties. It is important to recall that the *Manifesto*, while drafted by Marx, was "the product of an extended and intense but open debate among committed communist-internationalists" who were trying to fashion political organizations through which the collective efforts of the working classes to understand and confront the major problems of their time could cohere and have greater effect.[8] The eventual result was the mass working-class parties of the late nineteenth century; and so much did these become part of the political landscape that it is easy to forget that such autonomous political organizations of the subordinate classes were an entirely new historical phenomenon, and that it took the better part of a half-century, after the defeats of 1848, to make them a reality. By the time of the *Manifesto's* centenary in 1948, Social Democratic and Communist parties were among the leading forces on the world's political stage. Nevertheless, it was because these parties no longer embodied the radical legacy of the *Manifesto* that so many of the "1968 generation," only two decades later, not only rejected these particular parties, but eventually came to doubt the appropriateness of the "party" as a political form.

Yet most people who are active in political and social struggles today feel the need for something that will perform some essential tasks that used to be performed by parties. This confirms Cynthia Cockburn's premonition in the 1970s that, for all the exciting and energetic pluralism of the new community movements, there was something lacking; that their struggles, if conceived apart from "an arena of conflict between the dominant and exploited class," would be in danger of failing to cohere despite their proximity to each other

> within the working class and its near neighbours. . . . They shake out as tenants, ratepayers, teenage youth, house owners, swimming enthusiasts and

squatters. All are asked to compete and defend their special interests, while the class with real power remains untouched.[9]

The necessity of going "beyond the fragments," while not replicating the defects of the old parties or their sectarian offshoots, was already being argued brilliantly by Rowbotham, Segal, and Wainwright by the end of the 1970s;[10] but the "articulation" actually achieved between social movements and progressive trade unions—in forms that ranged from the Rainbow Coalition in the United States and the Action Canada Network in Canada to the Anti-GATT/WTO Movement in India and the Opposition to the Devastation Caused by the World Bank/IMF in Sri Lanka—have consisted mainly of "popular front"-style strategic networking between the top leaderships of the various organizations. What has, until very recently at least, been missing—and this has been increasingly felt by many social movement leaders themselves—is something that would be more than the sum of the parts, something which the Social Democratic and Communist parties did partly provide in their heyday.

This is, at one level, simply a matter of offering electoral alternatives. The century-long frustration that American political activists have experienced through being unable to translate political agitation and mobilization into meaningful electoral choices is now strongly felt elsewhere; the accommodation of the old Communist and Social Democratic parties in Europe to the neo-liberal agenda—epitomized now by "New" Labour in Britain—is giving activists there a taste of what the absence of a mass working-class party in the U.S.A. has meant throughout this century, and was witnessed in spades there again in the election of 2000.[11]

But it is much more than a matter of what to do on election day. It is about all the things Marx had in mind when he wrote that the "immediate aim" of all proletarian parties was the "formation of the proletariat into a class." These include providing activists with a strategic, ideological, and educational vehicle; a political home which is open to individuals to enter (rather than restricted, as today's social movement networking often is, to representatives of groups); a political community which explicitly seeks to transcend particularistic identities while supporting and building on the struggles they generate; and through all these things, serving as the incubator of a new social force, providing a structure but also an agency which expresses the preexisting range of identities while also expanding them—"helping to organize what it claims to represent," as Margaret Keck aptly put it in relation to the Workers' Party of

Brazil[12]—and which in doing so achieves the capacity to "make history." This, at any rate, is what Marx meant by "revolutionising praxis," by "the alteration of men on a mass scale"—and what a new socialist party today must be able to do.

The "formation of the proletariat into a class" is, moreover, not something that, once attempted and even partially accomplished, is then finished; the working class, once "made," is not "fixed and frozen," as imagined by traditionalists who cling to every cultural as well as socioeconomic encrustation—nor as imagined by modernizers (and "post-modernizers") who abandon the working class as hopelessly outdated and unchangeable and go in search of more fashionable agencies. New parties have already arisen and more will arise, profoundly conscious of how much they need to be different from the old Social Democratic and Communist parties if they are to form today's proletariat into a new class, a class once again capable of making history. But "making history" in what sense? A discriminating view of the *Manifesto* and its legacy is needed in this respect.

III

We need to ask, first of all, what the nature of the revolutionary message of the *Manifesto* was, as opposed to the way it has been understood, especially by its critics. It was certainly above all a revolutionary document, and it has always been taken as calling for a political revolution as a prelude to a social and economic one. But while the October Revolution has been seen as a response to its call, and Stalinism as a logical consequence, it is worth reminding ourselves that this is not true.

The revolution Marx called for (and thought inevitable) was a revolution in social relations. Marx, like all his contemporaries, had the example of the French Revolution sixty years earlier very much in mind, and thought a new political revolution—"the forcible overthrow of existing conditions"—would be necessary in order to achieve the social revolution in most countries, given the predictable resistance that would be offered by the bourgeoisie and its allies to any fundamental change in relations of production. Only in 1872—twenty-four years after writing the *Manifesto*—did he cautiously allow that in countries with long traditions of democracy (like the United States, Britain, and perhaps the Netherlands) the workers might "attain their goal by peaceful means."[13] In later writings Marx was also apt to put more stress on the possibility of revolution spreading to the capitalist heartlands from the system's unstable "extremities"; and, as Shanin and others have pointed out, since he was often impatient for action, he backed the revolutionary wing of the Russian populists against their proto-Menshevik opponents, even though this was not fully consistent with his analysis in the main body of his work, whether the *Manifesto* of 1848, or the *Grundrisse* written in the late 1850s, or *Capital* completed in the mid-1860s. What this did show, however, was that he did not believe that all peoples were fated to tread an identical path to socialism.[14]

Revolutions in the "periphery" would, evidently, also be more or less violent. Marx's attitude to this was practical. The right of revolution—"the only really historical right," as Friedrich Engels put it just before his death in 1895, "the only right on which all modern states rest"—was a democratic right, the right of the majority to make their own history; it would be exercised peaceably if possible, forcibly if not.[15] Marx's profoundest political commitment was to this democratic right, as his subsequent idealization of the Paris Commune of 1870 as exemplifying an unprecedentedly radical kind of democracy also makes clear; it was from the opponents of socialism that he anticipated violence, and not without cause.

Having said this, it remains true that there was also an unresolved tension in Marx's attitude, reflected in the concept of "proletarian dictatorship." On the one hand it meant, for him, "democracy carried to its fullest" (with the Commune as its example), in the sense of the majority class becoming the ruling class for the first time in history; on the other hand, it meant a period of centralized and repressive rule entailing strict measures to defeat the old ruling classes and prevent counterrevolution. Marx spent little time thinking about the risk that coercion might become institutionalized and overwhelm the democratic dimension of the revolution. Yet this was to become a tragically familiar pattern in the twentieth century. As Isaac Deutscher, reflecting on the October Revolution, put it:

Every revolutionary party at first imagines that its task is simple: it has to suppress a "handful" of tyrants or exploiters. It is true that usually the tyrants and exploiters form an insignificant minority. But the old ruling class has not lived in isolation from the rest of society. In the course of its long domination it has surrounded itself by a network of institutions embracing groups and individuals in many classes; and it has brought to life many attachments and loyalties which even a revolution does not destroy alto-

gether. . . . The revolution therefore treats its enemy's immediate neigh-
bour as its enemy. When it hits this secondary enemy, the latter's neigh-
bour, too, is aroused and drawn into the struggle. The process goes on like
a chain reaction until the party of the revolution arouses against itself and
suppresses all the parties which until recently crowded the political
scene.[16]

Evidently, the subsequent history of the twentieth century has produced
no easy answers to this conundrum. But it is no answer at all to take the
obduracy of capitalists and their allies as a sufficient reason for the majority to abandon their only "really historical right."

Even in the conditions of a capitalist democracy the question of how
the state's capacity for repression can be overcome by a mobilized
majority bent on exercising its historical right remains as difficult to
answer today as it was a hundred years ago when Engels, just before
he died, grappled with it in the text already quoted. Anticipating
Antonio Gramsci, Engels argued that in Europe the insurrectionary
strategies of 1848 had become obsolete by the nineteenth century's end.
The conditions of struggle had essentially changed, he noted, partly
due to technical reasons: the modern city with its broad boulevards, the
modern army with its firepower. But more fundamentally, the
conditions of struggle had changed because the conditions of
hegemony had changed. "Even in the classic time of street fighting . . .
the barricade produced more of a moral than a material effect. It was a
means for shaking the steadfastness of the military." By 1849, however,
when the bourgeoisie had everywhere "thrown in its lot with the
governments. . . . [T]he spell of the barricade was broken; the soldiers
no longer saw behind it 'the people' but rebels, agitators, plunderers,
levellers, the scum of society."[17] Now, almost fifty years later, Engels
was convinced that "an insurrection with which all sections of the
people sympathize will hardly recur; in the class struggle all the
middle strata will probably never group themselves round the
proletariat so exclusively that in comparison the party of reaction
gathered round the bourgeoisie will well-nigh disappear." But he did
believe that the growth of the mass working-class party in Germany by
1895 was such that, operating legally, it had a chance of winning over
the middle strata; and, in any case, "to shoot a party which numbers
millions out of existence is too much even for all the magazine rifles of
Europe and America."

> The time of surprise attacks, of revolutions carried through by small con-
> scious minorities at the head of unconscious masses, is past. Where it is a
> question of a complete transformation of the social organisation, the masses
> themselves must also be in it, must themselves already have grasped what
> is at stake, what it is they are going for, body and soul. The history of the last
> 50 years has taught us that. But in order that the masses may understand
> what is to be done, long persistent work is required.[18]

Unfortunately, Engels immediately went on to treat electoral successes
as evidence of this mass mobilization, as if the entry of Social Democrats
into national governments, or even the election of municipal councillors,
meant that the masses were really "in it."[19] A century of experience of the
"parliamentary road to socialism" has taught us better.

A further problem with the *Manifesto*'s legacy is that it says very little
about politics after the revolution, and this is also true of Marx's later
writings. His attitude was summed up in the position he ascribed to the
working-class Communards who, he said, had "no ready-made utopias,"
but knew they must pass "through long struggles, through a series of historic processes, transforming circumstances and men."[20] In this he was
surely right. But his resistance to blueprints kept Marx from addressing
the question of what kind of institutional structures socialist democracy
would require and left him open to the charge, advanced by a long line
of critics from Mikhail Bakunin onwards, that simply to declare "when
class distinctions have disappeared" political conflict would disappear
too ("the public power will lose its political character," as the *Manifesto*
puts it) was a perfect rationalization for the permanent dictatorship of an
elite ruling in the name of the workers.

This criticism plainly fails to appreciate the whole thrust of Marx's
approach; but it is true that for Marx simply to imagine a harmonious col-
laboration among all "the associated producers" was indeed to beg fundamental questions about the kind of democratic politics that would be
possible and necessary in a world from which the private ownership of
the means of production would have been abolished, but in which manifold other differences among people would remain. And it is also true
that Marx seriously overestimated, in the *Manifesto* and later, the extent to
which the class structure would be simplified, the "middle classes"
squeezed out and marginalized and the global working class itself
homogenized. Things were not going to be simplified in the way he
imagined.

But we have to keep a sense of historical proportion. The complex problems that were faced by the new mass working-class parties—including major divisions of interest within the working classes themselves, the rise of the professional middle class, and much else—could hardly be worked through in advance by Marx. In tackling these problems, however, the mass parties—the Communist and Social Democratic parties which so greatly influenced the history of the last century—failed to sustain Marx and Engels's distinctive political practice: the combination of social-scientific analysis, based on their materialist interpretation of history, with engaged political writing and speaking—pamphlets, lectures, articles, addresses, reports, letters—in which they tried to make current history intelligible to activists in such a way that they themselves could draw from the experience of their struggles the lessons they contained, and be better able to try to "make their own history." Instead, Social Democrats and Communists increasingly resorted to treating Marx's ideas as a text, a body of findings, either to be followed as dogma (subject to constant quasi-theological reinterpretation) in the case of the Communists, or to be rejected (after repeated revisions) in the case of the Social Democrats. And this was even more true of the numerous small revolutionary groups whose political impact has been marginal (even if their role in developing remarkable activists and intellectuals should not be underestimated).

It was to avoid this that both Marx and Engels often declared their opposition to all attempts to elevate their ideas into a "system," and insisted that their conception of history was "above all a guide to study" and that "all history must be studied afresh"; but very few people in either the Communist or the Social Democratic parties have done this in the way Marx and Engels did it themselves. As vehicles for socialism, however, these parties have in any case run their course; the true political legacy of the *Manifesto*—to develop a politics concerned above all with ensuring that the masses really are "in it"—remains to be taken up again by others.

IV

To say this is to go against the current of much so-called leftist thought and practice over the past two decades. After what can now be seen as a very brief spell of attempting to renew Marxism in the wake of 1968 we have gone through a period since the early 1980s when not only was the idea that "Marxism is over" quite widespread among people who still defined themselves as being on the left,[21] but the very idea of socialism as a systematic alternative to capitalism was dubbed an "anachronistic irrelevance."[22] The resulting vacuum has been filled by Social Democratic "modernizers" whose egalitarian commitments are even weaker than those of postwar Social Democracy in the West.

It is of the utmost importance to assess the reasons for this, as three major recent historical surveys of the twentieth century have sought to do. Eric Hobsbawm's *Age of Extremes* portrays the trajectory of socialism as largely determined by the necessary forced march to industrialization in that part of the underdeveloped world where Communist revolutions occurred. Capitalism's powerful tendencies to globalization eroded the determination and capacity of the authoritarian elite in control of those systems to avoid integration into the capitalist order; while the same forces of globalization also undermined the policies as well as the party and trade union organizations through which Social Democracy in the West had presided over the "golden age" of the mixed economy in the postwar era. Hobsbawm cannot see any alternative to the path followed either by the Communist or Social Democratic parties. The tragedy of the October Revolution was that it could produce only a ruthless, brutal command socialism. The tragedy of Social Democracy was that the Keynesian welfare state could not withstand the corrosive forces of capitalist globalization.

For all its brilliance, Hobsbawm's argument is also remarkably contradictory. He insists that the failure of Soviet socialism does not reflect on the possibilities of other kinds of socialism; yet he also contends "that it may well be that the debate which confronted capitalism and socialism as mutually exclusive and polar opposites will be seen by future generations as a relic of the twentieth-century Cold Wars of Religion." Insofar as this is the case, one might expect him not only to proclaim the virtues of the Social Democratic project, but also to provide some grounds for its revival. But far from doing this, he declares he has no solutions to offer, no way out of the process of the erosion of the nation-state and democratic politics by capitalist globalization, no way of halting the process wherein "human collective institutions had lost control over the collective consequences of human action."[23]

It is noteworthy that the actual policies and programs of the parties and labor movements of the Left figure hardly at all in Hobsbawm's text. The rise and fall of the golden age seem determined almost entirely by the dynamics and cycles of capital accumulation. This gap has been filled, however, by the publication of Donald Sassoon's *One Hundred Years of Socialism*, a work of almost 1,000 pages, warmly praised by Hobsbawm, which focuses on the Western European Left in the second half of the century. Sassoon writes very much from the perspective of the accommodation to capitalist globalization represented by the Blairite "modernisers" in Britain, the "renovadores" in Spain, the "riformisti" in Italy, the "nouveaux réalistes" in Belgium. He sees them as building on and completing the revisionist tradition, from Eduard Bernstein's *Evolutionary Socialism* at the end of the nineteenth century to Anthony Crosland's *Future of Socialism* and the Bad Godesburg program of the German SPD at the midpoint of the twentieth century. Summarizing his views in the *Guardian*, Sassoon writes that the abandonment of the old class politics and public ownership goals by today's modernizers finally delivers

> socialists of a utopian albatross. Capitalism is not a particular transitory historical phase in historical development but a mode of production. The task of socialists lies in devising a political framework which enables the advancement of certain values, such as justice and equality, while ensuring that the regulatory system does not seriously impair the viability of capitalism.[24]

Sassoon is right to connect Tony Blair to Bernstein, but there was nevertheless something very different about the old revisionists. They thought that capitalism was tending toward state collectivism and managerialism, and that this undermined the anarchic and inegalitarian tendencies of capitalist markets and confirmed and reinforced the reformist strategies of Social Democracy. But in recent decades capitalism has moved in the opposite direction from the one they expected and predicted. It is the arguments of the Marxist critics of revisionism, from Rosa Luxemburg to Ralph Miliband, who insisted that capitalism would eventually revert to a competitive and inegalitarian market logic, that are being confirmed today. All that is left linking today's modernizers with their revisionist predecessors is their accommodation to the dynamics of capitalism. Whereas Bernstein and Crosland had believed that this accommodation could yield a more planned and egalitarian social order, today's modernizers know (and they mince no words in saying so) that this means accommodating to an ever more competitive and market-driven one.

In light of the modernizers' claim to be free of all old illusions, it is worth recalling that much Social Democratic opinion in the 1950s was inspired by the same idea—the idea that it had become irrelevant to pose alternatives within the framework of "socialism versus capitalism." The difference lay in the optimistic register in which the theme of reconciliation between capitalist markets and socialist values was then expressed. Anthony Crosland's *Future of Socialism*, first published in 1956, famously encapsulated the thinking of a whole generation of Social Democratic leaders and intellectuals in Western capitalist countries. It opened with the argument that the postwar "transformation of capitalism" had, once and for all, proved the Marxist analysis of capitalism wrong. According to Crosland, the postwar world had witnessed three "fundamental changes in the social framework" which no act of parliament could undo: (1) in the political sphere, a "peaceful revolution" had transformed the state, so that "the capitalist class has lost [its] commanding position" with governments; (2) in social relations and social attitudes there had been a "decisive shift" of class power toward the working class at the expense of business; and (3) in the economy, there was a fundamental change in the nature of the business class whereby "the economic power of the capital market and the finance houses, and hence *capitalist* financial control over industry (in the strict sense of the word) are . . . much weaker. This change alone makes it rather absurd to speak now of a capitalist ruling class."[25]

In making this case, Crosland refused to adopt what he called "the current fashion" of sneering at Marx. Marx, in his view, was "a towering giant among socialist thinkers" whose work made the classical economists "look flat, pedestrian and circumscribed by comparison. . . . [O]nly moral dwarfs, or people devoid of imagination, sneer at men like that." That said, he was convinced that Marx's writings had "little or nothing to offer the contemporary socialist" because they related to "conditions that had long since passed." Yet it is obvious today that what Crosland took as fundamental conditions were in fact temporary—conditions that have long since disappeared. In almost every respect, the analysis of the *Manifesto* is today more relevant and less anachronistic than Crosland's text, written over a century later.

Yet despite the passing of the conditions on which Crosland built his case, today's modernizers are apt not only to sneer at Marx, but to denigrate anyone with the temerity to suggest the need for an anticapitalist strategy. The vacuum that modernization as a political project represents was revealed by Sassoon amidst a detailed discussion of the French Socialist party's retreat in the 1980s:

> To give up the ambition of abolishing capitalism . . . is not much of a strate-gy. Modernization as a slogan sounds appealing, but it has done so for over a hundred years. No party of the Left in post-war Europe (and hardly any party of the Right) has ever been against modernization. One suspects the watchword, devoid as it is of any practical content, is used purely symboli-cally: to be for modernization means to be for progress without abolishing capitalism.[26]

Yet this is precisely where Sassoon ends up. Like the modernizers, Sassoon directs his strongest criticisms at those who do not appear to be sufficiently "aware" of the limits global markets impose on an anticapi-talist strategy. To be sure, he does not want to join in "the supine endorse-ment of the neo-liberal glorification of the market" and he approvingly quotes John Maynard Keynes as saying that "capitalism is a beast to be tamed," but he offers no means of doing this, merely endorsing the mod-ernizers' strategies.

In sharp contrast, Gabriel Kolko's no less remarkable *Century of War* stresses the mistaken *choices* Communist and Social Democratic parties made, rather than treating their choices as inevitable, as Hobsbawm and Sassoon tend to do. Kolko attributes the mistakes to weaknesses of analy-sis as well as of organization and leadership:

> Their consistent failure to redeem and significantly (as well as permanently) transform societies when in a position to do so is testimony to their analytic inadequacies and the grave, persistent weaknesses of their leadership and organizations. It is this reality that has marginalized both social democracy and communism in innumerable nations since 1914, providing respites through the century to capitalist classes and their allies that otherwise would never have survived socialist regimes that implemented even a small frac-tion of the reforms outlined in their program.[27]

While this may bend the stick too far the other way, it is, indeed, only by coming to terms with these mistakes of analysis and strategy that we can begin to delineate an alternative to global capitalism. Social Democrats, no less than Communists, need to face up to their failed analyses and strategies and models, to come to terms with the fact that they were wrong in following Crosland in identifying the "golden age of capitalism" with "the future of socialism."

But the fact that Crosland was so obviously wrong does not make Marx right. To be sure, one increasingly finds today alert columnists once more affirming that Marx was right about the nature of capitalism, and the sneering dismissals of Marxist analysis that became so common in the 1980s are less often heard in the media now.[28] This kind of superficial "rediscovery" of Marx must not divert us, however, from addressing the real conundrums of socialism as they were experienced in the twentieth century; and we must also guard against any tendency to revert to that idiom of the revolutionary Left in which fundamental questions were systematically evaded, on the assumption that if the *Manifesto*, or Marx's other writings, didn't pose these questions, let alone solve them, they could be disregarded. Drawing on the legacy of the *Manifesto* today means treating it not as a sacred text, but first and foremost as an inspiration to construct a political agenda for our own time.

V

An agenda: hardly the term that comes most readily to mind for describing the *Manifesto*, certainly not its brilliant part 1, written in the style of an epic prose poem on the rise and impending fall of the capitalist world. Yet this was exactly the point: "more or less history has got to be related in it," as Engels prosaically noted (perhaps not yet aware of the full extent of his friend's literary powers), shortly before Marx was to begin writing.[29] In other words, the most fundamental political legacy of the *Manifesto* is that any serious agenda must first include a materialist analysis of contemporary history.

What this means for us now is, first of all, coming to a clear understanding of the twentieth century's passages through uneven development to "globalization." The *Manifesto* foreshadowed, with an accuracy that still astonishes, the "universal inter-dependence of nations" which it has been the business of our century to realize: "All old-established industries have been destroyed or are daily being destroyed ... dislodged by new industries ... whose products are consumed ... in every quarter of the globe. ... The bourgeoisie ... compels all nations, on pain of extinction, to adopt the bourgeois mode of production ... to introduce what it calls civilisation into their midst." What Marx could not specify, of course, was the precise pattern this complex and violent process would actually take in the twentieth century, now blocked, now rushing head-long, through world wars, television, electronic banking, and the ham-burger.

It has also taken a lot longer than he seems to have imagined; with world population increasing more than fivefold since Marx's time, it was only in the decades *following* the first centenary of the *Manifesto* (when world population had already reached 2.5 billion) that a majority of the world's people ceased to be peasants in the traditional sense and whole populations around the globe were transformed into urban or rural (semi-)proletarians.[30] This goes far toward explaining the spatial pattern of reform and revolution in the twentieth century. In Arrighi's insightful formulation, the "social power" which labor enjoys because it is indis-pensable to capitalist production was concentrated in the West and made reformism rewarding, while the immiseration which made for revolution (especially in the former Russian and Chinese empires) was concentrated at the "periphery."[31]

This was partly a question of imperialism, as Engels, Lenin, and many later theorists argued; cheap food and raw materials and other forms of surplus transfer from the periphery contributed significantly to the living standards of Western workers, and imperialist ideology and racism rein-forced bourgeois hegemony. Other factors were also involved, however. Down to the 1960s it remained possible for the organized Western work-ing class to make major gains through wage bargaining with employers who had limited opportunities to relocate, and to extract reforms from the governments of industrialized economies. It was not till after 1945 that the transnational corporation (TNC), developed in the interwar years, became generalized, and not until the 1980s that, with the aid of computerization, the TNCs realized their full potential for worldwide control of production and finance. Social changes at the periphery creat-ed more and more centers with the requisite externalities for advanced production (security, transport, communications, an elite of high-tech workers, and a supply of disciplined semiskilled wage labor); changes in the labor process reduced dependence on established labor forces, while a decline in the material element in manufactured goods and falling transport costs increasingly eroded older forms of "natural protection"; the end of the formal empires in the 1960s, followed by the end of the Soviet system, opened up the whole planet to capitalist penetration. The result of all these changes was that the extraction and realization of *rela-tive* surplus value finally became possible for capital on a global scale—if not exactly everywhere, at least somewhere in many parts of every continent and subcontinent—in a way that earlier forms of imperialism had not established.

The longer-run political implications of this, however, are very hard to read. What are the implications, for instance, of the fact that nearly *one billion* people around the world, according to the International Labor Organization (ILO), were unemployed or underemployed in the mid-1990s, at a time moreover when Chinese government reports were projecting *hundreds of millions* of "surplus" workers in rural areas by the year 2000, and just before East Asia, the region of the world that has been the preeminent magnet for the West's surplus capital, was plunged into crisis?[32] Or of the fact that whereas the International Monetary Fund (IMF) line of credit which the British government needed to prevent an economic collapse in 1976 was $4 billion (at the time the largest ever requested), the sum needed to do the same job for Mexico in 1994 was $48 billion, while for South Korea in 1997 even $60 billion was not enough. Experts cannot predict when or where the next financial crisis will strike, or the next natural disaster. When we contemplate all this we need to remember that it does not represent the planned outcome of a corporate agenda: there is a political project for capital, and it does involve driving down living standards in what used to be called the Second and Third Worlds as well as the First. But in the North as well as the South, capital is, as always, driven as much as it is driving. It is being driven by the unrelenting competition between capitals in each sector as well as by the global financial markets which not only impel capital to downsize, merge, reconfigure, restructure, and relocate, but also furnish the means of doing so: the increasingly dramatic and unpredictable results are anything but planned.

It was not only Social Democrats like Crosland who could not have been more wrong on the decline of the financial element in the capitalist class, but also all those, including John Kenneth Galbraith, who thought they saw a new technocratic industrial elite coming to manage the economies of the world. Instead, the *Manifesto's* image of the capitalist as "the sorcerer, who is no longer able to control the powers of the nether world whom he has called up by his spells" captures all too well the concerns increasingly expressed by significant elements of the international establishment—from advocates of the Nobel-laureate economist James Tobin's proposal for a tax on foreign exchange transactions to admirers of billionaire investor George Soros's musings about the pitfalls of unbridled self-interest in the open society—that some means must be found of regulating the chaos of contemporary capitalism. This is why the first item on the Left's agenda today has to be that of relating every national experience to the widest possible analysis of the accelerating and increasingly uncontrolled contradictions of the global accumulation process. What certainly will become clear, from such analyses, is that through the processes of globalization, the "social power" of Western labor has declined and impoverishment—or the threat and fear of it— has returned. The "Chinese walls" that are now being battered down by cheap goods are no longer only the precapitalist social structures at the periphery, but also those protecting high wages and welfare-state bene- fits of all workers—including those in the West—with no more than average skills from a global standpoint.[33] The world taken as a whole has indeed now begun to resemble the pattern Marx's logic led him to foresee, and the conditions that used to sustain Western workers' reformism are being undermined.

What might replace that reformism is very hard even to imagine. Throughout the postwar era everyone assumed that a return to mass unemployment would lead to a loss of legitimacy for capitalism; even the Western bourgeoisie delayed turning to unemployment as a means of stemming inflation and driving down the price of labor and, even when it did, it watched with apprehension to see how high unemploy- ment had to go before the back of wage militancy was broken. But the legitimacy of capitalism was not brought into question. Many workers saw that they were dependent on "the goose that laid the golden egg"[34] and accepted the case the goose's owners made for making it well again. They were unfortunately encouraged in this by post-Fordist intellectuals who saw in flexible specialization the path to a new regime of accumulation. Most leaders and activists were less prepared to accept the capitalists' arguments and insisted on the continued viability of the old Keynesian and corporatist arrangements; in effect, they struggled to defend the old managed capitalism. This should not have been surpris- ing: workers have often confronted new insecurities by appealing to idealized memories of earlier times, recalling "the shadowy image of a benevolent corporate state";[35] and in this they too were encouraged by some Social Democratic intellectuals who fostered the illusion that sta- bility could be had by clinging to (or imitating) Swedish or German or Austrian corporatism.

After two decades, however, we are at a new conjuncture. Neither the dream of a post-Fordist future nor that of a safe return to the neo-corporatist past is any longer tenable; even during the American boom of the late 1990s, it became more and more obvious that there would be no magic moment when prosperity is felt to be safely restored, unaccompanied by constant demands for still further rounds of sacrifice. Yet at the same time struggles to bring back the Keynesian welfare state have less and less meaning for young people who never knew it, or even for their parents who have ceased to believe in it. It inevitably took some time for the dynamics of neo-liberalism to become familiar and to be seen as normal phenomena of capitalism in the era of globalization, but it has happened. On the other hand, to understand neo-liberalism objectively does not necessarily induce fatalism. On the contrary, a good many workers, as we have seen, are recognizing that they are willy-nilly trapped in a class struggle and are once again blaming the economic system for their situation.

That said, what is still absent is any concrete notion of an alternative system. People in the former Communist countries are learning firsthand that capitalist streets are not necessarily paved with gold;[36] but they, like many workers in the old Third World, have no other model of well-being than that of the Western consumer portrayed by the media. Yet there can still be no other way forward for working people anywhere than once more building movements oriented to ending the rule of private property—beginning with imposing effective controls on capital mobility through cooperation between national governments with a popular mandate to do so, and democratizing control over the major means of production, distribution, communication, and exchange.

And here the historic failure of Bolshevism weighs like a nightmare on the brains of the living. The Russian and Chinese revolutions and their aftermaths dominated the last century; their brute achievements in face of the bitterest odds, the courage and intelligence they mobilized and consumed, the hopes they raised and ultimately disappointed, the immense human costs—the memory of all this is now an extra barrier that the anticapitalist struggle has to overcome. Giving our goals their proper name—full democracy—will not prevent them from being called Communist. But the effect of that association will not forever be negative if we can figure out how to make our commitment to democracy genuine and our goals for it viable.

VI

"To win the battle of democracy": this is what the *Manifesto* saw as the first step in the revolution, the primary condition for establishing the political supremacy of the working class.

In the established liberal democracies opinion polls show that representative party politics have never been more despised, and the connection between genuine democracy and an equitable distribution of social and economic power is becoming clear in a way not seen, perhaps, since the struggles for franchise extension in the last century. This is hardly surprising. Not only have national governments enhanced the power of "market forces" to determine their citizens' economic fates, but as extreme inequality has been restored and welfare-state protections have been stripped away, they have also done their best to close down avenues for popular forces to oppose the process, let alone reverse it. Presidential decrees of dubious constitutionality override parliamentary majorities; legislation curtailing democratic rights is pushed through, contrary to preelection promises; the powers of local government are usurped; the powers of the police are extended, the powers of juries curtailed; and political parties—including, now, the old Social Democratic parties (including those called Socialist or Labour) and the new "Democratic Left" ex-Communist ones—are themselves "modernized," i.e., power is taken away from their mass membership and given to small groups of professional politicians ("people who make a business of politics") and their market-savvy, media-oriented advisers.[37]

Disillusion has also rapidly overtaken the much-touted globalization of "liberal democracy," the so-called "third wave" democratization announced by Samuel Huntington and other apologists for neo-liberalism. As often as not it has turned out to mean "no more than a military despotism and a police state, bureaucratically carpentered, embellished with parliamentary forms" (as Marx said of 1875 Germany).[38] And in any case, international agencies are ready to intervene to ensure that elections do not get in the way of the interests of global capital: within a few short weeks in November–December 1997 the IMF extracted public undertakings from all the leading candidates in the South Korean presidential elections *before* the poll that they would abide by the liberalizing conditions of an IMF loan—without which an economic disaster was categorically promised.[39] Perry Anderson's comment is, if anything, an understatement: "Democracy is indeed now more widespread than ever. But it is also thinner—as if the more universally available it becomes, the less active meaning it retains."[40]

A further dimension of the emasculation of democracy everywhere is the importance of the mass media. Here the legacy of the *Manifesto* is not of much help. Marx recognized that "the class which has the means of material production at its disposal, has control at the same time over the means of mental production, so that thereby generally speaking, the ideas of those who lack the means of mental production are subject to it."[41] But he also thought a revolutionary class could create its own means of mental production; and while for a time they did so with their publishing houses and newspapers, he did not foresee the way mass-circulation newspapers would become essentially vehicles for selling advertisements, and would in this way eventually bankrupt progressive newspapers that could not raise equivalent advertising revenue.[42] Nor could he foresee how this would be repeated on an even more spectacular scale with radio and television after other means of communication—and especially the public meeting, which was still the key popular medium of communication in Marx's time—had become so much less effective.

The fact is that in most countries of the world the main conversation of society now takes place through a medium—television—from which issues of public concern are increasingly displaced in favor of entertainment and sport, and from which, when public affairs are discussed, Left perspectives are often deliberately excluded.[43] This change—whereby not only has public conversation been commodified, but a medium has been developed that increasingly gives a monopoly of public conversation to capital—has to be one of the most politically critical developments of the last century; yet the Left has still fully to register its immense significance and develop a commensurate response. Possible solutions exist: broad public access to mainstream media and to the Internet is not the stuff of fantasy but a democratic necessity, for which institutional models already exist in various countries in Europe, in particular.[44] It is high time to make it a nonnegotiable element in a mass campaign for the restoration of democratic rights.

But this is only a beginning. Contrary to the interested arguments of the "professional representative" class (as Raymond Williams aptly called it), periodic elections—absolutely fundamental as they are—are anything but the only practicable democratic institution that a complex modern society requires. There is a rich legacy of genuinely democratic theory—and of practical experience, from the Paris Commune through

Italian Council Communism to the "social movement" organizations and experiments (East and West, South and North) of our own times—that has still to be assimilated. The range of possibilities is vast, including various kinds of monitoring, reporting, and accountability without which elections alone are ineffective as a means of controlling power; deliberative democratic procedures (as in "citizens' juries") that preempt the distortion of democratic debate by adversarial rhetoric; various forms of democratic management (representative supervisory and executive boards, collective managements, job rotation, selection by lot); segmented, coalitional forms of organization; "socialized" information systems and institutions of the kind proposed by Diane Elson to tame the market—the list could be extended almost indefinitely.[45]

The Left must make itself the legitimate champion of this legacy by embodying it in its own practice and driving its significance home to the widest possible public. We need to expose at the same time the way so much local grassroots popular activity is coming to be structured and appropriated by today's modernizing elite (including the World Bank working through nongovernmental organizations). The capitalist class will undoubtedly not relinquish the power they have recently reestablished behind their pseudo-democratic façade without a bitter fight; but the first necessity is still to articulate a convincing, practicable, and consistent conception of genuine democracy to set against it. If the point of drawing on the legacy of the *Manifesto* is indeed "to exaggerate the given task in the imagination, rather than to flee from solving it in reality, to recover the spirit of revolution, rather than to set its ghost walking again,"[46] then bringing to life these visions of radical popular democracy must also be at the very top of an agenda for socialist renewal.

The Social Democratic parties—not to mention the Bolsheviks—failed to do this precisely because the political forms they created, or adapted to, sapped the "spirit of revolution." It was because Marx was so sensitive to the danger of bureaucracy sapping the spirit of revolution that he made so much of what the Paris Commune suggested about workers discovering new radical democratic means of avoiding this. Yet the notorious statism of socialism in the last century was also perhaps inscribed, it must be said, in the *Manifesto*'s own conception of what the proletariat would need to do, at least in the short run, when it achieved power, above all in the stress it placed on the *centralization* of control over credit, communications, and production in the hands of the state—not only to divest the bourgeoisie of its power, but also in order "to increase the total of productive forces as rapidly as possible."

What inspired so many Social Democrats and Communists in the twentieth century was precisely this idea that planning would be more efficient than markets. When, however, neither the Communists nor the Social Democrats found that planning production enabled them to displace capitalism ("bury" it, as Khrushchev said), they came to terms with it: the Communists through "peaceful coexistence" and "convergence," the Social Democrats through corporatism and the mixed economy. The radical democratic vision was sacrificed; and this eventually paved the way for the neo-liberal reaction. It was the neo-liberals, in successfully deploying the rhetoric of revolution to promote market freedom as the "common sense" of the era, who showed that capital, even at the end of the twentieth century, still retained the spirit of bourgeois revolution and the capacity to make the world in its image. But capital's idea of freedom brought to the fore once more the contradiction which had first surfaced during the French Revolution, between private capital and political equality.[47] It is this, together with the destructive social effect of global free markets—epitomized in Margaret Thatcher's notorious statement "that there is no such thing as society"—that makes the *Manifesto*'s charge that the bourgeoisie is no longer "fit to rule" seem so very contemporary: "society can no longer live under this bourgeoisie, in other words, its existence is no longer compatible with society."

Is it too much to hope that the Left can learn valuable lessons from neo-liberalism's sweeping victories over both neo-corporatist and central-command forms of planning? In his Preface to the 1888 English edition of the *Manifesto*, Engels wrote: "The very events and vicissitudes of the struggle against capital, the defeats even more than the victories, could not help bringing home to men's minds the insufficiency of their favourite nostrums, and preparing the way for a more complete insight into the true conditions of working-class emancipation."[48] The original New Left's critique of both Bolshevism and Social Democracy pointed in the right direction—that is, toward democracy over planning, and toward social revolution rather than coexistence. But the failure of the New Left either to transform the existing Social Democratic and Communist parties or to found viable new ones led a strong current of left-wing opinion to give up on both socialism and the working class in favor of a more diffuse, "decentered" conception of "radical democracy." This stance swept under the carpet the irreconcilability of democracy with private property that the French Revolution had itself so clearly brought to light—and this was something that could hardly be ignored in the era of globalization and neo-liberalism. The "free development of each" can only be "the condition for the free development of all" insofar as private property is abolished.

This, in other words, must come clearly back onto the agenda. Once again, as in the *Manifesto*, it must be made clear that this does *not* mean personal possessions, that socialism "deprives no [one] of the power to appropriate the product of society; all that it does is to deprive [anyone] of the power to subjugate the labour of others by means of such appropriation." And to this end we too need to put forward practical policies, as the *Manifesto* did with its ten-point program, that can begin to make "inroads on the rights of property," the kinds of measures "which appear economically insufficient and untenable, but which in the course of the movement, outstrip themselves, necessitate further inroads upon the social order."[49]

It is sobering to note how far the measures they put forward are still relevant today. For any sane environmental policy, the relevance of the passages that have to do with land policy, especially the one which calls for "the improvement of the soil generally in accordance with a common plan" is quite clear. Equally relevant is the *Manifesto*'s proposal for "a heavy progressive or graduated income tax," given the massive redistribution of income and wealth from the poor to the rich over the past twenty years. And the unprecedented power which capital mobility now places in the hands of the bourgeoisie, not to mention the financial instability that accompanies it, makes the *Manifesto*'s call for credit control no less relevant, and moreover prefigures the proposals for capital controls that are now being put forward even on the liberal and Social Democratic Left, not just by Marxist political economists writing in the *Socialist Register*.[50] Contemporary proposals for the radical redistribution of working time and lifelong education are also prefigured in the *Manifesto*'s calls for the "equal liability of all to labour" and "combination of education with industrial production." The legacy of the *Manifesto* is very much present, in other words, in the most sophisticated socialist economic proposals being advanced today, such as Greg Albo's ten-point program for achieving "egalitarian, ecologically-sustainable reproduction" through measures directed at "expanding the scale of democracy while reducing the scale of production."[51]

The struggle to implement these measures must be both national and global; and this too is very much part of the *Manifesto's* legacy. While it called on the workers of the world to unite, it also argued that "the proletariat of each country must . . . *first* of all settle things with its own bourgeoisie"—because to accomplish anything, the workers "must *first* acquire political supremacy," which meant winning power in the nation-state. But then as now, too, "united action, of the leading . . . countries at least, is one of the *first* conditions for the emancipation of the proletariat."[52] It is inconceivable, for example, that effective capital controls can be put in place without such cooperation; yet this implies a wave of national struggles that will commit the leading states to those strategies.

This multiple set of conditions explains the superabundance of "firsts" in the *Manifesto*. Yet all these first steps and conditions are themselves conditional on yet another, even more primary: the "formation of the proletariat into a class." The various kinds of wrong-headed socialists so mordantly criticized in Part 3 of the *Manifesto* had one common fault in Marx's eyes: that of seeing socialism in terms of the introduction of measures "for the benefit of the working class" by people "outside the working-class movement . . . looking rather to the 'educated' classes for support."[53] The priority Marx attached to the "formation of the proletariat into a class" needs to be understood in terms of his commitment to the *self*-emancipation of the workers. But this did not mean merely the formation of unions and parties that would express the particular interests of workers. "The basic thought running through the *Manifesto*," as Engels later put it, was that the class oppression and conflict that has marred all previous human history could be ended only once humanity reached "a stage where the exploited and oppressed class (the proletariat) can no longer emancipate itself from the class which exploits it (the bourgeoisie), without at the same time for ever freeing the whole of society from exploitation, oppression and class struggles."[54]

The working classes' lack of credibility as general emancipators in our time not only explains why the feminist and ecology movements, engaged in struggles crucial to human emancipation, have often defined themselves in opposition to the working class; it also explains why, for the first time in a century, and despite the rise of the new social movements, we lack a sense that there is an alternative to capitalism. The separation of the social movements from working-class politics, unfortunate but understandable, tragically became crystallized into dogma by a generation of intellectuals. Edward Thompson noted in the *Socialist Register* as early as 1973 that there were real reasons for this dismissal of the working class as an agent of general emancipation, but he also noted that the "writing off did damage to intellectual growth itself." He went on to say, in his famous "Open Letter to Leszek Kolakowski":

> You appear to share this instant dismissal, writing: . . . "Let us imagine what the 'dictatorship of the proletariat' would mean if the (real, not imaginary) working class took over exclusive political power now in the U.S." The absurdity of the question appears (in your view) to provide its own answer. But I doubt whether you have given to the question a moment of serious historical imagination: you have simply assumed a white working class, socialized by capitalist institutions as it is now, mystified by the mass media as it is now, structured into competitive organizations as it is now, without self-activity or its own forms of political expression: i.e. a working class with all the attributes of subjection within capitalist structures which one then "imagines" to achieve power without changing either those structures or itself: which is, I fear, a typical example of the fixity of concept which characterizes much capitalist ideology.[55]

Of course, the question of how the alteration of people on a mass scale can come about is a huge one, to which there is no ready-made answer. But, to repeat, classes are never frozen and fixed, they are constantly changing; and there is good reason to look forward to—and work for—developments through which working classes will increasingly acquire a broad emancipatory outlook, a spirit of revolution expressive of the full range of identities they comprise. In any case their potential power can now be fully realized only if, far from trying to ignore or efface these differences, working-class organizations express and gain strength from the plurality of identities that make up the proletariat. The recomposition of the proletariat that has been going on in recent decades before our eyes needs to be soberly examined from this perspective.[56] What is certainly clear is how little help the parties that once based themselves on the working classes have been in this respect. Nothing speaks more clearly than this to the need for new ones.

For the moment we might seek inspiration from the remarkable Communist-internationalists of the 1830s and 1840s who were then trying to fashion appropriate organizations through which working people could develop themselves. After the leaders of League of the Just were expelled from France in 1839, they made their way to London, where Karl Schapper, Heinrich Bauer, and Joseph Moll founded the German Workers' Educational Society. We could do worse today than emulate their efforts, as advertised on one of the Society's posters:

> The main principle of the Society is that men can only come to liberty and self-consciousness by cultivating their intellectual faculties. Consequently, all the evening meetings are devoted to instruction. One evening English is taught, on another, geography, on a third history, on the fourth, drawing and physics, on a fifth, singing, on a sixth, dancing and on the seventh communist politics.[57]

Notes

1. "Ultimately, when stubborn historical facts had dispersed all intoxicating effects of self-deception, this form of Socialism ["petty-bourgeois socialism"] ended in a miserable fit of the blues" (Karl Marx, "The Manifesto of the Communist Party," in Karl Marx, *The Revolutions of 1848: Political Writings,* Marx Library Series, vol. 1, ed. David Fernbach (New York: Vintage, 1974), p. 90. On "new times" see Stuart Hall and Martin Jacques, eds., *New Times: The Changing Face of Politics in the 1990s* (London: Lawrence and Wishart, 1989), a collection of articles published by *Marxism Today* in the late 1980s. The book ended by suggesting that Mikhail Gorbachev's *perestroika* was an inspiring example of the politics needed for "new times," and *Marxism Today* closed soon after Gorbachev's fall. On "radicalism of the center" as articulated by the Tony Blair leadership of the Labour Party, see Leo Panitch and Colin Leys, *The End of Parliamentary Socialism: From New Left to New Labour* (London: Verso, 2001), esp. ch. 11. On the "third way," see Anthony Giddens, *The Third Way: The Renewal of Social Democracy* (Cambridge, U.K.: Polity, 1998).

2. On these "new populations" at the end of the twentieth century, see Nigel Harris, *The New Untouchables: Immigration and the New World Worker* (London: Penguin, 1996).

3. Boris Kagarlitsky, "The Unfinished Revolution," *Green-Left Weekly* (Sydney, Australia), 5 November 1997.

4. It was noteworthy that by 1997 Social Democratic parties were in office in twelve of the fifteen states of the EU.

5. Giovanni Arrighi, "Workers of the World at Century's End," *Review* 19,3 (Summer 1996): 339–40.

6. "Fighting the Class War," *The Economist,* 27 September 1997.

7. "The Downsizing of America," *New York Times,* 5 March 1997.

8. See Rob Beamish, "The Making of the *Manifesto*," in Leo Panitch and Colin Leys, eds., *The Socialist Register 1998* (London: Merlin, 1998), pp. 218–39.

9. Cynthia Cockburn, *The Local State* (London: Pluto, 1977), p. 118.

10. Sheila Rowbotham, Lynne Segal, and Hilary Wainwright, *Beyond the Fragments* (London: Merlin, 1979).

11. Writing in the mid-1980s, when he was a close adviser to Jesse Jackson, Vicente Navarro chastised "post-Marxists" whose proposals for "a constantly shifting pattern of alliances . . . [were] but a recycling of the old pluralist-interest groups' theories that have been the dominant form of political discourse and practice in the US for many years. The emergence and importance of social movements in the US—the main trademark of US political behaviour and mass mobilization—are a direct consequence of the absence of class-based practices by the dominated classes. . . . This is not to deny the enormous importance for the left to be sensitive to forms of exploitation other than class exploitation, nor to ignore the importance of establishing coalitions with strata outside the working class. . . . The operational meaning of this awareness is not, however, the mere aggregate of the demands of each component of the 'people.' Class practices are not the mere aggregate of 'interest group' politics. . . . This was, incidentally, the main problem with Jesse Jackson's 'rainbow coalition' . . . with [its] heavy emphasis on the rights of blacks without providing enough linkage with other components of the working class." "The 1980 and 1984 Elections and the New Deal," in Ralph Miliband et al., eds., *The Socialist Register 1985/6* (London: Merlin, 1986), pp. 199–200.

12. Margaret Keck's account of the Workers' Party of Brazil (PT) in the 1980s offers a rich portrait of what this entails in our own time: "The PT's origins were deeply influenced by the perception of widespread mobilization around social demands in the late 1970s; in the early 1980s, as it became clear that local organization around specific equity demands did not automatically translate into a societal movement, the party was placed in the ambiguous position of having to help organize what it was claiming to represent." *The Workers' Party and Democratization in Brazil* (New Haven: Yale University Press, 1992), p. 242.

13. "We know that heed must be paid to the institutions, customs and traditions of the various countries, and we do not deny that there are countries, such as America and England, and if I was familiar with its institutions, I might include Holland, where the workers may attain their goals by peaceful means. That being the case, we must recognise that in most continental countries the lever of the revolution will have to be force; a resort to force will be necessary one day to set up the rule of labour"; "Speech on the Hague Congress," in David Fernbach, ed., Marx Library Series, vol. 3, *The First International and After* (New York: Vintage, 1974), p. 324.

14. See Teodor Shanin, *Late Marx and the Russian Road* (London: Routledge, 1983).

15. Friedrich Engels, 1895 Preface to Marx's *Class Struggles in France*, in Karl Marx and Friedrich Engels, *Selected Works*, vol. 1 (Moscow: Foreign Languages Publishing House, 1962), p. 135.

16. Isaac Deutscher, *The Prophet Armed* (Oxford: Oxford University Press, 1954), pp. 338–39.

17. 1895 Preface to *The Class Struggles in France*, p. 132.

18. Ibid., p. 134.

19. For an excellent discussion of the unfortunate use made of this in the German SPD, see Guglielmo Carchedi, *Class Analysis and Social Research* (Oxford: Blackwell, 1987), ch. 1.

20. Karl Marx, "The Civil War in France," in David Fernbach, ed., Marx Library Series, vol. 3, *The First International and After: Political Writings* (New York: Vintage, 1974), p. 213.

21. A phrase that Ronald Aronson repeats like a mantra in his *After Marxism* (New York: Guilford, 1995).

22. John Gray, "Socialism for the Unconverted," *The Times Higher Education Supplement*, 6 October, 1995.

23. Eric Hobsbawm, *Age of Extremes: The Short Twentieth Century* (London: Michael Joseph, 1994), pp. 564–65.

24. "Why the Left Lost Utopia," *Guardian*, 24 November 1996.

25. Anthony Crosland, *The Future of Socialism*, rev. ed. (New York: Schocken, 1963), pp. 7–16.

26. Donald Sassoon, *One Hundred Years of Socialism* (London: I.B. Taurus, 1996), pp. 558–59.

27. Gabriel Kolko, *Century of War* (New York: New Press, 1995), p. 457.

28. See John Cassidy, "The Next Thinker: The Return of Karl Marx," *New Yorker*, 20 October 1997.

29. Engels wrote to Marx on 23–24 November 1847, just before the London Congress of the Communist League which commissioned Marx to write the *Manifesto*: "As more or less history has got to be related in it . . . I am bringing what I have done here [Paris] with me; it is in simple narrative form, but miserably worded, in fearful haste. I begin: What is Communism? And then straight to the proletariat—history of its origin, difference from former labourers, development of the antithesis between proletariat and bourgeoisie, crises, conclusions." Karl Marx and Friedrich Engels, *Selected Correspondence* (Moscow: Foreign Languages Publishing House, n.d.), pp. 52–53.

30. See Hobsbawm, *Age of Extremes*, pp. 289–93; and Michael Kidron and Ronald Segal, *The State of the World Atlas* (London: Penguin, 1995), pp. 28–29; but especially Henry Bernstein, ""The Peasantry" in Global Capitalism: Who, Where and Why?" in Leo Panitch and Colin Leys, eds., *Working Classes/Global Realities: The Socialist Register 2001* (London: Merlin, 2000), pp. 25–52.

31. Giovanni Arrighi, "Marxist Century, American Century: The Making and Remaking of the World Labour Movement," *New Left Review* 179 (1990): 29–63.

32. See International Labor Organization, *World Employment 1996/97* (Washington, D.C.: ILO, 1996). A projection of 370 million "surplus" rural workers by the year 2000 appeared in the *China Daily* on 2 December 1997, citing a report by the State Council issued on 11 June 1997.

33. As the *Manifesto* puts it: "The cheap prices of its commodities are the heavy artillery with which [the bourgeoisie] forces the barbarians' intensely obstinate hatred of foreigners to capitulate."

34. This is a metaphor Marx himself was wont to use, albeit more aptly in relation to Russian agriculture. See Shanin, *Late Marx*, p. 115.

35. "Luddism must be seen as arising at the crisis-point in the abrogation of paternalist legislation, and the imposition of the political economy of *laissez-faire* upon, and against the will and conscience of, the working people. . . . True enough, much of this paternalist legislation had been in origin not only restrictive, but, for the working man, punitive. Nevertheless, there was within it the shadowy image of a benevolent corporate state, in which there were legislative as well as moral sanctions against the unscrupulous manufacturer or the unjust employer, and in which the journeymen were a recognized "estate," however low, in the realm. . . . These ideals may never have been much more than ideals; by the end of the eighteenth century they may have been threadbare. But they had a powerful reality, none the less, in the notion of what *ought* to be, to which artisans, journeymen, and many small masters appealed." E. P. Thompson, *The Making of the English Working Class* (London: Penguin, 1968), p. 594.

36. In September 1997 the Russian duma reported that life expectancy had fallen far below the levels of other industrialized countries; per capita consumption of meat, milk, and fish had fallen by about a third between 1990 and 1996, the rate of illness among schoolchildren had increased fivefold and only 10 per cent of high-school graduates could be considered healthy, with 40 percent chronically ill. *Toronto Star,* 13 September 1997.

37. In North America, Engels wrote, "each of the two major parties which alternately succeed each other in power is itself in turn controlled by people who make a business of politics, who speculate on seats in the legislative assemblies . . . or who make a living by carrying on agitation for their party and on its victory are rewarded with positions." Introduction to Marx's *Civil War in France,* in Robert C. Tucker, ed., *The Marx-Engels Reader* (New York: Norton 1972), p. 535.

38. Karl Marx, "Critique of the Gotha Programme" ("Marginal Notes on the Programme of the German Workers' Party"), in Fernbach, ed., *The First International and After,* p. 356.

39. Report on Business, *Globe and Mail,* 4 December 1997.

40. Perry Anderson, *A Zone of Engagement* (London: Verso, 1992), p. 356.

41. Karl Marx and Friedrich Engels, *The German Ideology* (New York: International Publishers, 1947), p. 39.

42. James Curran and Jean Seaton, *Power Without Responsibility: The Press and Broadcasting in Britain* (London: Fontana, 1981).

43. See, e.g., Brian McNair, *News and Journalism in the UK* (London: Routledge, 1994); and Douglas Kellner, *Television and the Crisis of Democracy* (Boulder: Westview, 1990).

44. For rich analyses of existing and possible ways of restoring the media to democracy, see James Curran, "Mass Media and Democracy Revisited," in James Curran and Michael Gurevitch, eds., *Mass Media and Society* (London: Arnold, 1996); and Don Hazen and Julie Winokur, eds., *We the Media: A Citizen's Guide to Fighting for Media Democracy* (New York: New Press, 1997).

45. On citizens' juries see John Stewart, Elizabeth Kendall and Anna Coote, *Citizens' Juries* (London: IPPR, 1994); on the idea of a socialized market, see Diane Elson, "Market Socialism or Socialization of the Market?" *New Left Review* 172 (1988): 3–4; on the GLC and democratic "deepening" in a Swedish women's edu-

cation center, see Hilary Wainwright, *Arguments for a New Left* (Oxford: Blackwell, 1994), ch. 5–7; on democratic management in the workplace and the state, see, respectively, Michael Albert and Robin Hahnel, *Looking Forward: Participatory Economics for the Twenty First Century* (Boston: South End Press, 1991), and Gregory Albo, David Langille, and Leo Panitch, eds., *A Different Kind of State: Popular Power and Democratic Administration* (Toronto: Oxford University Press, 1993).

46. Karl Marx, "The Eighteenth Brumaire of Louis Bonaparte," in David Fernbach, ed., Marx Library Series, vol. 2, *Surveys from Exile: Political Writings* (New York: Vintage, 1974), p. 148.

47. See Frederic L. Bender's excellent introduction to his edition of *The Communist Manifesto* (New York: Norton, 1988), esp. pp. 3–4.

48. Frederick Engels, Preface to the 1888 English edition of the *Manifesto*, in Bender, ed., p. 47. His claim that lessons had been learned, coinciding as it did with the rise of industrial unionism and mass working-class parties, was quite valid.

49. The measures were advanced as only "generally applicable": they would be "different in different countries." And when Marx and Engels a quarter of a century later wrote their first preface to the *Manifesto* (for the 1872 German edition), they insisted that "no special stress" should be laid on the measures proposed, and that the whole "passage would, in many respects, be very differently worded today." See Bender, ed., *The Communist Manifesto*, p. 43.

50. See William Greider, "Saving the Local Economy," *The Nation*, 15 December 1997, as well as the declaration and memorandum by twenty-five European economists, *Full Employment, Social Cohesion and Equity for Europe: Alternatives to Competitive Austerity*, May 1997. In the *Socialist Register*, among others essays, see especially Jim Crotty and Gerald Epstein, "In Defence of Capital Controls," in Leo Panitch, ed., *The Socialist Register 1996* (London: Merlin, 1996).

51. Gregory Albo, "A World Market of Opportunities? Capitalist Obstacles and Left Economic Policy," in Leo Panitch and Colin Leys, eds., *The Socialist Register 1997* (London: Merlin, 1997), esp. pp. 27–39.

52. The text actually says "leading civilized countries." Without wishing to burke the question of how far Marx's use of Hegel's concept of "world-historical" nations (in which the principle of "freedom" had been most fully realised, etc.) involved assumptions of a racialist nature, we have omitted the word "civilized" in the quotation in order to focus on the main point, which remains valid—the need for joint action by the leading or major economic powers.

53. Friedrich Engels, Preface to the 1888 English edition, in Bender, ed., *The Communist Manifesto*, p. 48.

54. Friedrich Engels, Preface to the 1883 German edition in Bender, ed., *The Communist Manifesto*, pp. 45–46.

55. E. P. Thompson, "An Open Letter to Leszek Kolakowski," in Ralph Miliband and John Saville, eds., *The Socialist Register 1973* (London: Merlin, 1973), pp. 84 and 99–100 n. 69.

56. For this, see the essays in Leo Panitch and Colin Leys, eds., *Working Classes/Global Realities: The Socialist Register 2001*. Marx's observations on the con-

temporary study of social and economic history are worth recalling: "Much research has been carried out to trace the different historical phases that the bourgeoisie has passed through. . . . But when it is a question of making a precise study of strikes, combinations and other forms in which the proletarians carry out before our eyes their organisation as a class, some are seized with real fear and others display a *transcendental* disdain." *The Poverty of Philosophy* (Moscow: Foreign Languages Publishing House, 1956), p. 196.

57. Quoted in Bender's introduction to the *Manifesto*, p. 10.

5

Globalization and Left Strategies

Alice never could quite make out, in thinking it over afterwards, how it was that they began: all she remembers is, that they were running hand in hand, and the Queen went so fast that it was all she could do to keep up with her: and still the Queen kept crying "Faster! Faster!," though she had no breath left to say so.

The most curious part of the thing was, that the trees and the other things round them never changed their places at all: however fast they went, they never seemed to pass anything. . .

*"Well, in **our** country," said Alice, still panting a little, "you'd generally get to somewhere else—if you ran for a long time as we've been doing."*

*"A slow sort of country!" said the Queen. "Now, **here**, you see, it takes all the running **you** can do, to keep in the same place. If you want to get somewhere else, you must run at least twice at fast as that!"*

—*Lewis Carroll*, **Through the Looking Glass**

I

Think of the Red Queen's garden as capitalism. The bourgeoisie's relentless search for markets and profits brings about faster and faster changes in production and space, industry and commerce, occupation and locale, with profound effects on the organization of classes and states. It is through this ferocious process of extension and change that capitalism is preserved and reproduced. Now think of Alice, frantically running alongside the Red Queen, as the labor *movement*, or the social *movements*, or the broadly defined "Left." For all the running they did in the twentieth century, for all the mobilization and reform, even the moments of revolution and national liberation, the world today is most certainly still very much capitalist, indeed it would seem ever more so. Of course, this does not mean the world is unchanged from what it was, and this is partly due to the effect of those who have contested and thereby insulated themselves somewhat or even modified the vast transformations wrought by the bourgeoisie. But the institutions of the Left, not least the once powerful Communist and Social Democratic parties, increasingly could not even keep pace and lost more and more initiative to the forces of capitalist change. Their original ambition *to get somewhere else*, to a social order beyond capitalism—that is, to socialism, however conceived—more or less gradually gave way to attempts at adaptation and accommodation to the dynamics of capitalist change. Yet the only result has been that they became more and more ineffective in their attempts to tame the market, and the social forces they had once mobilized and spoken for have become more than ever the victims of ruthless capitalist change.

It has become quite commonplace to recognize that some fundamental rethinking is required on the left. But all too often such rethinking is still cast in terms of grabbing hold of the bourgeoisie's hand and trying to run faster and faster to match the pace of changes set by contemporary capitalism. This involves a fundamental strategic misconception. If effective forms of strategy ever are to reemerge on the left, they will have to be less about keeping up with or adapting to capitalist change, but rather more about developing the capacity to mobilize more broadly and effectively *against* the logic of competitiveness and profit in order eventually *to get somewhere else*, that is, to an egalitarian, cooperative, and democratic social order beyond capitalism. To run, even twice as fast, on capitalism's terms will not in fact lead somewhere else at all.

These considerations are especially germane in light of the challenge posed by what has come to be known as "globalization," where we have witnessed the apparent subordination of the domestic economies of even advanced capitalist social formations in recent decades to the competitive logic and exigencies of production, trade, and finance undertaken on a world scale. The most acute observers have recognized that the tendency to globalization, as Robert Cox says, is never complete, and that there is nothing inevitable about its continuation: "Any attempt to depict it must not be taken teleologically, as an advanced stage towards the inevitable completion of a latent structure. Rather it should be taken dialectically, as the description of tendencies that, as they become revealed, may arouse oppositions that could strive to confound and reverse them."[1] Most accounts of globalization, however, do see the process as irreversible, and in this perspective the predominant strategic response becomes one which invariably tends to see the strategies, practices, and institutions of the Left as perhaps having been appropriate to an earlier "national" stage of capitalism but as having now been rendered outmoded and outdated by globalization. Just like Alice before she stepped through the looking glass, it is as though the Left used to be able to get somewhere else by running on the terrain of the nation-state, but now that capital had escaped the nation-state, the Left will have to learn to run with the bourgeoisie across the terrain of the globe.

This approach has been well-represented by David Held, for instance, for whom globalization implies a distinctively new "international order involving the emergence of a global economic system which stretches beyond the control of a single state (even of dominant states); the expansion of networks of transnational linkages and communications over which particular states have little influence; the enormous growth in international organization which can limit the scope for action of the most powerful states; the development of a global military order ... which can reduce the range of policies available to governments and their citizens." Since this new global order has apparently escaped the control of democratic institutions located at the national level, Held concludes that this means that "democracy has to become a transnational affair." Strategic priority must be given to "the key groups, agencies, associations and organizations of international civil society," extending their capacity as agencies for democratic control through an appropriate recasting of the territorial boundaries of systems of accountability, representation, and regulation, fortified by entrenched transnational bills of social, economic, and civil rights.[2]

While characterizations of globalization as a qualitative new phase of capitalism such as these depart sharply from those who have understood capitalism as a world system from its inception, in terms of the implications of globalization for the institutional capacity and strategic focus of the Left, the dilemma is precisely the same one as posed long ago by world system theorists. Thus Wallerstein:

> While the multiple political organizational expressions of the world bourgeoisie—controlling as they did *de facto* most state structures—could navigate with relative ease the waters of murky geographical identity, it was precisely the world's workers' movements that felt obliged to create national,

that is, state-wide, structures, whose clear boundaries would define and limit organizational efforts. If one wants to conquer state power, one has to create organizations geared to this objective. Thus, while the world bourgeoisie has, when all is said and done always organized in relationship to the world economy . . . the proletarian forces—despite their internationalist rhetoric—have been far more nationalist than they claimed or their ideology permitted. . . . [T]hese movements are caught in a dilemma. They can reinforce their state power, with the advantage of holding on to a foothold in the interstate system, but they face the risk of making the detour the journey, in Hobsbawm's phrase. Or they can move to organise transnationally, at the great risk of losing any firm base, and at the risk of internecine struggle, but it may be that power is only truly available at the world level.[3]

Even those less inclined to reduce the tradition of socialist internationalism to mere rhetoric, nevertheless still see the prime cause of the weakness of the Left today in terms of internationalism having "changed sides," as Perry Anderson put it:

The new reality is a massive asymmetry between the international mobility and organization of capital, and the dispersal and segmentation of labour that has no historical precedent. The globalization of capitalism has not drawn the resistances to it together, but scattered and outflanked them. . . . The age continues to see nationalisms exploding like firecrackers across much of the world, not least where communism once stood. But the future belongs to the set of forces that are overtaking the nation-state. So far, they have been captured or driven by capital—as in the past fifty years, internationalism has changed sides. So long as the Left fails to win back the initiative here, the current system will be secure.[4]

There are a number of problems with this way of approaching the Left's strategic dilemmas in the face of globalization. The premise that globalization is a process whereby capital limits, escapes, or overtakes the nation-state may be misleading in two senses. First, there is often an overestimation of the extent to which nation-states were capable of controlling capital in an earlier era; it is as if the Left's mode of practice was adequate in relation to the nation-state and thus encourages a similar mode to be adopted at the global level: the problem is just one of running faster on the new terrain. But even for those not given to such illusions, there is a tendency to ignore the extent to which today's globalization both is authored by states and is primarily about reorganizing, rather than bypassing, states; it promotes in this sense a false dichotomy between national and international struggles and diverts attention from the Left's need to develop its own strategies for transforming the state, even as a means of developing an appropriate international strategy.

II

Any attempt to reassess Left strategies in the context of globalization must begin with the understanding that although the nature of state intervention has changed considerably, the role of the state has not necessarily been diminished. Far from witnessing a bypassing of the state by a global capitalism, what we see are very active states and highly politicized sets of capitalist classes hard at work to secure what Stephen Gill (primarily focusing on the European Union but pointing to much broader tendencies of this kind) aptly termed a "new constitutionalism for disciplinary neo-liberalism."[5] Not only with the General Agreement on Tariffs and Trade (GATT) and its successor the World Trade Organization (WTO) at the world level but also with similar treaties at the regional level, states act as the authors of a regime which defines and guarantees, through international treaties with constitutional effect, the global and domestic rights of capital. This process may be understood in a manner quite analogous to the emergence of the so-called laissez-faire state during the rise of industrial capitalism, which involved a very active state to see through the separation of polity from economy and guarantee legally and politically the rights of contract and property.[6] We are living through something like this in our own time: capitalist globalization is a process which also takes place in, through, and under the aegis of states; it is encoded by them and in important respects even authored by them; and it involves a shift in power relations within states that often means the centralization and concentration of state powers as the necessary condition of and accompaniment to global market discipline.

The North America Free Trade Agreement (NAFTA), which came into effect on 1 January 1994, and its predecessor the U.S.–Canada Free Trade Agreement (FTA), which came into effect five years earlier, are especially worth examining as key instances of constitutionalizing neo-liberalism. Far more important than the reduction in tariffs, as President William Clinton himself repeatedly intoned, were the guarantees NAFTA provided for American investment in Mexico and Canada. As Ian Robinson put it in one the best analyses of the deal, international trade agreements like NAFTA not only "prohibit discrimination between national and foreign owned corporations [but also] create new corporate private property rights, possessed by both national and foreign investors. . . . It will function as an economic constitution, setting the basic rules governing the private property rights that all governments must respect and the types of economic policies that all governments must eschew."[7]

NAFTA's investment chapter proscribes attempts by governments to establish performance requirements on foreign TNCs and defines investor rights which are protected under the agreement very broadly to include not only majority shareholders but minority interests, portfolio investment, and real property held by any company incorporated in a NAFTA country regardless of the country of origin. The Monopolies and State Enterprises chapter requires public enterprises not only to operate "solely in accordance with commercial considerations" and to refrain from using anticompetitive practices such as "the discriminatory provision of a monopoly good or service, cross-subsidization or predatory conduct" (all of which amounts to the bread and butter of TNCs themselves), but also requires public enterprises to minimize or eliminate "any nullification or impairment of benefits" that investors, broadly defined as above, might reasonably expect to receive under NAFTA. The Intellectual Property Rights chapter, which grants up to twenty years of protection to a vast array of trademarks, patents, semiconductor and industrial designs, trade secrets, satellite signals, etc., goes furthest of all to "extend existing property rights by quasi-constitutionally protecting them against future democratic governments with the threat of trade sanctions . . . even though the effect of these rights is to restrict rather than enhance the free flow of ideas across national boundaries. . . ."[8]

Taken together, these various provisions have the effect of redesigning the Mexican and Canadian states' relation to capital to fit the mold made in the American metropole by establishing and guaranteeing state defense of "new private property rights that go well beyond those recognized in Canadian and Mexican law, if not that of the United States."[9] What is particularly important to stress, however, is that this is not something imposed on the Canadian and Mexican states by American capital and state as *external* to the latter; rather it reflects the role adopted by the Mexican and Canadian states in representing the interests of their bourgeoisies and bureaucracies as these were *already penetrated* by American capital and administration. As John H. Bryan, Jr., president of Sara Lee

Corp., put it, the "most important reason to vote for NAFTA is to lock in [Mexico's] reforms."[10] This was all the more pressing insofar as there was a widespread awareness among North American elites (long before the Chiapas revolt on the day NAFTA came into effect) of popular discontent with the neo-liberal policies Mexico had adopted over the past decade, and a concern that any eventual opening up of Mexico's limited democracy might promote a left alternative to the Partido Revolucionario Institucional (PRI) government. Shortly before the passage of NAFTA, the Report on Business of Canada's leading newspaper the *Globe and Mail*, quoted Alvaro Cepeda Neri from Mexico City's *Jornada*: "The booty of privatisation has made multimillionaires of 13 families, while the rest of the population—about 80 million Mexicans—has been subjected to the same gradual impoverishment as though they had suffered through a war."[11]

But the Mexican state was not only acting in terms of the interests of its domestic bourgeoisie, nor even just concerned with providing further security guarantees to American capital in Mexico. It was also, in Nicos Poulantzas's apt terms, "taking responsibility for the interests of the dominant capital"[12] by endorsing NAFTA as an exemplary "staging post" for a renewed American imperialism throughout Latin America, as well as a model for a similar constitutionalizing of neo-liberalism on a global scale. The chairman of Saloman, Inc. did not mince his words when he said that the defeat of NAFTA "would be a slap in the face to all leaders in the Western Hemisphere who have chosen the capitalist road over government-controlled economies."[13] Indeed, if, as the Foreign Affairs Committee chairman in the U.S. House of Representatives, Lee Hamilton, put it, "the question is U.S. leadership in the world," it is notable that the greatest threat to NAFTA came from the opposition within the United States itself. The side deals on the environment and labor undertaken by Clinton were designed to allow for the necessary compromises within the American social formation: this succeeded to the extent that it divided the environmental movement; if the labor side deal failed to do the same, it was because, not surprisingly, it did not go as far as the environmental side deal and did not allow Canadian or American groups affected by NAFTA to challenge the nonenforcement of Mexican labor laws.

As for Canada, the FTA that preceded NAFTA was designed not to inaugurate but rather to constitutionalize, formalize, and extend Canada's dependence on the United States in a world now marked by economic instability amidst rampant financial speculation and strong trade rivalries. Far from wanting to prove their entrepreneurial virility by taking the risk of becoming globally competitive, Canadian domestic capital sought to minimize the risk that Americans, when in protectionist mood, might treat them and their exports and investments as merely "foreign." In turn, the Canadian government promised to give up those weak devices it had heretofore retained as a means of negotiating the scope of Canadian dependency. Margaret Atwood (following Antonio Gramsci) used a very Canadian metaphor to describe what the Brian Mulroney government had done in entering into the FTA: the beaver was noted in medieval bestiaries for biting off its own testicles when frightened and offering them to its pursuer.

It was a mark of how deep the lines of American imperialism ran in Canada that every issue, from social policy to defense policy to Quebec's status in Canada was interpreted during the course of the 1988 federal election through the prism of the pros and cons of the FTA. All sides of the debate took the position that the free trade agreement was a historic departure, an epochal turning point for Canada. Either it would finally free Canadian business from the fetters of tariffs and regulation, expose it fully to the rigor of competition, lay open a vast continental market for exports and investment. Or it would mean the end of Canada as we had known it for 121 years, shifting our economic axis southward, imposing the rule of business, destroying the welfare state, undermining Canadian culture, subverting national sovereignty. Both views were misleading. The outcome of what became known as "the free trade election" marked not a new chapter, but rather the punctuation mark on a very long historical sentence of economic and cultural integration with American capitalism.

Canada's particular status as a rich dependency in the American Empire rested on the fact that like the United States, and partly due to its geographic and cultural proximity to the United States, the development of capitalism in Canada was predicated on a class structure which facilitated capitalist industrialization.[14] A high-wage proletariat and a prosperous class of small farmers drew American capital to Canada not only in search of resources, and not at all in search of cheap labor, but to sell to a market distinctly similar to the American. The national tariff designed to integrate an east-west economy and protect Canadian industry from competition from the south (and the migration of Canadian workers to the south) had the paradoxical effect of inducing the first American TNCs to jump the tariff barrier by establishing Canadian subsidiaries and sell to Canada's (and sometimes through Canada to the British Empire's) mass market. They were welcomed with open arms by the state as good corporate citizens and funded by Canada's substantial and powerful financial capitalists. Through the course of the first half of the twentieth century, Canada moved from formal colonial status as a privileged white dominion in the old British Empire to a formally independent, but in reality quite a dependent status in a new kind of imperialism amidst a degree of direct foreign (American) ownership unparalleled anywhere on the globe.

Yet this status was still a privileged one, and Canadians shared in the spoils that went with American hegemony in the postwar order. Any dependent country has a degree of autonomy: This was especially true of a rich one with a substantial industrial proletariat not as easily subjected to the same pressures as American workers to accede to imperial demands of unswerving loyalty in a Cold War and therefore more open to socialist political ideas and mobilization. Canada's welfare state, however poor a cousin to those in northern Europe, eventually came to surpass what the New Deal had inaugurated in the United States. This gave Canada a badge of civility compared with American society. Some public corporations and regulatory bodies took on the additional role of protecting what residual autonomy Canadian economy and culture could retain. But in doing this, they did not so much challenge the fact of, as negotiate the scope of, Canada's dependency.

What most opponents of the FTA were really objecting to was the whole dependent path of Canadian development: they wanted to avoid a punctuation mark being put at the end of the long sentence of dependence. To defeat the deal would be to leave open the possibility of a "nevertheless" or a "however"—which might yet be written at some point in the future. They were encouraged by the emergence of a visible strain of anti-Americanism, even of anti-imperialism. An indigenous cultural community had long been straining to define Canadian identity in the face of dependence. The labor movement, once a strong if subordinate sponsor of continentalism, had also experienced a shift toward Canadianization as the American labor movement proved ever weaker and more abject in the face of economic instability. And considerable domestic ecology, peace, and feminist movements had emerged, often with socialists in leadership positions, and with greater influence in Canadian political life than such movements had in the United States.

The anti–free trade forces were encouraged as well by the fact that the Canadian electorate showed no great enthusiasm for the Reagan and Thatcher type of neo-liberal state model. Just as the 1980s began, Canadians had opted for a Liberal platform which promised to install a "fair tax" system rather than supply-side economics and to foster a Canadian capitalist class with distinctive national goals and ambitions through the National Energy Programme (NEP) and a strengthened Foreign Investment Review Agency. It had indeed been in reaction to all this, as well as to cries for protectionism in the U.S. Congress, that the business community launched the free trade initiative and pursued it with such remarkable unanimity. When the NEP was established, Canadian capitalists, no less than American ones, were determined not only to get rid of it at the first opportunity, but to disable permanently such interventions by the state. They feared that popular pressures were pushing the state to become, not the handmaiden to business it had usually been, but a countervailing power to it. Not just fear was at play here, but also greed: Some elements of Canadian business had become full players on a continental plane while others harbored ambitions that they too might reap substantial profits if Canada embraced its continental destiny. This demonstrated that the point had long passed when business in Canada was interested in "reclaiming" the Canadian economy.

The continuing political dominance of business, despite the mood of the electorate and the volubility of progressive forces, was seen when opposition from a unified capitalist class destroyed the tax reforms advanced in the 1981 budget, and when the Liberal government responded to the recession of 1981–82 by removing the right to strike from some one million of the three million organized workers in Canada. Yet the ideological impact of neo-liberalism still remained limited. In 1984 even the Conservatives sensed that they could not get elected on a Thatcher-Reagan platform. Mulroney ran a typically Canadian brokerage campaign promising everything to everybody and declaring the welfare state a sacred trust. This did not make it a sacred trust, of course, given the powerful business interests to which the government was beholden. But it emboldened people to defend the welfare state as soon as the Tories tried to undo it.

The decision to go for the FTA, under considerable pressure from the Business Council on National Issues (a powerful lobby which grouped together the most powerful domestic and American corporations), thus took on a double purpose: to make permanent the dominance of business by formalizing continental integration in the face of American protectionism and Canadian economic nationalism; and to introduce Reaganomics by the back door of the free market ethos and provisions of the free trade deal. A popular coalition, funded by the labor movement and led by the leadership of the above-mentioned "new social movements," marshaled against the FTA with remarkable fervor and determination to force the free trade election of 1988. But it must be admitted that this coalition, and much less the opposition parties, never made clear what their alternative really was. The experience with the 1980–84 Liberal government showed that a policy for more economic independence and social justice could not rely on the cooperation of business. Yet the anti–free trade coalition was afraid to spell out the conclusion that the alternative had to involve fundamental challenges to capital's power and radically democratizing the state. They were afraid to do so because the Canadian people had been so little prepared for such a departure, with the limitations of the NDP (Canada's Social Democratic party) in this respect particularly glaring.

Alongside a trenchant critique of the details and implications of the FTA, the anti–free trade coalition took a different tack. And it proved a shrewd one. They chose to mythologize the Canadian state as if it had always been a repository of Canadian independence and social justice. This was myth indeed. But nationalisms are built on myths, and this one became uncontested in the election with remarkable ideological consequences. The small badge of civility which a welfare state lends to Canadian social life in comparison with the American laid the basis for Canadian national identity to be defined in the 1988 election in almost Scandinavian terms, where pride in the welfare state was rather more justified. In this context, the outcome of the free trade election was, despite the narrow victory by the Tories, and the subsequent introduction of the FTA, rather ambiguous. Certainly, the victory of the business forces confirmed the historical trend toward continental integration. An exclamation mark had been added to Canada's historical sentence of dependence.

Paradoxically, the election also confirmed the absence of an ideological mandate to carry through Reaganomics in Canada. The Tories and the business community accepted the anti–free trade forces' definition of patriotism as at least involving a defense of the welfare state. The freedom to trade and invest by business was bought at the ideological cost of pledging allegiance to medicare and other social programs. Insofar as the popular coalition forged during the campaign against free trade set the terms of the debate and forced their opponents to adopt a defense of the welfare state as a central element in the definition of "Canadianism," they provided a strong ideological basis for defensive struggles. The challenge for the Left remained to enlarge the framework of struggle. A defense of the welfare state promises only stalemate so long as the power and mobility of capital remains untouched. Over a decade later, in the context of Canada's reinforced dependency amidst global economic instability and financial speculation, a clear alternative to free trade and unbridled capitalist competition still remains to be articulated.

III

Unfortunately, the "progressive competitive" strategy adopted by the mainstream parties of the center-left in the 1990s, while certainly abandoning a strategy centered on the defense of the welfare state, does not amount to much of an alternative either. For a considerable period through the 1970s and well into the mid-1980s, a large portion of the Left refused to acknowledge that the crisis of the Keynesian/welfare state was a structural one, pertaining to the very nature of capitalism and the contradictions it generates in our time. Their response to the crisis, clearly visible in the Canadian free trade debate, was to point to relatively low unemployment levels in Sweden as evidence of the continuing viability of tripartite corporatism in sustaining the Keynesian/welfare state.[15] This involved, however, ignoring or downplaying the very contradictions and conflicts that were undermining even the Swedish model, and eventually this naïve stance was displaced by an attempt to emulate those countries which were most successful in the export-led competitive race. But rather than allow right-wing economists, with their neo-liberal logic of deregulation, free markets, privatization, and austerity, to dictate the terms of the race, these parties by the late 1980s began to take up the "progressive competitiveness" strategy advanced by many intellectuals on the left (from Social Democrats to leftist liberals to a good many erstwhile Marxists) whereby labor and the state were urged to take the initiative and seize the hand of business in making the running toward competitive success.

At the core of the strategy, still largely inspired by a different facet of Swedish corporatism, was the idea that the state should support and guide both workers and capitalists toward high-tech/high-value-added/high-wage production. The key to this was to be public policies which promoted the widespread training of a highly skilled, highly flexible, and highly motivated labor force and encouraged enterprises to take full advantage of recent technological developments in micro-electronics, to the end of producing high-quality commodities at high productivity levels through flexible production methods. Founded on an acceptance of the irreversibility of globalization, but convinced that its connection with neo-liberalism was only a matter of the ideological coloration of politicians too closely attached to right-wing economists, this approach still wanted to give strategic priority to the state. Once shorn of an ideology of free markets as the premise of state policy in the process of globalization, the "progressive competitiveness" strategy expected the state to be able to sustain a substantial social wage if it explicitly connected welfare and education to the public promotion of flexible production and technological innovation in those particular sectors which could "win" in a global export–led competitive race. Relative prosperity (clearly based on an extension of the advantages of relative over absolute surplus-value extraction) would fall to those states which could guide capital and labor to adopt this "smart" com-petitiveness strategy. With all its emphasis on training, this was indeed a strategy which was precisely about *learning* how to run twice as fast amidst globalization.

That such a strategy is both chimerical and dangerous for the left was already demonstrated in North America first by the NDP government elected in Ontario in 1990, and then by the left-wing Democrats like Robert Reich who went to Washington with Clinton in 1992 as secretary of labor. As Gindin and Robertson put it in 1992:

> There are those who . . . believe that we can take on the challenge of com-petitiveness *and* retain our socialist values; indeed they believe that compet-itiveness will create the very economic success essential to sustaining social programs. . . . The framework for competitiveness they invite us to accept is ultimately dangerous. . . . Once it is accepted, its hidden aspects. . . such as attacks on social programs—quickly reassert themselves. Once we decide to play on the terrain of competitiveness, we cannot then step back without paying a serious price. Having legitimated the importance of being compet-itive (when we should have been mobilizing to defend our social values), we would be extremely vulnerable to the determined attacks that will inevitably come in the name of "global realities." . . . The competitive model ultimate-ly asks how the *corporate sector* can be strengthened. Our perspective asserts

that it is the very strength of that sector that limits our freedom and belittles the meaning of "community."[16]

The progressive competitiveness strategy presented a program of vast economic readjustment for both labor and capital, with blithe disregard for how, in the interim, the logic of competitive austerity could be avoided; it presumed that unemployment was primarily a problem of skills adjustment to technological change rather than one aspect of a crisis of overproduction; it fostered an illusion of a rate of employment growth in high-tech sectors sufficient to offset the rate of unemployment growth in other sectors; it either even more unrealistically assumed a rate of growth of world markets massive enough to accommodate all those adopting this strategy, or it blithely ignored the issues associated with exporting unemployment to those who did not succeed at this strategy under conditions of limited demand (and with the attendant consequence this would have for sustaining demand); it also ignored the fact that capital can adapt leading technologies in low-wage economies, and the competitive pressures on capital in this context to push down wages even in high-tech sectors and limit the costs to itself of the social wage and adjustment policies so central to the whole strategy's progressive logic in the first place. It is hardly surprising that Greg Albo in this context came to the conclusion that even "the progressive competitiveness strategy will be forced to accept, as most social democratic parties have been willing to do, the same 'competitive austerity' as neo-liberalism."[17]

Robert Cox, terming this strategy "state capitalist," saw it as the only possible medium-term alternative to the "hyper-liberal" form of state yet made it quite clear that it was "in effect, grounded in an acceptance of the world market as the ultimate determinant of development":

> The state capitalist form involves a dualism between, on the one hand, a competitively efficient world-market-oriented sector and, on the other, a protected welfare sector. The success of the former must provide resources for the latter; the sense of solidarity implicit in the latter would provide the drive and legitimacy for the former. . . . In its most radical form, state capitalism beckons toward an internal socialism sustained by capitalist success in world-market competition. This would be a socialism dependent on capitalist development, i.e. on success in the production of exchange values. But, so its proponents argue, it would be less vulnerable to external destabilization than attempts at socialist self-reliance were in weak countries.[18]

Cox saw this option ("with or without its socialist coloration") as largely limited to late industrializing countries (such as France, Japan, Germany, Brazil, South Korea) with strong institutional and ideological traditions of "close coordination between the state and private capital in the pursuit of common goals." He was well aware that this type of state capitalism, while incorporating that portion of the working class attached to the world-market-oriented sector or employed in the welfare services sector, would nevertheless exclude many people ("disproportionately the young, women, immigrant or minority groups, and the unemployed") who would remain in a passive relationship to the welfare services and without influence in policymaking. Amidst anomic explosions of violence from these groups, Cox foresaw that the state capitalist alternative's "historic bloc would be thin" and that this might entail the kind of repression and insulation from democratic pressures which would particularly make illusory the prospects the state capitalist strategy holds out for an "internal socialism." Still, Cox, like so many others on the left, took the position that state capitalist strategies in Japan and Europe constituted "the only possible counterweights to total globalization at the level of states." He held out particular hope that the European Community, where the "unresolved issue over the social charter indicates a stalemate in the conflict over the future nature of the nation state and of the regional authority" might yet bring to the fore "a capitalism more rooted in social policy and more balanced development," one reflecting the continuing influence of Social Democratic and older conservative traditions. Given the limited medium-term options of those on the left who were looking for an alternative that would go beyond choosing between rival forms of capitalism, Cox urged them to look positively upon "the ideological space that is opened by this confrontation of hyper-liberalism and state capitalist or corporatist forms of development."[19]

Yet what is the evidence of such a confrontation? There was an unfortunate tendency exhibited here to turn juxtaposed ideal-types, constructed for the purposes of analytic clarity, into real-world confrontations for which there is all too little evidence. The institutional and ideological structures that were pointed to as the basis for a state capitalist progressive competitiveness alternative to neo-liberal globalization were in fact being subsumed as subsidiary sponsors of globalization in manner quite analogous to the way Cox saw tripartite institutions of national economic planning as having become subsidiary elements in adjusting domestic economies to the world economy in the postwar order. Both in Europe and in North America, ministries of labor (and the tripartite forums and agencies they sponsor) as well as ministries of welfare and education, were being restructured to conform with the principles of global competitiveness, but their capacity to retain their links to the social forces they represent in the state rested on their ability to tailor this reconstruction along the lines of progressive competitiveness principles.

In this way, key social groups that would otherwise become dangerously marginalized as a result of the state's sponsorship of global competitiveness may become attached to it by the appeal a progressive competitiveness strategy makes, especially through the ideology and practice of training, to incorporating working people who are unemployed and on welfare (or who soon might be) as well as the leaders of the unions, social agencies, and other organizations who speak for them. Insofar as they are successful in this, moreover, ministries of welfare, education, labor, regional development, etc., may prevent their further loss of status in the hierarchy of state apparatuses and even recapture some of their previously foregone status. Insofar as it undertakes no greater challenge to the structure of the state or to the logic of global competitiveness than that of insisting that more, rather than less, state economic orchestration can be a more effective, and at the same time a more humane handmaiden to competition, the progressive competitiveness strategy ends up being not an alternative to, but a subsidiary element in, the process of neo-liberal capitalist restructuring and globalization.

In North America, the most often cited guarantee that the progressive competitiveness strategy would not coalesce with the logic of neo-liberalism was the European Social Charter. It was constantly pointed to as a model for other international agreements which would constitutionalize a high level of labor rights, social standards, and corporate codes of conduct. On this basis, for instance, Robinson argued: "If globalization can mean more than one thing . . . then the irreversibility of globalization no longer necessarily leads to neo-conservative economic and social policy prescriptions. In this light, national competitiveness, too, can mean more than one thing, depending upon whether it is achieved by cutting labour and environmental costs to TNCs, or promoting technological innovation and reducing the social, political, and environmental externalities associated with largely unregulated global market competition."[20] This approach almost always involved vastly inflating the applicability and significance of the European Social Charter, or, where its weakness was acknowledged (as Robinson did), it failed to inquire whether the reason "the most powerful labour movements in the world have made only very limited progress towards an adequate EC social dimension" was because of its incompatibility with even the progressive competitiveness strategy of global competitiveness.

Proponents of the European model would have done well to have paid attention to Alain Lipietz's chilling account of how the moderate European Social Democrats "set up a Europe of traders and capital," hoping that a social dimension would follow, but failing to understand that they had already "thrown away their trump cards by signing the Single Act of 1985":

> A single market for capital and goods without common fiscal, social and ecological policies could not fail to set off a downward competition between member states, each needing to bring its trade into balance. To deal with the threat of "social dumping," Jacques Delors counted on a push *after the event* by unions in peripheral and social democratic countries to impose common statutory or contractual bases throughout the community. This has not happened, despite the (half-hearted) protestations of the European parliament. . . . [A]ttempts to harmonise VAT failed . . . [and] lack of harmonization on capital taxation is much more serious. . . . Even more serious was the surrender over social Europe. In September 1989, the European Commission proposed an insipid Social Charter. . . . In December 1991, at Maastricht[,] . . . legislative power in Europe was handed over to coordination by national governments; a state apparatus on auto-pilot. Social Europe was once more sacrificed, and reduced to a "zero-Charter," with Britain opting out. . . . In essence, as it is presently emerging, Europe will be unified only for the sake of capital, to allow it to escape from state control; that is, from the tax authorities and from social legislation.[21]

It is, of course, not really an escape from state control. Lipietz's account would make no sense if it were. The governments of Europe are not trying to assert a control over capital at the nation-state level while at the same time trying to forswear control at the regional level. The states, including the Social Democratic–led ones, as Lipietz avers, are the political authors of the Europe of traders and capitalists. Of course, they reflect capital's domination in each social formation in doing so, but it must also be said that the notion that this capital is ready to sustain, as the basis of regional trade rivalries, a rival state capitalist form "rooted in social policy and territorially balanced development" is belied by all the facts before us. Indeed, Cox may have been closer to the mark when he suggested in 1987 that the decline of American hegemony and the competitive pressures in the world system were acting on all states in such a way as to encourage an "emulative uniformity."[22] But his expectation at that time that this might involve common "adoption of similar forms of state-capitalist development geared to an offensive strategy in world markets and sustained by corporatist organization of society and economy" only rings true if we see state capitalism, as we have suggested, not as an alternative to "hyperliberalism" but rather as a subsidiary element sustaining progressive competitiveness, even in Europe. As Albo noted, "it is not the Anglo-American countries who are converting to the Swedish or German models but Germany and Sweden who are integrating the 'Anglo-American model.'"[23]

IV

It would indeed appear that there is no way of honestly posing an alternative to neo-liberal globalization that avoids the central issue of the political source of capitalist power, globally and locally: the state's guarantee of control of the major means of production, distribution, communication, and exchange by private, inherently undemocratic banks and corporations. It is inconceivable that there can be any exit from today's crisis without a planned reorientation and redistribution of resources and production on a massive scale. Yet how can this even be conceived as feasible, let alone made a basis for political mobilization?

We need to recognize, first of all, that those who want to install a "transnational democracy" in the wake of the nation-state allegedly having been bypassed by globalization simply misunderstand what the internationalization of the state really is all about. Not only is the world still very much composed of states, but insofar as there is any substance to democracy at all in relation to the power of capitalists and bureaucrats, it is still embedded in political structures which are national or subnational in scope. Those who advance the nebulous case for an "international civil society" usually fail to appreciate that capitalism has not escaped the state but rather that the state has, as always, been a fundamental constitutive element in the very process of extension of capitalism in our time.

Sol Picciotto, who himself wants to give strategic priority to "international popular organisation" as the best way forward, is nevertheless cor-

rect to warn against "naive illusions that social power exists quite inde-
pendently of the state" and calls for "more sophisticated analyses of the
contradictions of the state and the ways they can be exploited to build the
strength of popular movements, while remaining aware that the national
state is only a part of the overall structure of power in a global capitalist
society."[24] The international constitutionalization of neo-liberalism has
taken place through the agency of states, and there is no prospect what-
soever of getting to a *somewhere else*, inspired by a vision of an egalitarian, democratic, and cooperative world order beyond global competitiveness, that does not entail a fundamental struggle with domestic as well as
global capitalists over the transformation of the state. Indeed, the contemporary era of the globalization of capital may have finally rendered
the distinction between national and foreign capital more or less irrelevant as a strategic marker for the Left. The two-centuries-old search for a
cross-class "producer alliance" between labor and national capital as an
alternative to class struggle took shape in recent years in the form of the
progressive competitiveness strategy, but its weaknesses were very
quickly revealed in the context of the globalization of capital.

It is necessary to try to reorient strategic discussions on the left toward
the democratic transformation of the state rather than toward *transcending the
state* or trying to fashion a *progressive competitive state*. At the most general level this means envisaging a state whose functions are not tied to
guaranteeing the legal, social, and economic infrastructure for capitalism.
We have seen how the internationalization of the state entails a turning of
the material and ideological capacities of states to more immediate and
direct use, in terms of both intranational and international dimensions, to
global capital. The first requirement of strategic clarification on the left
must be the recognition that it must seek the transformation of the material and ideological capacities of states so that they can serve to realize
popular, egalitarian, and democratic goals and purposes. This does *not*
mean attempting to take the state as it is presently organized and structured and trying to impose controls over capital with these inappropriate
instruments. Nor does it mean trying to coordinate such controls internationally while resting on the same state structures. The point must be
to restructure the hierarchy of state apparatuses and reorganize their
modus operandi so as to develop radically different material and ideological
capacities.

"One of principal tasks of the capitalist state," David Harvey has
noted, "is to locate power in the spaces which the bourgeoisie controls,

and disempower those spaces which the oppositional movements have the greatest potential to command."[25] The Left needs to take this lesson out of the book of capital to the end of relocating power to the benefit of progressive social forces. The same might be said about the important role the state can play in the distribution of time as an aspect of power. Radical proposals coming forward on the left today for a statutory reduction in the working day to as little as four hours are not only directed at coping with the appalling maldistribution of employment in contemporary capitalism, but are best conceived as also establishing the conditions for the extension and deepening of democracy by providing the time for extensive involvement in community and workplace decision making.[26]

To emphasize the continuing importance of struggles to transform the state does not mean that territorial boundaries within which claims to state sovereignty are embedded ought to be seen as immutable. The integration of national with international capital upsets the old bases for national capital's unity; and at the same time regional discontents with state policies which are increasingly articulated with the needs of the global economy have provided fertile ground for a resurgence of old nationalisms with a separatist purpose. Right-wing nationalisms, and the parochialisms and intolerances they both reflect and engender, must be combated on every front. But it is not always necessary for the Left to oppose the breakup of an existing state, just as it is not wise to dismiss out of hand attempts at international rearticulation of sovereignties through the creation of regional federations. The question is only whether the locus of power is thereby shifted to those spaces wherein democratic and inclusive movements which are oppositional to capital can expand their space and powers through such a reorganization of sovereignties.

For instance, while left-internationalists usually shake their heads in dismay at the apparent stupidity of Quebec leaving the Canadian federation at the very moment when France should be joining a federal Europe, it is by no means necessarily the case that the existing Canadian federal state lays a firmer foundation for democratic challenges to capital than would close and amicable cooperation between an independent Quebec and a restructured Canadian state. Indeed, more might be expected from two nation-states each of whose *raison d'état* was expressly more egalitarian and democratic in purpose rather than binational and territorial (*Ad Mare usque ad Mare*, it has often been pointed out on the Canadian Left, does not quite match *Liberty, Equality, and Fraternity* as a symbolic national expression of *raison d'état*). Nor should it be necessarily thought that a federal Europe must be one that necessarily extends democratic powers rather than disperses them more thinly in relation to a greater centralization of state powers oriented to fulfilling capital's needs on a continental terrain. Moreover, a federal state composed of the *existing* states of Europe is one that continues to rest on the *modus operandi* of these states. As every Canadian knows, capitalist forces are as capable of playing off the units of a federation against one another and against the center, as they are of doing so with sovereign nation-states; indeed the process may be more easily obscured behind an interminable debate over the division of constitutional powers.

Lipietz, while taking his "starting point that the struggles and social compromises are still settled at the level of the old-established nations of Europe" averred that he would have liked to see social and political uni-fication as quickly as possible insofar as it would be democratically struc-tured so as to overcome the condition of competitive austerity. But he admitted that while it was "better to have a Europe which is progressive (in the alternative sense of the word) than a France, a Sweden, etc., which are progressive in isolation . . . the present dilemma does not lie here. We are asked to choose between a Europe of *possibly* alternative states, and a united Europe which is liberal-productivist. My response is that if this is the choice, the first solution is better." Lipietz admitted that in the short term it was unrealistic to expect a united Europe to be based on anything other than "liberal-productivism." And it would be no less unrealistic to expect that this could change in the future without a prior change in the configuration of social forces and restructuring of state apparatuses in the member countries.[27]

A "possibly alternative state" to those sponsoring globalization amidst competitive austerity today would have to be based on a shift toward a more inwardly oriented economy rather than one driven by external trade considerations. This in turn would have to mean placing greater emphasis on a radical redistribution of productive resources, income, and working time than on conventional economic growth. This could only be democratically grounded, as Albo puts it, insofar as "production and ser-vices [were] more *centred* on local and national needs where the most legitimate democratic collectivities reside."[28] Democratically elected eco-nomic planning bodies at the local level, invested with the statutory responsibility of engineering a return to full employment in their com-munities and funded through direct access to a portion of the surplus that at present is the prerogative of the private financial system to allocate, should be the first priority in a program for an alternative state.

This alternative could not be realized without at least some trade controls and certainly not without quite extensive controls over the flow of capital. (Indeed, it is improbable that such capital control can be realized without bringing the financial system within the public domain and radically reorganizing it in both its structure and its function. This used to be known, when the Left was still innocent about its terminology, as the "nationalization" of the banks.) Of course, this would necessarily require interstate cooperation to install managed trade (rather than autarky) and to make capital controls effective. Have we then gone through this exercise only to come full circle—right back to the internationalization of the state? Certainly not. International agreements and treaties between states will most certainly be required, but they will have the opposite purpose to the constitutionalizing of neo-liberalism: They will be explicitly designed to permit states to effect democratic control over capital within their domains and to facilitate the realization of alternative economic strategies.

The feasibility of this alternative scenario rests entirely on conditions that still remain to be established. It is all too easy to predict the immense pressure and exertion of naked power that would emanate from international capital and dominant states on a country that was even near the point of embarking on such a strategic alternative; all too easy (and, of course, intentionally or unintentionally demobilizing) because what it ignores are the prior material and political conditions that would bring the possibility of change onto the historical agenda. Some of these are material in the economic-technical sense of the term. Thus, even the technical feasibility of short-term capital controls is an open question today. Yet the instability of the world financial system is such that we are likely to see the "discovery" of means of control and regulation, whether before or after an international financial collapse. But it is, above all, the political conditions that need to be created. The impact of domestic and external resistance is unpredictable in abstraction from the character, strength, and effectiveness of the social forces that will mobilize within states and put the alternative on the agenda. Cox was extremely insightful on this when he insisted at the end of *Production, Power, and World Order* that once "a historical movement gets underway, it is shaped by the material possibilities of the society in which it arises and by resistance to its course as much as by the ... goals of its supporters." Yet this is why he also insisted that "critical awareness of the potentiality for change ... concentrates on the possibilities of launching a social movement rather than on what that movement might achieve. ... In the minds of those who opt for change, the solution will most likely be seen as lying not in the enactment of a specific policy program as in the building of new means of collective action informed by a new understanding of society and polity."[29]

This will happen within states or it will not happen at all, but it will not happen in one state alone while the rest of the world goes on running with the bourgeoisie around the globe. Alternatives arise within international political time: the movement-building struggles arise in conjunctures which are more than ever "determined on a world basis."[30] Movements in one country have always been informed and inspired by movements abroad; all the more so will this prove to be the case as opposition builds to the evils globalization is visiting on peoples all around the globe, increasingly also in the developed capitalist countries. There is no need to conjure up out of this an "international civil society" to install a "transnational democracy." Rather we are likely to witness a series of movements arising that will be exemplary for one another, even though national specificities will continue to prevail. It is to be hoped, of course, that these movements will as far as possible exhibit solidarity with one another, even though international solidarity movements cannot be taken for alternatives, rather than as critical supplements, to the struggles that must take place on the terrain of each state.

There has been a stifling tendency on the left in recent decades to draw facile lessons from previous failures of attempts to escape from the logic of globalization. The limits faced by the Alternative Economic Strategy in Britain in the mid-1970s and the French socialist program at the beginning of the 1980s are particular favorites employed to "prove" that capital has the unchallengeable power to escape the state. But was there even the political will in these cases, let alone the movement or the material conditions, to try to escape the control of capital? François Mitterand had learned to "speak socialist," in the immortally cynical words of Gaston Defferre, but what failed in 1981–82 was primarily an attempt at a Keynesian reflation at a very inopportune moment rather than the far more radical assault on capitalism that had been envisaged in the *Programme Commune*.[31] And while U.S. Secretary of State William Rodgers harbored "cosmic" fears in 1976 that Tony Benn might precipitate a policy decision by Britain to turn its back on the IMF, which might in turn lead to the whole liberal financial system falling apart, Rodgers quickly found he could count on the support of the rest of the Labour Cabinet, let alone the Treasury and the Bank of England and the MI5.[32] It is time the Left stopped reading its own faulty memory of such past moments into all potential futures. It would seem that the last word, like the first, belongs to *Through the Looking Glass*:

> "That's the effect of living backwards," the Queen said kindly; "it always makes one a little giddy at first—"
>
> "Living backwards!" Alice repeated in great astonishment. "I never heard of such a thing!"
>
> "—but there's one great advantage in it, that one's memory works both ways."
>
> "I'm sure *mine* only works one way," Alice remarked. "I can't remember things before they happen."
>
> "It's a poor sort of memory that only works backwards," the Queen remarked.

Notes

1. Robert Cox, *Production, Power, and World Order* (New York: Columbia University Press, 1987), pp. 253, 258.

2. David Held, "Democracy: From City-States to a Cosmopolitan Order?" *Political Studies* 40 (Special Issue, 1992): 32–34. For Held's most recent formulations, which give more emphasis to the "transformation" of states, see Held et al., *Global Transformations: Politics, Economics, Culture* (Stanford: Stanford University Press, 1999).

3. Immanuel Wallerstein, *The Politics of the World-Economy* (Cambridge, U.K.: Cambridge University Press, 1984), pp. 10–11. Italics in original.

4. Perry Anderson, *A Zone of Engagement* (London: Verso: 1992), pp. 366–67.

5. Stephen Gill, "The Emerging World Order and European Change," in Ralph Miliband and Leo Panitch, eds., *New World Order? The Socialist Register 1992* (London: Merlin, 1992).

6. See Phillip Corrigan and Derek Sayer, *The Great Arch: English State Formation As Cultural Revolution* (Oxford: Basil Blackwell, 1985); and Alan Wolfe, *The Limits of Legitimacy* (New York: Free Press, 1977).

7. Ian Robinson, *North American Free Trade As If Democracy Mattered* (Ottawa: Canadian Centre for Policy Alternatives, 1993), p. 3. Two other excellent analyses were Christian Deblock and Michele Rioux, "NAFTA: The Dangers of Regionalism," *Studies in Political Economy* 41 (1993): 7–44; and Ricardo Grinspun and Robert Kreklewich, "Consolidating Neoliberal Reforms: 'Free

Trade' As a Consolidating Framework," *Studies in Political Economy* 43 (1994): 33–61.

8. Robinson, *North American Free Trade*, p. 20.

9. Ibid., p. 20.

10. *Business Week*, 22 November 1993, p. 34.

11. *Globe and Mail*, 1 November 1993.

12. See Nicos Poulantzas, *Classes in Contemporary Capitalism* (London: New Left Books, 1974), p. 66.

13. *Business Week*, 22 November 1993, p. 35.

14. See Leo Panitch, "Dependency and Class in Canadian Political Economy," *Studies in Political Economy* 6 (1981): 7–33.

15. See the critique of this position in my *Working Class Politics in Crisis* (London: Verso, 1986), esp. chs. 4–6; and in my "Tripartite Experience," in Keith Banting, ed., *The State and Economic Interests* (Toronto: University of Toronto Press, 1986).

16. Sam Gindin and David Robertson, "Alternatives to Competitiveness," in Daniel Drache, ed., *Getting on Track: Social Democratic Strategies for Ontario* (Montreal: McGill-Queens University Press, 1992), pp. 32–33, 39. Emphasis in original.

17. Greg Albo, "Competitive Austerity and the Impasse of Capitalist Employment Policy," in Ralph Miliband and Leo Panitch, eds., *Between Globalism and Nationalism: The Socialist Register 1994* (London: Merlin, 1994), p. 157.

18. Robert Cox, *Production, Power, and World Order*, pp. 292–94.

19. See Robert Cox, "Global Perestroika," in Miliband and Panitch, ed., *New World Order?* esp. pp. 31 and 41; and Cox, *Production, Power, and World Order*, esp. pp. 292 and 297–98.

20. Robinson, "North American Free Trade," p. 44.

21. Alain Lipietz, *Towards a New Economic Order* (Oxford: Oxford University Press,1992), pp. 156–59.

22. Cox, *Production, Power, and World Order*, pp. 298–99.

23. Albo, "Competitive Austerity," p. 168.

24. Sol Picciotto, "The Internationalisation of the State," *Capital and Class* 43 (1991): 60.

25. David Harvey, *The Condition of Postmodernity* (Oxford: Basil Blackwell, 1989), p. 237.

26. See Ernest Mandel, *Power and Money* (London: Verso, 1992), esp. pp. 202; and Andre Gorz, *Critique of Economic Reason* (London: Verso, 1989), p. 159.

27. Lipietz, *Towards a New Economic Order*, p. 135.

28. Albo, "Competitive Austerity," p. 164.

29. Cox, *Production, Power, and World Order*, pp. 394–95.

30. Poulantzas, *Classes in Contemporary Capitalism*, p. 67.

31. See Daniel Singer, *Is Socialism Doomed?* (Oxford: Oxford University Press, 1988).

32. See Leo Panitch and Colin Leys, *The End of Parliamentary Socialism: From New Left to New Labour* (London: Verso, 1997), esp. ch. 6; and Leo Panitch, "The New Imperial State," *New Left Review* 2,2 (March/April, 2000): 12–13.

6

Bringing Class Back In: Reflections on Strategy for Labor

I

To speak of strategy *for labor* needs some justification today. Class analysis went out of intellectual fashion almost two decades ago; and class politics has been increasingly displaced as the pivot of party political discourse and electoral mobilization. Class, as we have been so often reminded, is not everything.

But nor is class nothing, and the costs of marginalizing class in the intellectual and political arena are becoming increasingly severe, especially in the context of globalization—which is another word for the reach of American imperialism, the power of financial markets, the spread of capitalist social relations, the intensification of exploitation, and a vast growth in social inequality. An extensive process of what looks like classic proletarianization is taking place in many countries of the so-called developing world; and in the advanced capitalist world the decline in the size of the traditional industrial labor force is accompanied by the proletarianization of many service and professional occupations and the spread of more unstable, casual, and contingent employment. These are developments that can only be comprehended through a revival of class analysis; and they may also provide the grounds for new strategies for labor which transcend the limits of the old forms of class politics.

The discourse of "civil society" has made a strong bid to displace the discourse of class on the left. It is intended to present a more inclusive and pluralistic approach than the old class politics in that it identifies those social forces which are the fount of political freedom and progressive change. But one of the ironies of this discourse's claim to inclusivity is that it has often left labor out, having afforded almost no vantage point for observing that arena of nonfreedom within civil society, the workplace, where most people, in selling the right to determine what they do with their time and abilities, enter an authoritarian relationship with an employer within which freedom of speech and assembly are considerably attenuated.[1] Moreover, despite the central importance which the discourse of civil society properly gives to associational autonomy from the state, there has been a remarkable silence in most of the civil society literature regarding state attacks on trade unions over the past two decades—making organizing harder and decertification easier, restricting or removing the right to strike, and so on. It sometimes even appears that trade unions have a better appreciation of what is entailed in securing freedom of association than many contemporary nongovernmental organizations (NGOs): contrast the financial dependence on government grants of so many NGOs with the trade unions' traditional sensitivity (famously articulated even by such nonradical labor leaders as Samuel Gompers) to the danger posed by state funding for associational autonomy.

To be fair, the labor movement's capacity to collect dues (often institutionalized in collective bargaining arrangements) is not open to NGOs and new social movements. Yet this very fact has made some of these movements rely on the labor movement for the funding of various campaigns. It is unfortunately the case that trade unions often use their financial clout to narrow or moderate these campaigns; but this precisely speaks to the need for a new strategy for labor. It is now obvious—it always should have been—that there is nothing inevitable about the working class becoming a transformative agency. Not only reformist and revolutionary, but even reactionary practices have issued from the working classes. But what is also true is that, unless a very substantial part of the labor movement becomes involved, no fundamental socioeconomic change can be realized.

This is why even as harsh a critic as Andre Gorz had returned by the 1990s to thinking again about a strategy for labor—as he had originally done in his famous book of that name in 1964—despite having famously bid "farewell to the working class" in the interim. The very success of the new social movements—whose specific campaigns were not only to "mold the consciousness of a growing number of people" but contained

the promise of "a wider, more fundamental struggle for emancipation"—
had brought out the necessity for this:

> The fact that the trade-union movement is—and will remain—the best orga-
> nized force in the broader movement confers on it a particular responsibili-
> ty; on it will largely depend the success or failure of all the other elements in
> this social movement. According to whether the trade-union movement
> opposes them or whether it seeks a common alliance and a common course
> of action with them, these other elements will be part of the left or will break
> with it, will engage with it in collective action or will remain minorities
> tempted to resort to violence.[2]

A new strategy for labor would mean altering labor movements themselves in fundamental ways, but what Gorz came to see was that the
trade unions' indifference or hostility to the new social movements was
neither foreordained nor unchangeable. As he put it: "The attitude
towards the other social movements and their objectives will determine
[the labor movement's] own evolution."

That this may be an opportune moment to address new strategies for
labor is suggested not only by the strikes in so many countries in recent
years; or by surveys that show rising class awareness even in the United
States where working-class self-identification has historically been very
low.[3] What is much more important than these instances of conflict and
consciousness is the fact that *labor is changing in ways that make it a more
inclusive social agent*. The main developments here have been women's
massive (re)entry into the labor force and changing patterns of migration,
both of which have recomposed the working classes of many countries
and made them into very different classes in both objective and subjective
terms than they were even a quarter-century or so ago. Working classes
have, of course, always been made up of many diverse elements: What is
significant is the way the old labor movements are being changed by the
recomposition of the working classes in our time.[4]

The image many people, including many on the left, have of labor is
outdated. Feminism and environmentalism, even gay-rights activism,
have had a visible effect within the labor movement—and the discourse
and, in many cases, the practice of unions reflects this. Of course, these
changes are very uneven around the globe, and there is substantial vari-
ation even within each national labor movement, and sometimes even
within each union. Sexism, racism, and homophobia continue to be seri-

ous problems, and hostility to environmental issues among those unions whose members' jobs are directly affected remains strong. Even among those which have learned to "talk the talk," unions often have far to go in actually assigning priority to these issues—and tensions can be severe when change goes so far as to induce a clash of priorities. Yet it is also true that there is far more pluralism in today's working classes than is allowed for in the perspectives of those who find it convenient to essentialize labor as male, white, and straight. This new pluralism is one of the main reasons new strategies for labor are needed.

The case to be argued here for a new strategy for labor in no way implies that what the new social movements do is somehow less important. On the contrary, if we concentrate on strategy for labor it is only because, with Gorz, we think the enormous potential of the new social movements for social transformation will only be realized if labor finally takes enthusiastically on board the key emancipatory themes raised by the other movements. But at the same time, the new social movements themselves can hardly ignore their own need for strategy for labor. The experience and possibilities of feminism in relation to labor, and the challenge that this entails not only for unions but also for a feminism that wants to speak to immigrant "maids" as well as their professional "mistresses" is clearly crucial for both movements.[5] Nor can the issue of strategy for labor in the environmental movement be ignored: This is seen in the internal debates that go on within environmental groups over whether the priority often attached to high-profile campaigns as necessary for fundraising among the well-to-do comes at the expense of addressing the environment as a matter of public health in working-class communities.[6]

If the working classes of every country have always been diverse, then the fact that they are becoming more so in our time ought to be a source of strength—and it will be the task of new strategies for labor in unions as well as political and social movements to unleash that strength. The notion of solidarity would never have made any sense if the working classes were homogeneous to begin with. The organization within unions of caucuses, conferences, and committees among women or minority members is a healthy development precisely because it allows additional space within the union for capacity-building among those who have suffered most from discrimination or marginalization. Solidarity as a process has always been about, not ignoring or eliminating, but *transcending* working-class diversity—and this has meant gaining strength via forging unity of purpose out of *strategies of inclusiveness* rather than repressing diversity. At the core of all the failures of past labor strategies lay the inability to build solidarity in this sense as effectively as possible.[7] The challenge is to discover (and to overcome resistance to attempts to discover) how to build fully inclusive labor movements which are democratically structured in such ways as to encourage the development of the capacities of *all* members of the working class in as many facets of their lives as possible.

II

But to say new strategies are needed does not get us far in determining what they should be. Social movement activists have rightly been wary that many traditional labor attitudes and old strategies are recipes for failure and that the labor movement's clinging to them, even if sometimes clothed in new language, is a major factor in blocking social change. The most favored labor strategies have indeed turned out be failures, partly due to changing conditions represented under the symbol of globalization, but also partly due to fundamental flaws in the strategies themselves, flaws which were already visible under the old conditions.

In speaking of this, one should not only count the obvious failures of the Communist parties and insurrectionary Left; or the no less obvious limitations of the American "service" model of trade unionism. Many people on the left today take as their benchmark of success the European Social Democratic labor movements, especially in building the democratic "mixed economies" in the postwar era. But the latter's own failures, if less immediately obvious, are perhaps for that very reason the most important to come to understand. From today's perspective of the defeat of the mixed economy by neo-liberalism, these failures need to be measured above all in terms of the long-run effects of Social Democratic labor movements having lulled themselves into ideological stupor and organizational inertia for three decades with illusions of the humanization of capitalism. In the wake of the postwar settlement and Cold War, unions took little or no responsibility for the education of their supporters on the nature of capitalism as a system or for the development of popular democratic capacities for challenging that system and for collective self-government in every walk of life. It was in good part because of this that the neo-liberal restoration proved possible in the face of the impasse of the Keynesian welfare state in the last quarter of the twentieth century.

The ruthless competitive dynamism of capitalism inevitably reasserted itself in the form of free trade and foreign direct investment, the ascendancy of financial capital, and "lean" production through job "flexibility" and casualization. Labor movements were unprepared for all this—and, worse, had not prepared their members and supporters with the organizational and intellectual resources to readily understand what was happening; nor had they been encouraged to imagine any alternative. No wonder the bourgeoisie at the end of the twentieth century was once again able to make the world in its own image.

This is not a matter of hindsight being easy. These failures were evident enough even in the heyday of the "mixed economy." They were uppermost in Gorz's mind when his *Strategy for Labour* was first published in France in 1964. Gorz took direct aim against those predominant labor strategies which offered

> no other perspective than that of increased *individual consumption*. In other words, they place the workers as a class on the tail end of the "consumer society" and its ideology; they do not challenge the model of that society, but only the share of the wealth which the society accords to the salaried consumer. They consciously bring into question neither the workers' condition at the place of work, nor the subordination of consumption to production; not even ... the diversion and confiscation of productive resources and human labor for frivolous and wasteful ends. . . . [It] is not that struggles over wages are useless; rather, it is that their effectiveness, insofar as mobilization, unification, and education of the working class are concerned, has become very limited. These struggles by themselves, even if they sometimes succeed in creating a crisis within capitalism, neither succeed in preventing capitalism from overcoming its difficulties in its own way, nor in preparing the working class sufficiently to outline and impose its own solutions. . . . On the contrary, the working class runs the risk of provoking a counteroffensive ... an attack leveled not only in the economic, but in the ideological, social and political realms; and the working class, because it did not also wage a fight in these spheres would be unable to respond with the necessary alertness and cohesion.[8]

With the inflationary dynamic which undid the postwar order already on the horizon, Gorz also warned against union adhesion to corporatist income policies, whereby they restrained their members' wage demands to try to stave off the crisis: "The incomes policy merely expresses the political will of organized capitalism to integrate the union into the system, to subordinate consumption to production, and production to the maximization of profit. The union cannot defend itself against this political will except by an opposite and autonomous political will which is independent of party and State."[9] Corporatist partnerships with capital and the state foreclosed strategies directed at "the socialization of the investment function," and without being able to challenge the determination of what was produced and how, the main effect of these corporatist arrangements could only be to subordinate union autonomy to Social Democratic governments which left "the power of the capitalist state intact." By virtue of not taking up structural reforms to challenge and change the structure of power in the capitalist order, the postwar nationalizations and welfare reforms would not only be absorbed by the system but increasingly undermined: "The only way the socialized sector can survive is by limiting capital's sphere of autonomy and countering its logic, by restraining its field of action, and bringing its potential centres of accumulation under social control ... (socialized medicine must control the pharmaceutical industry, social housing must control the building industry, for example), or else be nibbled away and exploited by the private sector."[10] Gorz clearly foresaw the main contours of the strategic failures of the labor movement that opened the way to the neo-liberal restoration.

Yet as the "new world order" represented by neo-liberal globalization began to take shape, many of those who had earlier shown some indication of appreciating the problems Gorz had identified in European corporatism and Social Democracy now rushed to defend them as the only actually existing alternatives to neo-liberalism. A great deal of ink was spilled extolling the virtues of the Swedish or German or Austrian models even as unions in these countries were themselves increasingly internally divided by corporatism's effects over unevenly applied wage restraint and the loss of union autonomy. More significant still, given the real structure of power, even these "models" of corporatism were being abandoned by employers, bureaucrats, and politicians who had already redefined the parameters of economic management. In making the containment of inflation, not unemployment, the prime goal of economic policy, they had already given up on the strategy of securing the wage moderation of unions through corporatist negotiations on incomes policies, and had given priority instead to winning the confidence of financial markets with monetary policies designed to break union militancy through unemployment and job insecurity.

Nevertheless, the advocacy of social partnerships between capital and labor has remained the main leitmotif of most pragmatic and moderate labor leaders and liberal and Social Democratic intellectuals in the new era. Sometimes this has been boldly put forward by "making capitalism an offer it cannot refuse" wherein unions have been urged to present themselves as "being able to solve problems for capitalists which they cannot solve on their own."[11] This attempt to revive a social partnership strategy in the context of globalization was generally guided by the argument that the one thing unions could offer that capital wanted was higher productivity. This "supply-side" form of corporatism and the incorporation within it of strategies for "progressive competitiveness" had at its core what Bienefeld called the cargo cult of training ("if we train them the jobs will come"): partnerships between unions, capital, and state designed to train workers to become so productive that they could compete with low-paid labor abroad, or at least become so innovative that they could sustain the search for niche markets.[12]

The problems with this as a strategy for labor were manifold. First of all, there were the obvious ethical ones. It is as though, seeing a man on the street, hungry and homeless, you perceive his problem only in terms of his not being motivated enough, entrepreneurial enough, skilled enough to get a job, rather than seeing that something must be wrong with the system. This kind of logic is applied, in the progressive competitiveness framework, to whole sectors, regions, and economies. Even if such a strategy of export competitiveness were successful, its effect would be to export unemployment to the regions that are less successful. But the problems with such a strategy were also practical, embedded in the overproduction that must attend a global system where everyone tries to increase their exports and limit their imports through domestic austerity, and in the financial instability that attends capital movements in such a system.

In so far as Social Democracy by the early 1990s still had any distinctiveness in its economic strategies, it was reduced to advocating an active role for states and unions in advancing the export competitiveness of this or that particular capitalist economy. This strategy exaggerated considerably what national capital was willing to do, or could do, to achieve competitiveness, even while, as with the old corporatist strategy, this new one also sacrificed the autonomy of labor to this end. For this reason, the "supply-side" attempt to revive the corporatist approach, masquerading as a new strategy for labor, proved a dead end. With wage militancy and inflation having been broken by monetarism, and with the competitive dynamic of capitalism having already asserted itself in "free" capital flows as well as free trade, the offer of a deal that couldn't be refused was now usually met with a shrug or a blank stare. And when Social Democratic governments were elected, usually even before the new measures to implement corporatist "training" strategies were put in place, let alone could have much effect, these governments were quickly overwhelmed by the problems of short-term economic management. Since everything hinged on the goal of cooperating with capital, they invariably placated financial markets by limiting imports and stabilizing the currency through fiscal austerity. Where Social Democratic parties went so far as to accede to capital's insistence that the price of its cooperation was that Social Democracy jettison its own partnership with the unions, what we had left was Blairism—which prides itself on not conceiving its project as a strategy *for* labor at all, but rather a strategy for explicitly distancing itself from the labor movement.

It is worth noting, especially given this dénouement, that Gorz's original *Strategy for Labour* proceeded from the exact opposite premise from that of offering capital a deal it could not refuse—"one which does not base its validity and its right to exist on capitalist needs, criteria and rationales." The "structural reforms" he advanced were "determined not in terms of what can be, but what should be," and he based his strategy on "the possibility of attaining its objectives on the implementation of fundamental political and economic changes." These changes could be gradual, but the measure of structural reforms was that they effected "a modification of the relations of power"—strengthening workers' capacities to "establish, maintain, and expand those tendencies within the system which serve to weaken capitalism and to shake its joints."[13] In this way, a continuity could be "established between the objectives of present mass struggles and the prospect of a socialist society." The point was to build the kinds of organizations and to engage in the kinds of struggles through which workers might feel—"on all levels of their existence"— that elements of a desirable socialist society were actually discernible within their own world in the here and now. Compromises would still have to be struck, but this needed to be "understood explicitly for what it is: the provisional result of the temporary relationship of forces, to be modified in future battles."[14]

Of course, this was not the approach most unions adopted in the face of globalization. Yet some did: I am aware of no better example of the distinction between offering capital "a deal it cannot refuse" and Gorz's opposite strategic principle than that adopted by the Canadian Auto Workers union in the early 1980s—just as Gorz was (temporarily) bidding "farewell to the working class." The strategic principle the CAW adopted in the face of the big three auto companies demanding concessions from workers to meet the new global competition (leading to its break with its American parent "international" union, the UAW) was straightforward: "Competitiveness is a constraint, but it is not our goal."[15]

<h1 style="text-align:center">III</h1>

Even if the progressive competitiveness strategy is more clearly recognized today as a misguided response to globalization, it is nevertheless the case that no adequate new strategy for labor can evolve unless what is to be done about globalization is seriously addressed. It is first of all necessary to clear up some misconceptions. Globalization is not an objective economic process which labor needs to "catch up to," as so many seem to think. It is a political process advanced by identifiable interests for clear purposes. The failure to see the strategic political nature of globalization reflects an economism which needs to be overcome. Nation-states are not the victims of globalization, they are the authors of globalization. States are not *displaced* by globalized capital, they *represent* globalized capital, above all financial capital. This means that any adequate strategy to challenge globalization must begin at home, precisely because of the key role of states in making globalization happen. But labor's traditional goal of securing a progressive alliance with their national bourgeoisie under the aegis of the state is increasingly passé; for the state more and more represents a set of (domestic and foreign) internationally oriented capitalist classes.

What then is to be done? In order to answer this question we can usefully begin by looking again at the approach Gorz adopted in the mid-1960s with the European Economic Community (as it then was), since it presented problems for European unions that in many ways anticipated those now facing all unions under full globalization. Indeed, one of the most fascinating things about reading Gorz's *Strategy for Labour* now is to see how relevant his analysis of the European Common Market at the time remains for the development of labor strategies in the context of globalization today. Gorz saw the Common Market in the first years of its existence—with its "yearly average of 1000 'mergers and agreements' between companies of different nationalities"—as a prerequisite of a new kind of "monopoly expansion," wherein the nature of competition among big private corporations had shifted to the penetration of each others' interior markets. This entailed rationalization within and across sectors, but it also gave rise to overinvestment and overproduction, leading in turn to a further "thrust of industrial and especially financial concentration." Each state supported or sponsored its own big corporations, and as the financial risks entailed in this competitive mutual penetration of interior markets escalated, a degree of supranational planning at the European level was needed. Such planning, however, "obviously has nothing to do with real economic planning" since it was designed only to smooth out the contradictions of the competitive process in which "the capitalists' freedom of action remains untouched." If labor's goal was to attach union representatives to such supranational planning, it "would obviously make a fool's bargain. . . . Cut off from the working masses . . . the workers' representatives are under strong pressure to become technocrats, working out summit compromises which win a great deal less than mass action could have."[16]

The recent history of European economic integration chillingly confirms this. Capital's room for maneuver has been greatly expanded, and so has the "democratic deficit," embedding even further in the European Central Bank what each state's central banks had already represented in this respect. But as Andrew Martin and George Ross have demonstrated, what the European Trade Union Congress (ETUC) saw as its "breakthrough, beyond anything it could have reasonably expected" when it was suddenly embraced as a negotiating partner under Maastricht's Social Protocol, turned out to be only a breakthrough for the union bureaucracy in Brussels. The embrace "turned out very different from what enthusiasts had foreseen in the heady days of 1985 to 1990" and left the ETUC "essentially excluded from more fundamental matters of economic governance." This was reflected in the sheer weakness of the Social Chapter actually negotiated under Maastricht (especially insofar as matters concerning pay or the rights to organize and strike were entirely excluded). Even the much-vaunted subsequent protocol mandating European Works Councils in multinational corporations (which covered only some 10 percent of the European workforce in any case), left so much leeway to employers that it produced "less than a handful of agreements [which] provide for consultation more meaningful . . . than an 'exchange of views' after the fact." Despite some modest success in the area of parental leave benefits, there can be no escaping the fact that "the EMU macroeconomic policy regime has squeezed social policy between unemployment and convergence/stability pact criteria" to such an extent that capitalist "supply-side" strategies for greater labor market "flexibility" have come to take precedence over any positive new strategy for labor.[17]

Above all, what is confirmed in Gorz's prognosis is that labor's involvement in European integration has been "largely a top-down process." As Martin and Ross put it: "The ETUC has so far developed largely by borrowing resources from European institutions to gain legitimacy with its own national constituents . . . ETUC, in other words, has developed from the top rather than as a mass organization built from below out of a broader social movement." Moreover, since the promise of substantial gains from elite bargaining within European institutions has not materialized, the result has been that the European unions' position of "critical support" for Economic and Monetary Union "has so far put them in an excruciating political bind. It ties them to the particular version of the economic approach to political integration that has been pursued despite its social costs and rising popular disenchantment, including among union members."[18] Not surprisingly in this context, unions have relied on national collective bargaining and political structures to protect themselves as best they could. But the "competitive corporatism" they are still oriented to at this level, seen in various new "social pacts" that have been struck with employers and the state, has mainly to do with competitive adjustment (via the sacrifice of earlier labor market and welfare-state reforms as well as wage moderation) to the neo-liberalism embedded in European integration.

It is indeed significant that strategies for transnational collective bargaining have made so little headway since Charles Levinson made the case for it thirty years ago in the context of the spread of multinational corporations.[19] The reasons for this may partly be laid at the door of national-level trade unions bureaucrats, but much more important has been that the very purpose of globalization, from the perspective of business and the capitalist state, has been to bring about competition among workers, not foster centralized bargaining at a higher level. Notably, Gorz, unlike Levinson, did not advocate working "toward the unification and the centralization of a labor strategy . . . besides being impossible at present, [this] would only result in bureaucratic sclerosis." While it was necessary to try to "coordinate among the various sectoral, regional, or national strategies so they complement, not contradict each other," one had to primarily let each national struggle to "develop according to its own particular qualities" since it was from struggles at this level "that the labour movement principally draws its strength." This did not mean the class struggles ought to be isolated from the international arena; Gorz believed, rather, that it was increasingly possible to "trust in the contagious effect of each national victory." Isolated national victories would not be possible any longer, because in the context of the new international competitiveness, each national government, once forced by its labor movement to undertake a structural reform, would have to advance its adoption at the European level to ensure that the policy labor imposed in one state did not remain "a national peculiarity."[20]

IV

These considerations are very germane to the question of how labor should respond to further efforts to extend globalization today. It is time to question strategies—often borrowed from superficial accounts of the European Social Chapter—for securing the inclusion of labor rights in international trade treaties. Along the lines of the NAFTA labor and environmental "side agreements," this strategy is designed to constitutionalize minimum labor standards, as well as secure a place for labor representatives in the negotiation and administration of these treaties. Such a strategy may be useful for bringing terrible labor conditions and anti-union policies into public discussions of globalization, but at the same time, the very idea of attaching labor rights to such treaties also means endorsing the free trade and capital flows which these treaties are all about securing. Moreover, apart from what ideological effect they have, the difficulties of enforcing labor rights articulated in such side agreements are notorious.

What is most disturbing about this response to globalization, however, as Gerard Greenfield has especially pointed out, is how often it is used both by the International Confederation of Free Trade Unions (ICFTU) and national union leaders

> to justify the abandonment of collective action locally, and even nationally, as ineffective or irrelevant. Based on what they see as the inevitability of capitalist globalization and the weakness of organized labor, they are instead seeking a new set of compromises with global capital. Or to put it more accu-

rately, they are seeking a continuation of the old compromises with national capital at a global level.[21]

Insofar as this new strategy of global compromise displaces rather than supports militant workers' struggles, Greenfield argues, it is not only misguided, but positively harmful. This is not to say that the institutions of globalization don't have to be engaged with by unions; the question is what priority they assign to this and what they seek from such engagement. In a discussion document prepared for developing union strategy for the World Trade Organization's (WTO) round of multilateral negotiations that was supposed to have begun in Seattle at the end of 1999, Greenfield articulated, in direct contrast with the ICFTU's "strategy for inclusion," a new "strategy for exclusion." This meant that, in addressing the content of international economic treaties, unions and their allies could follow the principle of immunity ("freedom from") rather than of rights ("freedom to") along the lines of those labor law regimes which established that organizing attempts or strikes were protected from punishment or legal prosecution by the employer. This would take the form of demanding the exclusion of particular sectors, or particular biological resources (such as seeds), from WTO agreements and would go along with demands for the immunity of workers' and farmers' organizations from repression when their states face unfair trading practices through the WTO's complaint mechanisms. This defensive aspect of the strategy, designed to limit the damage caused by such agreements, can accompany a more general strategic challenge to the whole process entailed in these negotiations, above all to the secrecy of the negotiations which "reflects an inherent hostility towards democracy and democratic processes among WTO technocrats, government advisors and the powerful corporate interests they represent." Greenfield goes on:

> This problem is not simply resolved by getting unions a chair at the negotiating table. Whatever is decided will still be decided behind-the-scenes anyway. . . . Past experience has shown that getting a seat at the table sometimes places far too much emphasis on representing labor, rather than organising labor. . . . More important is the task of breaking down walls to these behind-the-scenes deals in a way that organises and mobilises our members along with a broader alliance of democratic forces. Clearly this requires a public education and mobilisation campaign to achieve what WTO technocrats and TNCs do not want—a critical awareness among working people of *what is being done to them.*[22]

The negotiated exclusion strategy advanced by Greenfield was thus explicitly conceived as secondary and subsidiary to a primary strategy of mobilization against the institutions of globalization themselves. This is what actually came to the fore at Seattle, where the initiative was taken away from those trying to get a seat at the table in a such a surprising and stunning fashion that it may be counted as a turning point. To be sure, what happened on the streets of Seattle was not spontaneous combustion—a lot of planning was involved by a great many NGOs and unions. And it followed on the impressive activities already undertaken in the same year by People's Global Action, a new alliance formed in February 1998 by some 300 delegates from movements in 71 countries on the basis of their common rejection of the WTO and other trade liberalization agreements. Their self-described "confrontational attitude" was based on the perception that lobbying cannot "have a major impact in such biased and undemocratic organizations [as the WTO], in which transnational capital is the only real policy-maker." The Global Day of Action they sponsored in the world's financial centers on 18 June 1999 was an important, if much less noticed, prelude to what took place in Seattle six months later.

The sight of steelworkers declaring solidarity with anarchists on the streets of Seattle was a heady one. The multiplicity of voices and slogans was bewildering and frustrating to those "progressive" negotiators, whether from the Third World or the First, whose main priority is the strategy of global compromise. "It's not clear what they want—they want so many different things," was the complaint often heard. The mutterings of officials in the French royal court in 1789 must have been much the same. One measure of the truly radical nature of these kinds of protests is just this—they aren't putting forward a series of demands that can be negotiated within the given institutional frameworks of globalization: They really are building critical awareness among people of "what is being done to them"—and are galvanizing a great deal of attention and support as a result.

Unfortunately, immediately after Seattle the political initiative against globalization within the United States swung back to those leaders of the American unions who, by the time of the protests against the International Monetary Fund (IMF) and the World Bank in Washington, D.C., four months later, were prepared to narrow the issue down to whether the U.S. Congress should endorse China's inclusion in the WTO. The problem was not so much that of protectionism per se (any serious attempt to challenge globalization entails "protection" for local and national communities); it was rather what can only be called the *chauvinist* protectionism and *imperial* condescension that lay behind the demand that the American state should not be giving the Chinese masses the "benefit" of access to its markets until labor rights were enforced in China. The whole discourse was framed in terms of appealing to the American state to play its "proper" world role as a democratic and benevolent good guy against the Chinese state. The absence of a strong alternative vision, and the danger of not having one, was revealed in the astonishing support which key American NGO leaders gave to the AFL/CIO's narrowly conceived campaign against China's inclusion in the WTO.[23] They contributed in this way to legitimating the WTO as something really worth getting into, even as they mobilized for the Washington demonstration against the other institutions of globalization, the IMF and the World Bank.

Lost in the rhetoric in the debate on China after Seattle were two main things: first, the enormous concessions China is making to foreign capital to get into the WTO;[24] and second, the fact that the struggle for labor rights is not external to China but is being conducted within it (as it is in all developing countries), including by the millions of Chinese workers who, by official estimates, undertook over 120,000 strikes in 1999 alone.[25] If the AFL/CIO really wants to help Chinese workers, it will campaign for the exclusion of those provisions in the WTO that will result in tens of millions of Chinese workers losing their jobs when public enterprises are robbed of their "subsidies"; and it will take direct action itself by providing the level of resources and support to those struggling to build independent trade unions in China that it provided in the 1980s to Solidarity in Poland (of course it was encouraged in this at the time by the American state—as it will not be regarding Chinese independent unions now).

But can much better be said of those Third World elites who themselves employed the charge of imperialism against those who called for labor rights to be included in the WTO? We should have no illusions either about Third World leaders and their technocratic advisers who are ready and willing to set aside labor rights in their anxiety to ensure at all costs that foreign capital comes their way rather than leaves them marginalized in the new world capitalist order. It is misleading to speak, as Samir Amin does today, of the "political authorities in the active peripheries— and behind them all society (including the contradictions within society itself)—hav[ing] a project and a strategy" for national economic development which stands in "confrontation with globally dominant imperialism."[26] He includes in the active peripheries China, Korea, and India as well as unnamed others in Southeast Asia and Latin America and contrasts these with "marginalized peripheries" which are "the passive subjects of globalization." But while the ruling classes and political elite of India, Korea, and especially China are definitely not merely the "passive subjects" of globalization as they actively maneuver for a place in the new global order, it is also patently clear that only a major transformation in class relations in each of these countries will lead to anything like a "confrontation with globally dominant imperialism." For Third World state elites who really want to take an anti-imperial stand, a good place to start, rather than clamoring for a seat at the table of the imperium, would be to stop their repression of domestic class struggle and their denial of freedom of association.

A sustained mobilization against the institutions of globalization will have to eventually offer a strategic vision for a different order. Until such a vision gains some currency, legitimacy will continue to be lent to the institutions of globalization by many labor, NGO, and Third World elites who see no practical alternative to them. No such vision has yet emanated from the mobilizations that gave us Seattle, although the World Social Forum held in Porto Alegre, Brazil, in January 2000 (attended by delegates from 120 countries) signaled the widespread desire for one. Andrew Ross previously noted that "the capacity to organize dissent and resistance on the international scale" has been considerably enhanced by the "undeniable asset" of the Internet, but the "new informational landscape" has also "magnified the gulf between the temporality of activists—based on urgency around mobilization—and the temporality of intellectuals—based around the slower momentum of thought and theoretical speculation. Many forms of radical thought require a patient process of germination that is antipathetic to the new speed of information circulation."[27] To be sure, the contribution that even Left intellectuals see themselves as making is mostly limited to offering narrow-gauge policy advice to their states which internalizes the politics of compromise (as such, Left intellectuals bear some responsibility for the dead end to which competitive corporatism and progressive competitiveness have led). The seeds of an alternative vision have more often been planted by the activist groups themselves, such as by the People's Global Action organizational philosophy of "decentralization and autonomy" which implies inward-oriented development strategies ("localization") rather than export competitiveness. But for this glimmer of an alternative to make sense to people it needs to be made much clearer what this can mean and what its implications are for strategy.

V

The key long-term condition for an alternative to globalization is democratic investment control within each state—the opposite goal to that of multilateral international negotiations. This must mean going beyond the type of quantitative controls on the inflow and outflow of capital allowed under Bretton Woods, let alone beyond the Tobin tax on capital flows being advanced by many today. A campaign for qualitative democratic capital controls is required, one which puts on the agenda what international investment is for and should be for, rather than governments themselves either taking a piece of the action (shades of tobacco and alcohol taxes) or just managing short-term capital flows in relation to currency stability, as they did prior to globalization. Nor can we pretend that controls over foreign investment can be divorced from the need for democratic control over private *domestic* investment. This will not be adequately addressed by notions of "pension fund socialism" or labor investment funds which offer tax breaks to the workers that put their money in them.[28] Far from giving the labor movement control over jobs and the direction of the economy, such funds as now exist generally lack even the capacity to control any particular project, and many of them adopt no investment criteria other than profitability, or even require that the jobs created be unionized ones. Moreover, at the same time as shifting the risk of investment to workers' savings, these schemes envelop workers in the world of the stock markets and tax accountants (investors *should* be taxed and regulated, not subsidized, which is what accountants seek to achieve). And perhaps most important, approaching the issue of control over investment in this narrow way reinforces the conventional notion that the money in the banks is legitimately the capitalists' to do with as they please.

But how does the notion of democratic investment control get on the agenda in a world where even pension fund socialism sounds radical? We should not initially approach this in terms of getting this on the *state's* policy agenda. We need to recognize that the *first step in a new strategy* is to get labor movements to think again in terms that are not so cramped and defensive, *to think ambitiously again*, and then, once mobilized in such frame of mind, to make radical demands on the state of this kind. I have found the following argument effective in talks with trade unionists and social movement activists.[29] We still have in Canada directly elected local school boards which are vested with the statutory responsibility of providing everyone under eighteen in their catchment area with a place in the school system; and they are provided by higher levels of government with the funds, or the means of taxation, to accomplish this. Why do we not have directly elected "job development boards" or "economic planning boards" at the local level which are vested with the statutory responsibility of providing everyone in their catchment area with gainful paid employment? They wouldn't have to provide the jobs directly but could vet and fund proposals for *new* projects (to avoid displacing other workers). They would have to be given, like the school boards are, the funds, or the taxing powers, to accomplish this. There is no question it would be very costly if it were to be done properly. So how to fund it? The only really effective way to fund it would be to establish such control over the banks and other financial institutions as would allow for a considerable portion of the surplus that passes through their hands (*our own money*) to be designated for distribution to the elected local boards. This should be done centrally and the money distributed by higher levels of governments to each planning board to ensure regional parity.

When I present this argument, because it begins with a democratic reform related to job insecurity, there is usually strong assent by the time I get to the control over the financial system as being the condition for making this happen. It is necessary to make it clear that this is not a matter of "socialism in one city"—it is a structural reform (political as much as economic) which needs to be implemented across the board. And there is no sense ignoring the likelihood that unless the mobilization capacity of the labor movement and other social movements is enhanced considerably, it will be real-estate agents and property developers who will get elected to the local boards. Moreover, such a municipal scheme for the democratic control of investment would have to be synchronized with councils in each sector of the economy to discuss the regional and national allocation of resources in and across the sectors (in contrast to the notion of industrial democracy at the level of single companies which would leave workers balkanized and sustain competition between them). In the public sector, such councils would include public employees, the consumers of public goods and services, and the recipients of social assistance, involving thereby a democratization of the state in ways that meet social needs, which are now defined and provided on the terms set by political patronage and bureaucratic administration.

At this stage, this proposal is mainly about getting labor movements and working people generally to think about how to develop their capacities to the point where this kind of structural reform could be meaningfully put on the political agenda. This brings us to *the second dimension of a new strategy for labor*—the need for a strategy for *transforming labor itself.* Nor is it only new radical demands, like democratic investment control, that bring this to the fore. Even reforms that are currently on the agenda, such as the reduction of work time, face limits that are internal to labor. The 35-hour legislation passed in France, for instance, quickly ran into the type of agreement struck in the engineering sector with the bulk of the unions. The goal of job creation was frustrated by offsetting the loss of four hours a week by "annualizing" and raising the ceiling of "normal" time worked over a full year as well as by doubling the limit on annual overtime. In doing this, this agreement not only reduced the likelihood of companies having to hire more workers or pay more overtime as a result of the 35-hour law, but also met employers' demands for "flexibility"—and this aspect of the agreement was incorporated into the second round of legislation, as a way of accommodating capital.[30]

This only shows that the scandal of work polarization—whereby at one end full-time employees are working over 50 or 60 hours a week, while at the other end, casual employees are working under 20 hours—also cannot be overcome without the transformation of unions themselves, from the local level to that of national confederations to the ICFTU. This must partly involve the shift in the balance of union activity more toward organizing than servicing that many people in the American labor movement are now talking about (although the ability to service can never be divorced from any serious organizing drive); and it partly must involve the spread of "social movement unionism" along the lines articulated in Kim Moody's important book, *Workers in a Lean World.*[31] In both respects, the goal must be to make unions more inclusive not only in terms of their members' racial, ethnic, and gender identities, but also in terms of being more inclusive of their members full-life experiences as more than "just workers." This will need to be reflected in collective bargaining priorities, but it will also mean thinking hard about the limits of unions in relation to all the spaces and places working people currently interact outside of work, and interrogating the degree of democracy and developmental capacity-building that they might enjoy if such centers of working-class life could be appropriately restructured. Unions have a major role to play in this, but this is also where movements conceived in broader social and political terms are still so badly needed and could still have enormous potential if only they were ambitious and committed enough.

To speak of a strategy for labor, then, is not initially about laying out a detailed set of policies for democratizing the economy and the state but for *refounding, reorganizing, and democratizing the labor movement itself* in order to make clear what new capacities workers and their unions need to develop to start to change "the structure of power." Among those in the labor movement who are developing strategies for challenging the WTO and free trade, there are all too few like Gerard Greenfield, who has also perceptively addressed the irony of mass mobilizations of workers for militant protests and strikes in East Asia which "articulate political demands for democracy and democratic reform in society at large but without promoting democratic processes within the collective action or organization itself."[32] The same point needs to be made about unions in the advanced capitalist countries, like the American, which have rediscovered the importance of putting more resources into organizing drives, and even active rank-and-file member involvement in recruiting new members, but don't connect this with the issue of internal union democracy. As Mike Parker and Martha Gruelle have put in their Labor Notes handbook, *Democracy Is Power*:

> The organizing model is a big step forward from the servicing model, but it can have limitations. In practice, some union leaders encourage member *involvement* without member control. They expect to turn member involvement on and off like a faucet. That way, leaders can keep tighter control of a possibly volatile situation. When the rank and file await their marching orders from clever staffers or officials, there's less likelihood they'll undertake tactics that step outside conventional boundaries, or threaten deals made elsewhere.[33]

Of course, there is a deeper union culture involved here—a dialectic between rank-and-file deference and pride in the leader who can talk tough with an employer (or a president or a party leader or a media talk-show host) and the paternalism of even a radical reform leadership which, as Parker and Gruelle put it, "may genuinely have the members' interests at heart, but believe the ranks are best served if the leaders maintain control."[34] Which precise constitutional mechanisms are technically best for maximizing accountability and democratic decision making is not the issue here; the point is to measure these mechanisms in terms of the contribution they make to developing democratic capacities for members to overcome deference, for leaders to pass on expertise (rather than hoard it like their personal capital), and for more frequent changes of leadership to be made possible. Above all, debate needs to be encouraged, rather than avoided, even over the most potentially divisive issues. The problem of avoiding debate—whether due to impatience, intolerance, or avoidance of tough questions—once again emerges out of a dialectic in which members' attitudes as much as leaders' inclinations are entwined. As Bill Fletcher (the most creative and radical staff member brought into the AFL/CIO under the new John J. Sweeney regime) has put it:

> The emphasis on dialogue is essential. The aim is not to talk *at* workers, but rather to encourage debate. The object of debate is to promote the consciousness of workers. But here we come up against some fundamental problems. Some in the labor movement argue that workers must come to understand their economic interests as workers and must therefore not be distracted by "wedge issues," i.e., divisive issues around race, gender and the like. Others argue that while economic interests are of critical importance, the working class does not see things only through the narrow prism of economics. Class itself is configured racially, ethnically, and by gender in the United States. So workers cannot be inoculated against divisive or wedge issues. Class consciousness cannot be built unless they deal with such issues and take a position on them. History demonstrates time and again the folly of attempting to live in denial of their centrality to class struggle.[35]

This relationship between democracy and class consciousness is, in other words, especially important in terms of those changes in the working class that are turning labor into a more inclusive social agent. Similarly, the most effective way to extend union organization to the unorganized is to identify democratic capacity building among old as well as new members as the main goal. And what matters for this is the development of leadership just as much as the development of membership. Katherine Sciacchitano, on the base of a wealth of organizing experience, has recently expressed this:

> For frontline organizers, then, the crucial link between union campaigns and movement building is not just militancy. As one organizer said, you can take workers through mobilization after mobilization—but if they play no role in

building and debating strategy they won't necessarily learn anything. Movement building requires understanding how learning and organization takes place at the bottom. This means frontline organizers, educators and labor intellectuals alike beginning a process of open reflection about failures as well as successes. . . . Most of all, it means paying attention to workers'— not just organizers'—accounts of organizing. . . . It also suggests we need to develop and train staff . . . not just to educate leaders and committee members to mobilize co-workers, but to educate them to develop the group as a whole. The development of staff and leaders as educators is the missing link needed to support democratic decision making, participation, and organizing by members.[36]

Of course, the type of radical strategy for labor articulated by Gorz, and echoed here for our own time, is unmistakably a socialist one. This is appropriate at a time when the label anticapitalist is not only commonly attached by the establishment media to demonstrations like those in Seattle and Washington, but is openly embraced by the participants themselves. There is indeed a growing sense of the need to think not only in terms of class once again, but also to think about the question of socialist political organization again. This is heard not just among political activists in the labor movement as well as the other social movements, most of whom have worked together for years in coalition campaigns, but especially among the new generation of young activists who have emerged in the anticorporate "no logo" and sweat-shop campaigns as well as in the burgeoning protests against the institutions of globalization.[37] The alienation from party politics remains, but there is an oft-heard lament that something more than coalitions and campaigns is needed, some sort of organization within which to discuss and develop what an anticapitalist strategy would seriously amount to. This is the *third necessary element in a new strategy for labor*.

In Canada this has given rise to discussions followed by some tentative moves toward what is being called a "structured movement" that has clearly touched a nerve among many activists.[38] It would not be a party, but it would be more than the kind of coalition among movement activists on a specific issue that we have become familiar with in recent years. Its immediate emphasis, sensitive to this historical moment of uncertainty on the left, would be transitional: to create the spaces and processes for collectively working out how to combine daily activism with the need for a broader alternative politics; and to increase the likelihood, through organizing the impressive commitments to radical change that already exist, that such energies will be organizationally cumulative rather than dissipated. The "structured movement" would neither take people away from the broad-based coalitions and organizations that concentrate on campaigns against the institutions of globalization, nor would it seek to undermine Social Democracy's electoral project. It would have a different project, a much longer-term one oriented to developing a genuinely alternative vision and program to neo-liberal globalization— and a genuinely alternative practice, especially one that demonstrated the kind of leadership qualities and democratic and capacity-building processes discussed here.

Social Democratic parties today seem incapable of doing this—but the question of whether new ones will be needed or old parties might yet somehow be changed is something best left to the future when some measure of the progress made by the structured movement may be taken. One of those measures will have to be whether the type of strategy for labor sketched here gets enriched and developed and taken up in the unions as well as the other social movements. But no less important a measure will eventually be how many trade union activists will be prepared to join such a new "structured movement." There was a time when local and even national labor leaders were prepared to risk trying to bring those whose confidence they had earned in the industrial arena with them into socialist political organizations; a significant change in labor movement culture among both leaders and members would have to take place in Canada before this would be likely to happen again on any scale. But there is no alternative but to try.

Of course, in each country the landscape of political culture and organization is different. Those who are trying to build a "structured movement" in Canada will have much to learn from places like Brazil where the landscape two decades ago was already such that labor leaders could carry many of their members with them in building the Workers' Party, explicitly as a party of a new alternative type to the old Communist and Social Democratic ones. The time-scales within which strategies for change are conceived in the North and South may of course be very different. For example, in El Salvador after the end of the civil war, one of the main leaders, Fecundo Guardado, expressed his worry that the Farabundo Martí National Liberation Front (FMLN) had too short a time horizon, regarding the elections that were to take place at the end of the decade (for which Guardado himself would eventually be chosen as the

FMLN's presidential candidate) as the long-term goal for which the party had to prepare itself. In Guardado's view, this was a mistake. This period up to the next election was really the short term, and the most the FMLN could hope for was to hold onto the activist base it had developed during the civil war and effectively turn it into the membership of a mass party. The medium term was 2010, when the party might hope to develop that membership politically and gather within it such additional new elements as would establish it as the strongest political force on the Salvadoran political stage. The long term was 2020, by which point it might be hoped that the FMLN would have established such a hegemonic presence in Salvadoran society that it could get elected with the expectation of really doing something. Notably, however, Angela Zamora, director of the FMLN's educational program at that time, reacted to the idea of such a patient strategy with dismay. Indeed, she indicated she would have to think about leaving the party if it adopted such a time scale. After the sacrifices the people she had worked with had made through the long civil war, they needed immediate reforms and she felt she couldn't look them in the eye and tell them they'd have to wait another two decades, as Guardado's strategy implied they would.[39]

The strategy for labor discussed here has clearly been conceived, as was Gorz's, in the context of experience in the North. The kind of patient time horizon outlined by Guardado makes a great deal of sense for a new "structured movement" in a rich country like Canada, but one can certainly see why by no means everyone would agree it makes sense for El Salvador. Yet at the same time, as Guardado's long-term strategy suggests, many of the same problems faced by labor in the North, and which will require a long-term patient strategy to change, are by no means exclusive to it. Sexism, intolerance, fragmentation, undemocratic mobilization processes, the hierarchy built into "labor aristocracies" in every country, organizational dialectics that reinforce member deference on the one hand and leader egotism on the other—all these problems are as common, and will take as long to change, in the labor movements of the South as in those in the North. To take another important southern example: even in the midst of the general upsurge of working-class militancy and self-confidence that accompanied the liberation from apartheid and the democratic election of the new African National Congress (ANC) government in South Africa, the fragmentation in the labor movement was notable. This was seen in the lack of contact—and to some extent even concern—on the part of activists in the metal workers union,

National Union of Metalworkers of South Africa (NUMSA), not only with the 7,000 black nurses in the Eastern Cape who were fired (by a Communist provincial prime minister) in 1995 for going on strike, but even with the municipal workers on strike in Johannesburg the same year.[40] Such fragmentation between public and private sector unions is of course notorious in the North; but it is also very significant that it was so evident at such a historic moment even in the labor movement, which perhaps more than any other in our time, was living proof that solidarity was a viable practice and not just a song.

These sobering reflections are appropriate to the conclusions we need to come to about the *fourth strategic dimension of a new strategy for labor: a new internationalism*. But what exactly does internationalism mean for labor in this era of globalization? There is no sense pretending that problems that are deeply embedded in, and reflect the weaknesses of, each national movement will somehow magically be resolved through transnational collective bargaining with the multinationals and international campaigns against the political institutions of globalization. Sam Gindin is right when he says that international labor bodies can

> make constructive contributions to our struggles. They are useful vehicles for exchanging information and analysis and mobilizing acts of solidarity and support. But here, too, we should be clear about their limits. Strategic international coordination is dependent on the strength of national movements. For example, what kind of internationalism can we expect among the United States, Mexico, and Canada if the American labor movement can't yet organize its own South; if the Mexican labor movement doesn't yet have a common union across workplaces within a single company like GM; if the Canadian labor movement hasn't yet been able to achieve major organizing breakthroughs in its own key private service sectors?[41]

Nor is there any sense pretending that, in the South as much as in the North, anything other than class struggles of the most trenchant kind at the level of each state can shift the global political terrain. Certainly the notion that without a major shift in the balance of class forces in the leading capitalist states, campaigns to reform the IMF or World Bank or even the ILO can amount to anything significant is nonsensical. The importance of shedding the illusion that globalization displaces the nation-state is that we are then able to perceive the way states have become responsible for taking charge of the complex relation of international capital to the domestic bourgeoisie; and to appreciate that states do this in ways that still reflect the specific features of class struggle and political and ideological forms that remain distinctively national even as they are increasingly influenced by, and express themselves within, conjunctures determined globally. Hugo Radice correctly notes that "the asymmetry between labour and capital in their degree of transnationalisation makes workers more a passive object of globalisation than an active contestant."[42] But if this is so, it is mainly because of the asymmetries of power between capital and labor at the *national* level, and can't be changed without change at this level. Radice also contends that the dead end of progressive competitiveness is yet another instance of "the failure of progressive nationalism itself." But here again the main answer can only lie in transformations in the class relations at the national level. Insofar as labor remains satisfied with being—and with being capable of being no more than—a subsidiary partner of a national bourgeoisie, nationalism can be no more progressive than this, as Radice discerns. But in the context of the increasing inability, indeed with very few exceptions the increasing lack of interest, on the part of domestic bourgeoisies to chart a course of development beyond that determined by globally dominant imperialism in this conjuncture, such a partnership is no longer on offer in any case. This is precisely why a new strategy for labor has such importance and promise today.

If internationalism is conceived in a way that is an alternative to, or a substitute for, changes that are necessary at the national level the results can only be negative, if not disastrous. There can be little tolerance for the kind of invocations of global working-class unity that, as was first made so tragically clear in 1914, has always produced more rhetorical heat than effective transnational solidarity and understanding. The most effective internationalism at this stage is for each labor movement to try to learn as much as possible from others about the limits and possibilities of class struggles that are still inevitably locally based. When the mayor of Porto Alegre comes to Toronto to talk about the democratic "popular budget" the Workers' Party runs in that Brazilian city,[43] we need to see less of the glossy brochures that are designed to convince Coca-Cola to invest there, and to be given more detail on how it is that workers and not real-estate agents and property developers predominate at the community meetings that compose the popular budget process: This is something that we do not know how to ensure in Canada. And when Canadian trade unionists and Left intellectuals go abroad and talk about the union and social movement coalitions that organized the successive one-day general strikes across Ontario's cities, they need to be candid about the tensions and divisions that soon brought this exciting mobilization to an end with a whimper.[44]

What is needed is the kind of internationalism that reinforces the space for, and that contributes to building the strategic and material resources for, working-class struggles in each country. In this respect labor movements in the North were much indebted to the Workers' Party in Brazil and Congress of South African Trade Unions (COSATU) in South Africa, among others, in the last two decades of the twentieth century for the inspiration and guideposts they provided in developing new strategies for labor. Those of us in the North can try to repay this political debt by throwing all our weight behind campaigns that would commit each leading capitalist state to a policy of cancellation of Third World financial debt: This is the most practicable immediate reform that can be won from the institutions of globalization today. We can repay this debt even more by working toward a long-term transformation of working-class culture in each of the rich capitalist countries, so that unions can really do more than "place workers as a class on the tail end of the consumer society," to use Gorz's formulation. Apart from ecological sanity, what is at stake here is the possibility of developing the kind of internationalism that alone will allow for the massive material redistribution from the rich countries to the poor ones that any progressive alternative global capitalism must entail.

The world's working classes have changed and the world's labor movements will change with them. There can be no doubt that the greatest challenge will be to learn how to "reinvent solidarity" in this era of globalization. Winning international support for local struggles is as important, or indeed more important, than ever. But the most open and trenchant discussion of each movement's weaknesses and ongoing problems must also be the focus of transnational strategic discussions. This is especially needed now because advances made—and defeats suffered—by labor and its allies in any one state will have a greater exemplary effect than ever. In this era of globalization, it will be through converging and coordinated national pressures that successful new strategies for labor will have significant effects at the international level. A new labor internationalism that appreciates this is what is needed if working people are to develop the confidence and capacity to build a better tomorrow out of the great many popular struggles in evidence around the world today.

Notes

1. Some of the "associational democracy" literature does explicitly try to marry the concerns of community groups and unions, although usually in a manner that would tie this "third sector" to the state in neo-corporatist "social capital" and "stakeholding" arrangements. See Alan Zuege, "The Chimera of the Third Way," in Leo Panitch and Colin Leys, *Necessary and Unnecessary Utopias: The Socialist Register 2000* (London: Merlin, 1999) esp. pp. 102–5.

2. Andre Gorz, *Critique of Economic Reason* (London: Verso, 1989), pp. 231–33. Cf. *Farewell to the Working Class* (Boston: Southend Press, 1982). Gorz's original *Strategy for Labor: A Radical Proposal* (Boston: Beacon, 1967) was originally published as *Stratégie Ouvrière et Néocapitalisme* (Paris: Éditions du Seuil, 1964).

3. See Chapter 4.

4. A personal anecdote may exemplify some of what I mean by this. About ten years ago, while on a flight returning to Toronto, I struck up a conversation with the young woman seated beside me. We chatted amiably about the differences in growing up in Winnipeg in her time and mine, but when I ventured to ask her what she did for a living, she said "I'd rather not tell you." When I assured her that I was quite broad-minded, she eventually laughed and relented, telling me that she was a postal worker, but that she was reluctant to tell strangers about it because it usually led to recriminations about the strikes her union had been engaged in. Since she supported these, she would either get into a fruitless argument with a stranger or have to suffer the recriminations in silence. She then proceeded to tell a fascinating story about how she got active in her union. She had been hired by Canada Post straight out of high school and had been put to work on the "docks" of the central postal terminal where the bags of mail arrive and are shifted to various sorting stations. She was one of the first women to be assigned this kind of heavy manual work, but she felt comfortable with it, except for the fact that there were no women's toilets in the dock area and she had to make a very long trek to the other side of the terminal whenever she needed to go to the bathroom. She mentioned this to the foreman one day, who responded: "Well, you'll just have to learn to stand up and pee at the urinal like the rest of the guys." To this point, she had nothing to do with the union; indeed she came from an antiunion family and refused to go to the union's orientation session for new workers. But this comment from her foreman led her to seek out her shop steward, whose positive support began a transformation in her attitude to the union. She was now chief steward of the Winnipeg local of the Canadian Union of Postal Workers.

5. Brigitte Young, "The 'Mistress' and the 'Maid' in the Globalized Economy"; and Rosemary Warskett, "Feminism's Challenge to Unions in the North: Possibilities and Contradictions," both in Leo Panitch and Colin Leys, eds., *Working Classes/Global Realities: The Socialist Register 2001* (London: Merlin, 2000), pp. 315–27, 329–42.

6. Charles Graypo and Bruce Nissan, eds., *Grand Designs: The Impact of Corporate Strategies on Workers, Unions, and Their Communities* (Ithaca: ILR Press, 1993).

7. There is wealth of outstanding labor history on this. See, most recently, Paul Buhle, *Taking Care of Business: Samuel Gompers, George Meany, Lane Kirkland and the Tragedy of American Labor* (New York: Monthly Review Press, 1999).

8. Gorz, *Strategy for Labor*, p. 26.

9. Ibid., p. 17.

10. Ibid., p. 99.

11. Joel Rodgers and Wolfgang Streek, "Productive Solidarities: Economic Strategy and Left Politics," in David Miliband, ed., *Reinventing the Left* (Cambridge, U.K.: Polity, 1994), p. 134.

12. Fred Bienefeld, "Is a Strong National Economy a Utopian Goal at the End of the Twentieth Century?" in Robert Boyer and Daniel Drache, eds., *States Against Markets* (London: Routledge, 1996), pp. 429–31; and his earlier "Capitalism and the Nation State in the Dog Days of the Twentieth Century," in Leo Panitch and Ralph Miliband, eds., *Between Globalism and Nationalism: The Socialist Register 1994* (London: Merlin, 1994), p. 115.

13. Gorz, *Strategy for Labor*, pp. 7–8.

14. Ibid., p. 181.

15. Sam Gindin, "Notes on Labor at the End of the Century," in Ellen Wood et al., eds., *Rising from the Ashes* (New York: Monthly Review Press, 1998); and his *Canadian Auto Workers: The Birth and Transformation of a Union* (Toronto: Lorimer, 1995).

16. Gorz, *Strategy for Labor*, pp. 152–53.

17. Andrew Martin and George Ross, "The Europeanization of Labor Representation," in Martin and Ross, eds., *The Brave New World of European Labor* (New York: Berghahn Books, 1999), pp. 312–39.

18. Ibid., pp. 352, 358.

19. Charles Levinson, *International Trade Unionism* (London: Allen & Unwin, 1972).

20. Gorz, *Strategy for Labor*, pp. 187–89.

21. Gerard Greenfield, "The ICFTU and the Politics of Compromise," in Wood et al., eds., *Rising from the Ashes*, p. 180. Cf. Peter Waterman, "International Labour's Y2K Problem," unpublished paper delivered at the ILO/ICFTU Conference on Organised Labour in the 21st Century, 15 November 1999. Available on the Internet at http://www.antenna.nl/~waterman/.

22. Gerard Greenfield, "Union Responses to Negotiations on the WTO Agreement on Agriculture: A Strategy of Exclusion," discussion paper for International Union of Food and Allied Workers Associations (IUF), 7 May 1999.

23. Including Ralph Nader as well as Lori Wallach, director of Public Citizen's Global Trade Watch campaign. See Moses Naim, "Lori's War," *Foreign Policy* 118 (Spring 2000): 29–55, and John Nichols, "Now What? Seattle Is Just a Start," *The Progressive* 64, 1 (January 2000): 16–19.

24. Within China, an important critique of the negative effects of entry to the WTO in terms of increased unemployment, economic dependence on foreign companies, American "hegemony" and "double standards" has been put forward by Dr. Han Deqiang. His book, *Collision*, with a print run of 10,000 copies, has reputedly attracted significant attention from concerned officials and academics across China. Another important and influential critique, focusing on the enor-

mous social inequalities that will be generated, has also been set out by Shaoguang Wang of the Chinese University of Hong Kong in his unpublished paper, "Openness, Distributive Conflict, and Social Insurance: The Social and Political Implications of China's WTO Membership," March 2000.

25. See John Pomfret, "China Reports Big Surge in Labor Unrest during 1999," *San Francisco Chronicle*, 24 April 2000.

26. Samir Amin, "The Political Economy of the Twentieth Century," *Monthly Review*, June 2000, p. 9.

27. Andrew Ross, *Real Love: In Pursuit of Cultural Justice* (New York: New York University Press, 1998), pp. 26–27. See also Naomi Klein's very perceptive examination of the mode of organizing these types of protests: "The Vision Thing," *The Nation*, 10 July 2000, and her account of the Porto Alegre meeting, "A Fete for the End of the End of History," *The Nation*, 19 March 2001.

28. See Henry Jacot's critique of Robin Blackburn's proposals in this vein in "The New Collectivism?" *New Left Review* 2,1 (January–February 2000): 122–30. For the definitive critique of labor investment funds in Canada, see Jim Stanford, *Labour Investment Funds* (Toronto: CAW, 1999); and his *Paper Boom* (Toronto: Lorimer, 1999), esp. ch. 15.

29. I first set out this argument in "A Socialist Alternative to Unemployment," *Canadian Dimension* 20,1 (March 1986): 40–41.

30. See Robert Graham, "Unions Split over 35-Hour Week," *Financial Times*, 14 October 1998; and "Turning Back the Clock," *Financial Times*, 29 July 1999. For a perceptive look at the complex union politics behind work-time reduction in Germany as well, see Stephen J. Silva, "Every Which Way but Loose: German Industrial Relations Since 1980," in Martin and Ross, eds., *Brave New World*, esp. pp. 99–100.

31. See Kim Moody, *Workers in a Lean World: Unions in the International Economy* (New York: Verso, 1997).

32. Gerard Greenfield, "Organizing, Protest and Working Class Self-Activity: Reflections on East Asia," in Leo Panitch and Colin Leys, eds., *Working Classes, Global Realities: The Socialist Register 2001*, p. 242.

33. Mike Parker and Martha Gruelle, *Democracy Is Power: Rebuilding Unions from the Bottom Up* (Detroit: Labor Notes, 1999), p. 26.

34. Ibid., p. 2.

35. Bill Fletcher, Jr., "Labor Education in the Maelstrom of Class Struggle," in Wood et al., eds., *Rising from the Ashes*, p. 119.

36. Katherine Sciacchitano, "Unions, Organizing, and Democracy: Living in One's Time, Building for the Future," *Dissent*, Spring 2000, pp. 75–81.

37. See Naomi Klein, *No Logo: Taking Aim at the Brand Bullies* (Toronto: Knopf, 2000).

38. See Sam Gindin, "The Party's Over," *This Magazine* (Toronto), November–December 1998, pp. 13–15, and the subsequent debate in various issues of *Canadian Dimension* in 1999.

39. Both these statements were made as personal communications to me when I was in El Salvador in January and February 1995 to help the FMLN inaugurate a new intraparty educational program.

40. These observations are based on discussions with NUMSA activists while I was in South Africa in October 1995 to participate in a series of joint CAW/NUMSA educational seminars.

41. Sam Gindin, "Notes on Labor at the End of the Century," in Wood et al., eds., *Rising from the Ashes*, p. 202.

42. Hugo Radice, "Responses to Globalisation: A Critique of Progressive Nationalism," *New Political Economy* 5,1 (March 2000): 14–15.

43. For an account of this visit, see Judy Rebick, *Imagine Democracy* (Toronto: Stoddart, 2000), ch. 2. For an excellent account of the budget process and its history, see Boaventura de Sousa Santos, "Participatory Budgeting in Porto Alegre: Towards a Redistributive Democracy," *Politics and Society* 26, 4 (December 1998): 461–510.

44. For sober assessments, see Marcella Munroe, "Ontario's 'Days of Action' and strategic choices for the Left in Canada," *Studies in Political Economy* 53 (Summer 1997): 125–40; Marsha Niemeijer, "The Ontario Days of Action—The Beginning of a Redefinition of the Labour Movement's Political Strategy?" paper presented at the Fourth International Working Conference of the Transnational Information Exchange (TIE), on "The Building of a Labour Movement for Radical Change," Cologne, 16–19 March 2000; and Janet Conway, "Knowledge, Power, Organization: Social Justice Coalitions at the Crossroads," *Studies in Political Economy* 62 (Summer 2000): 43–70; see also Tony Clarke et al., "Forum: Assessing Seattle," *Studies in Political Economy* 62 (Summer 2000): 7–42.

7

Transcending Pessimism:
Rekindling Socialist Imagination

"We're free. . . . We're free." The last words of Arthur Miller's masterpiece, *Death of a Salesman*, are uttered, sobbing, by Linda Loman over her husband Willy's grave. Weary and penniless after a life of selling "a smile and a shoeshine," overwhelmed by feelings of emptiness and failure, yet mesmerized by the thought that his life insurance will provide his estranged son with the stake that might induce him to compete and "succeed," Willy Loman's suicide famously symbolizes the tragic dimension of the relentless competitiveness at the heart of the American capitalist dream. "He had the wrong dreams. All, all, wrong," this son laments at the grave side, even as his other son dedicates himself to "beat this racket" so that "Willy Loman didn't die in vain. . . . It's the only dream you can have—to come out number-one man." At the end Linda stands over the grave alone. Telling Willy that she had just made the last payment on their mortgage, a sob rises in her throat: "We're free and clear. . . . We're free. . . . We're free."[1]

When first uttered on stage in 1949, at the start of the Cold War, these words spoke to the ambiguity of the freedom represented by the "free world." In 1999, when Linda cried "we're free" at the end of *Death of a Salesman*'s fiftieth-anniversary revival on Broadway, she seemed to embody the angst of an entire world enveloped by the American dream at the end of the twentieth century. One can everywhere sense the anxiety—an anxiety as omnipresent as "globalization" itself—that has emerged with accumulating awareness of the enormous odds against actually "beating this racket" and escalating doubts about the worth of a life defined by the freedom to compete.

At the same time, however, we still live in an era of foreclosed hope in the possibility of a better world. What makes the tragedy of Willy Loman so universal now is that even people who wonder whether the capitalist dream isn't the wrong dream see no way of realizing a life beyond capitalism, or fear that any attempt to do so can only result in another nightmare. Overcoming this debilitating political pessimism is the most important question anyone seriously interested in social change must confront.

As people search for what direction to take under these conditions, it helps to know that others before have faced the same problem. How to make "the defeated man . . . try the outside world again" was precisely the question that impelled Ernst Bloch in the 1930s to write his magnum opus, *The Principle of Hope.*[2] Pessimism—"paralysis per se"—was the first obstacle to be confronted:

> people who do not believe at all in a happy end impede changing the world almost as much as the sweet swindlers, the marriage-swindlers, the charlatans of apotheosis. Unconditional pessimism therefore promotes the business of reaction not much less than artificially conditioned optimism; the latter is nevertheless not so stupid that it does not believe in anything at all. It does not immortalize the trudging of the little life, does not give humanity the face of a chloroformed gravestone. It does not give the world the deathly sad background in front of which it is not worth doing anything at all. In contrast to a pessimism which itself belongs to rottenness and may serve it, a tested optimism, when the scales fall from the eyes, does not deny the goal-belief in general; on the contrary, what matters now is to find the right one and to prove it. . . . That is why the most dogged enemy of socialism is not only . . . great capital, but equally the load of indifference, hopelessness; otherwise great capital would stand alone.[3]

Bloch's response was to try revive the idea of utopia. He insisted that even in a world where socialist politics are marginalized, we can still discover, if only in daydreams, the indestructible human desire for happiness and harmony, a yearning which consistently runs up against economic competition, private property, and the bureaucratic state. The "utopian intention," which was, for Bloch, the real "motor force of history," may be found in architecture, painting, literature, music, ethics, and religion: "every work of art, every central philosophy had and has a utopian window in which there lies a landscape which is still developing." Bending the stick against orthodox Marxism's traditional dismissal of "utopian socialism," Bloch's project was in good part to rehabilitate what Marx himself once called "the dream of the matter" which the world had long possessed. "The power of the great old utopian books," Bloch demonstrated, was that "they almost always named the same thing: Omnia sint communia, let everything be in common. It is a credit to the pre-Marxist political literature to possess these isolated and rebellious enthusiasms among its many ideological insights. Even if they did not seem to contain a shred of possibility . . . the society projected within them managed without self-interest at the expense of others and was to keep going without the spur of the bourgeois drive for acquisition." It was this literature which first established that one of the main prerequisites to realize "the leap of humanity out of the realm of necessity into the realm of freedom . . . is the abolition of private property and the classes this has produced. Another prerequisite is the consistent will towards the negation of the state in so far as it rules individuals and is an instrument of oppression in the hands of the privileged."[4] What made Thomas More's *Utopia* "with all its dross, the first modern portrait of democratic communist wishful dreams" was that

> For the first time democracy was linked here in a humane sense, the sense of public freedom and tolerance, with a collective economy (always easily threatened by bureaucracy, and indeed clericalism). . . . [T]he end of the first part of the "Utopia" states openly: "Where private ownership still exists, where all people measure all values by the yardstick of money, it will hardly ever be possible to pursue a just and happy policy. . . . Thus possessions certainly cannot be distributed in any just and fair way . . . unless property is done away with beforehand. As long as it continues to exist, poverty, toil and care will hang instead an inescapable burden on by far the biggest and by far the best part of humanity. The burden may be lightened a little but to remove it entirely (without abolishing property) is impossible."[5]

It was the abstractness of such utopian thinking, of course, that led Marx to insist on the crucial importance of analyzing "objective conditions." Bloch had no doubt about how necessary this was for "cooling down . . . totally extravagant abstractly utopian fanaticism" and for the development of the kind of practical consciousness that would allow the carrying through of the dream to reality through the transformation of social relations. But the unmasking of ideologies and illusions by what he called the "cold stream" of Marxism's "historical and current practical conditional analysis" had always to be mixed with the kind of appreciation of "subjective conditions" present in the "warm stream" of the Marxist tradition. "[F]ermenting in the process of the real itself," Bloch insisted, is "the concrete forward dream: anticipating elements are a component of reality itself. Thus the will towards utopia is entirely compatible with object-based tendency, in fact is confirmed and at home within it." The best kind of Marxism demonstrates that "enthusiasm and sobriety, awareness of the goal and analysis of the given facts go hand in hand. When the young Marx called on people to think at last, to act 'like a disillusioned man who has come to his senses,' it was not to dampen the enthusiasm of the goal, but to sharpen it."[6]

In recent years we have seen all too many disillusioned people on the left "coming to their senses" by abandoning the goal of socialism. Some have succumbed to a postmodernist pessimism, which has indeed proved to be "paralysis per se." Even more seem to have jumped from what Bloch called the "evils of putschist activism" all the way to Social Democracy's "third way," whose presumption that neo-liberal prescriptions of efficiency are compatible with social justice is the contemporary expression of what Bloch designated as one of the key hallmarks of ideology—"the premature harmonization of social contradictions" within the confines of existing social relations. Frustrated by their inability to change the world overnight through sheer activism, they have not so much abandoned the idea of change but, like the Greek mythic character Procrustes, who adjusted the size of his guests to fit the size of his bed, they have shrunk the meaning of change to fit what capital and the state will accommodate.

Yet it is increasingly apparent from the extreme limitations of the "third way" in practice that reviving the goal of socialism is necessary even to make small improvements in the current state of the world. As Bloch put it: "If the will-content of the goal is missing, then even the good probable is left undone; if the goal remains, however, then even the improbable can be done, or at least made more probable for later." Moreover, as against the kind of "third way" thinking that embraces the novelty, inevitability, and progressive character of globalization, "even a dash of pessimism" does not go amiss, for, as Bloch suggested, "at least pessimism with a realistic perspective is not so helplessly surprised by mistakes and catastrophes, by the horrifying possibilities which have been concealed and will continue to be concealed precisely in capitalist progress."[7]

But if such a healthy pessimism about capitalist progress is indeed growing as we enter the new century, what persists alongside it, even though repeated capitalist crises are anticipated by the Left, is a profound pessimism about the possibility of realizing any better world. This debilitating pessimism derives not only from the feeling that nothing can be done, or even that nothing other than capitalism is possible, but also from a fear, well-honed by twentieth century experience as well as ruling class propaganda, of the perverse consequences of the attempt to put utopian visions into practice. This is not surprising in light of the experience with Communist regimes in this century, where there occurred, as *The Principle of Hope* already suggested, "an undernourishment of revolutionary imagination" and "a schematic pragmatic reduction of totality" through an overemphasis on science and technology "such that the pillar of fire in utopias, the thing which was powerfully leading the way, could be liquidated."[8] "All the worse," as Bloch later wrote after his self-exile from East Germany, was that once it became clear that the "revolutionary capacity is not there to execute ideals which have been represented abstractly," the Communist regimes acted so as "to discredit or even destroy with catastrophic means ideals which have not appeared in the concrete." This stifled "transitional tendencies" within them which would have been able to move toward "active freedom only if the utopian goal is clearly visible, unadulterated and unrenounced."[9]

It must be said, of course, that Bloch's remarks only implicitly identified the weakest aspect of the classical Marxian legacy in this respect: the theorization of the role of the political in the transition to socialism. Marx's central concepts of the "dictatorship of the proletariat," "smashing the bourgeois state," and "the withering away of the state" all obscured rather than clarified the fundamental issues; and Marxists in the twentieth century did not go nearly far enough in overcoming the limits of this legacy.[10] Yet it is at the level of the political that transitions from one socioeconomic order to another are effected—or come to grief in the attempt.

But whether the socialist utopian goal can be revived must obviously depend on much more than a clarification and enrichment of socialist political theory. It will above all depend on agency, that is, on what human beings can still discover about their potential. For all the valuable insights, promising signposts, and rich hints even the "warm stream" of Marxism bequeaths, it must be said that the historical optimism in Marx that inspired generations of socialists came with an underestimation of the chasm between the scale and scope of the utopian dream and the capitalism-created agency honored—or saddled—with carrying it out: the working class. Between Marx's broad historically inspired vision of revolution/transformation and his detailed critique of political economy, there was an analytical and strategic gap—unbridgeable without addressing the problematic of working-class capacities—which later Marxists sometimes addressed but never overcame.[11] Nor has the problem been overcome by recent social movement theory. For the rethinking that is required must be more profound than just imagining that the problem can be resolved by substituting a plurality of new social movements for the old workers' movements. The compensatory stifling of ideals we saw in the institutions of the labor movement has also appeared in the new social movements. Every progressive social movement must, sooner or later, confront the inescapable fact that capitalism cripples our capacities, stunts our dreams, and incorporates our politics.

Where then can socialism, as a movement linking the present with the possible, once again find the air to breathe and space to grow? To answer this we need both to clarify the socialist "utopian goal" today and to develop a clearer sense of where our potential capacities to create that better world will come from.

The socialist "utopian goal" is built around realizing our potential to be full human beings. What separates this ideal from its liberal roots is not only socialism's commitment to extending this principle to all members of society, but also its insistence that the flowering of human capacities isn't a liberation of the individual from the social but is only achievable through the social. Ideals are always linked to some notion of justice and freedom. Notions of justice revolve around the egalitarianism of certain outcomes (like distribution of income or wealth) or the legitimacy of a process for reaching goals even if the ultimate results are unequal (equal access to opportunities). Notions of freedom generally divide into freedom from an external arbitrary authority (the state) or the freedom to participate in setting the broad parameters that frame the context of our lives (as in current liberal democracies). The socialist ideal does not exclude these other moral spaces but locates them on the specific terrain of capacities: capitalism is unjust and undemocratic not because of this or that imperfection in relation to equality or freedom, but because at its core it involves the control by some of the use and development of the potential of others and because the competition it fosters frustrates humanity's capacity for liberation through the social.

And what is especially important is that conceiving freedom and justice on the terrain of capacities leads beyond mere dreaming: It links the ideal to the possibility of change and so to what is politically achievable. This is what Bloch meant by "concrete utopias" which, always operating on the level of "possibility as capacity," incorporate the objective contradictions that create an opening for socialist goals ("capability-of-being-done"), the subjective element of agency ("capability-of-doing-other"), and therefore the possibility of changing ourselves and the world ("capability-of-becoming-other").[12]

These concrete utopias are not blueprints for a new order entirely external to this one. Communism, for Marx and Engels, was not "a stable state which is to be established, an *ideal* to which reality will have to adjust itself . . . [but] the real movement which abolishes the present state of things."[13] That "real movement" will live or die based on whether the necessary capacities and possibilities can first show themselves, in some substantive way, inside everyday capitalism. Terry Eagleton argues that "the only authentic image of the future is, in the end, the failure of the present."[14] This is indeed true. And the best measure of the failure of the present is its inability to redeem the glimpses of our potential afforded by our own experiences. In Barbara Kingsolver's novel *Animal Dreams*, a woman asks her lover: "Didn't you ever dream you could fly?" He answers: "Not when I was sorting pecans all day." When she persists and demands: "Really though, didn't you ever fly in your dreams?," he replies: "Only when I was close to flying in real life. . . . Your dreams, what you hope for and all that, it's not separate from your life. It grows right out of it."[15]

II

Despite what is sometimes alleged about the lack of attention paid to "alternatives" on the left today, there has actually been no shortage of attempts by progressive intellectuals in recent years to rethink and reformulate the utopian goal. While the institutional content of such alternatives extends beyond Social Democracy, many of those who advance these new utopias for our time do so in ways that, like today's Social Democracy, reflect a defeatism and thus an overcautious pragmatism. In the name of "getting real," these utopias limit either democratic expectations of the state or the scale of the economic transformations they consider, if not both. The result is what Bloch has referred to as "abstract utopias": a world too small to deliver on the large promises it holds out and a telling neglect of the politics of getting there. A number of recent books by prominent authors, each influenced by a different current of contemporary thought, have provided a rather clear perspective on the demoralized nature of much utopian thinking today and on why the real challenge before us is not to contract, but to expand, utopia's inspirational and visionary function.

The main concern of James C. Scott, in *Seeing like a State: How Certain Schemes to Improve the Human Condition Have Failed*,[16] is the "great state-sponsored calamities of the twentieth century" epitomized by Soviet collectivization and Tanzanian Ujamaa villagization of agriculture. Reflecting postmodernism's influence, Scott characterizes the utopian ideal not in terms of emancipation and liberation but rather in the negative terms of "aspirations to a finely tuned social control" driven by the work of "progressive, often revolutionary elites . . . who have come to power with a comprehensive critique of existing society and a popular mandate to transform it." In taking up the "utilitarian simplifications" which states employ to "map" societies, these elites repressed the complex, varied, and practical local knowledge which is the fount of human creativity. Borrowing from Kropotkin's famous declaration that "it is impossible to legislate for the future," Scott concludes that strategies for change must now be founded on "taking small steps," with preference, moreover, for the kind of interventions that "can be easily undone."[17]

This approach sensibly begins from the premise of incomplete knowledge in relation to "the necessary contingency and uncertainty of the future," and from "confidence in the skills, intelligence and experience of ordinary people." His rejection of detailed superrationalist blueprints is equally valid. But this only takes us back to Marx's own critique of abstract utopias for ignoring what Marx also saw as "the radical contingency of the future"—hence his refusal to write blueprints that might minimize the potential for humanity's creativity and inventiveness which could be unleashed in the process of transcending capitalist social relations. Scott allows, in passing, that "utopian aspirations per se are not dangerous." (He approvingly quotes Oscar Wilde's remark: "A map of the world which does not include Utopia is not even worth glancing at, for it leaves out the one country at which Humanity is always arriving.") Yet it is clear that he has a very limited awareness and appreciation of the "warm stream" of utopian (including Marxist) thought. And although he counterposes Rosa Luxemburg and Aleksandra Kollontai to Lenin, and acknowledges his debt to classic anarchists writers like Pyotr Kropotkin and Mikhail Bakunin, his own conception of social change is far removed from their revolutionary spirit.

The trouble with this all-too-common response to the socialist failures of the past century is not only its strategic but also its visionary inadequacy in relation to a global capitalism that Scott himself identifies as "the most powerful force for homogenization" today. Such passing comments hardly take the measure of global capitalism's ruthless remaking of societies in the name of efficiency, productivity, comparative advantage, and the rest. While Scott recognizes that the capitalist market, far from being "free" is "an instituted, formal system of coordination" which rests on that "larger system of social relations," his reversion to "the science of muddling through" and "disjointed incrementalism" provides no larger vision or strategy for a transcending of that system of social relations.[18] He appears to see "the private sector" as some sort of genial brake on the excesses of political leaders with utopian dreams, rather than as the alienated and socially destructive monster it is.

No progress can be made in this respect unless we can go beyond conceiving the future of the state only in terms of Foucauldian surveillance and Weberian bureaucratic rationality. Scott recognizes the positive role of certain institutions—especially ones that are "multifunctional, plastic, diverse, and adaptable," but he can't conceive of any beyond those local institutions ("the family, the small community, the small farm, the family firm in certain businesses") which have survived and adapted through history—and which he considerably romanticizes. His conception of the good state is entirely in terms of "negative freedom"—that liberal democratic state which allows space for activity outside of, and for resistance to, itself, and which "may in some instances be the defender of local difference and variety" against global capitalism. Although his argument against social engineering and in favor of local practical knowledge replicates Hilary Wainwright's important book *Arguments for a New Left*[19] (which he does not, however, cite), he shows, unlike her, little sense of the feminist, environmentalist, labor, and socialist consciousness and institutional practices in our time which have valued and fostered practical local knowledges, impelled by a vision of changing broader social relations, and sought to connect them to political parties, unions, and the local and national state. Not to romanticize these is one thing. To ignore them is to cut one's intellectual contribution off from those broader forces "fermenting in the process of the real" that might realize a better world.

An apparently more positive approach to reviving utopian aspirations has inspired the books published in Verso's Real Utopia Project, under the editorship of Eric Olin Wright, whose goals are to nurture "clear-sighted understandings of what it would take to create social institutions free of oppression [as] part of creating a political will for radical social changes to reduce oppression . . . [—]utopian designs of institutions that can inform our practical tasks of muddling through in a world of imperfect conditions for social change."[20] In a recent volume in that series, *Recasting Egalitarianism: New Rules for Communities, States and Markets*, Sam Bowles and Herb Gintis set out to bridge the democratization of the economy, expressed through a radical redistribution of capital assets, with what they view as the real-world need for raising productivity. This is utopia under the influence of supply-side economics.

Bowles and Gintis are, like Scott, sure that states can never be substantively democratized. While they readily assume that managers of firms will be subject to democratic accountability, they emphatically stress "the many unavoidable obstacles to citizen accountability over government actions" and they reject "the presumption that state managers and functionaries will faithfully carry out what an egalitarian citizenry would have them do."[21] On the other hand, they claim, again like Scott, that at the level of communities—families, residential neighborhoods, and the workplace—people can readily monitor each others' activities so as to guarantee reciprocity and trust (even if not altruism and affection) within the context of "structurally determined individual incentives and sanctions" to maximize economic efficiency. It is the reciprocity of fair trade in the market governed by individual material self-interest, rather than the substance of local democracy, that is determining, and this is why they also advocate school vouchers and private home ownership alongside the redistribution of capital assets to workers in enterprises.

Bowles and Gintis accept the doctrine that market competition is necessary for economic efficiency, but they claim that the unequal distribution of capital impedes productivity by imposing costs on the private sector in the form of work supervision and security in the face of labor indiscipline and lack of effort. If workers owned the capital assets of the firm they work in, while "the beneficial disciplining effects of market competition" between firms were maintained, then all the "behaviors critical to high levels of productivity—hard work, maintenance of productive equipment, risk-taking and the like" (p. 7)—would be forthcoming. Since conventional redistributive policies are passé in a global world where all

policies have to be "sensitive to the competitive position of each economy," then what is needed is a "productivity enhancing" (p. 15) redistribution of property rights in order to "strengthen the economy's competitive position" (p. 58). It is never made clear how Bowles and Gintis imagine
the redistribution of capital assets would come about—except that it
would not be mandated universally by government "fiat" (p. 48). It
seems likely that the authors have some kind of notion of pension fund
socialism in mind or that they expect that the banks would be induced to
lend workers the money to buy their firms at nonprohibitive rates of
interest. Whether banks are also to be worker-owned is not addressed,
but there is in any case to be "ample room for innovative private entrepreneurship," including that based on "venture capital" (p. 48).[22]

The main effect of this schema would be to ensure that competition
rather than solidarity was the goal—indeed the primary structural characteristic—of the working class itself. For the discipline of competition to
be effective, considerable inequalities in wealth and income among workers would necessarily have to be sustained, and it would be rooted in an
original arbitrary endowment based on which workers happen to "own"
General Motors as opposed to a small, asset-poor company—not to mention those who would suffer the effects of the bankruptcies and layoffs
that go with risk taking and competition.[23] Although Bowles and Gintis
do not situate their model in the 1980s debate about market socialism, the
attempt to "get real" involves incorporating so much capitalist rationality that the result, while perhaps "feasible," seems anything but utopian.[24]
A number of the critical contributions to that debate were very creative in
imagining what the institutions of a democratic economy, in which market relations were subordinated and marginalized, might look like; this
was especially true of those that stressed the importance of mechanisms
within each firm to attenuate the division of labor.[25] But Bowles and
Gintis seem to feel they don't have to delve too deeply into the actual req-
uisites of substantive democracy in worker-owned firms,[26] because what
really concerns them is to demonstrate that the external coercion of competitive markets, and the internal compulsion that will come from worker-
owners pressuring each other to work hard, will yield the main goal:
greater productivity and efficiency, greater even, they suggest, than what
current advanced capitalist structures might achieve.

Bowles and Gintis have no patience with a vision in which people are
primarily inspired by collective rather than individualist concerns.
Egalitarian projects, they claim, founder on a presumption of "overso-

cialized decision makers" that fail to take account of the "incentive structures of the relevant actors." As for why egalitarians should accommodate to an acquisitive morality rather than attempt to change it, their
answer is a familiar—reactionary—one: "we have no choice," they say,
because this morality, founded in "some combination of genes and culture," has an "inertial character."[27] For this, they wrongly appeal to
Barrington Moore's explanation of revolution and revolt in terms of people's outrage at the flouting of long-rooted conceptions of social justice
and reciprocity.[28] But Bowles and Gintis are not inviting people to revolt
against the capitalist value system: they are inviting them to buy into it.[29]

Roberto Unger's "anti-necessitarian" social theory—most recently
advanced in programmatic form in *Democracy Realized: The Progressive
Alternative*—seems to provide an antidote to Bowles and Gintis's dictum
that we are "trapped by the present in designing the future." Reiterating
a challenge he has put forth over the past two decades, Unger asserts:

> There is always more in us than there is in our contexts. They are finite. We,
> relative to them, are not. We can hope to diminish this disproportion
> between circumstance and personality by building institutional and cultur-
> al worlds that become more supportive of our context transcending powers.
> Such contexts may fortify our resources and powers of resistance, even as
> they invite their own revision.[30]

What has been so important about Unger's work has been his thinking
about the kind of reconfiguration of the state that would best facilitate the
radical democracy of the socialist utopian vision. As he put it in *False
Necessity* in 1987: "To understand the leftist as the person who values
equality over freedom and fraternity is to miss the main point of the leftist undertaking." This has meant, for him, stressing the need to go
beyond the redistributive programs of the Social Democratic welfare
state and to embrace a "vision of solidarity that simultaneously contributes to the enabling conditions for the [generalized] development of
practical capabilities." The greatest problem with Social Democracy
throughout the past century was not its gradualism, Unger has understood, but a reformism limited to policy outputs while leaving the institutional design of the state itself untouched. A different kind of state
could only be brought about through the "militant organization of the
oppressed, the poor, and the angry . . . [but] it is not enough for these sectors to mobilize, they must remain mobilized. They and their leaders

must use the favoring circumstances of crisis, revolution, and radical enthusiasm to establish economic and governmental institutions that help perpetuate in the midst of humdrum social routine something of the transitory experience of mass mobilization."³¹ A transformative state needs to see itself as engaged in a constant process of democratic experimentalism, developing new branches of government "friendly to the rise of popular engagement," endowed with the political legitimacy and practical capacity to facilitate the organization of the unorganized and disadvantaged, and operating under a system of public law which allows for state interventions to maintain these organizations as inclusive and internally democratic while at the same time leaving them "free from any taint of government control or tutelage."³²

The manifesto for change now presented in *Democracy Realized* still gives priority to strategies for institutional reform over redistributive reform. It seeks to deepen democracy and accelerate political change by removing the constitutional checks and balances, parliamentarist rules, and electoralist practices that maintain society at a low level of political mobilization and introducing constitutional reforms that expand direct democracy, encourage popular political engagement in the state, and "promote democratic experimentalism in all fields of social life."³³ Unfortunately, Unger's contribution to trying to conceptualize a different kind of state appropriate to a transformative democratic strategy is considerably weakened by its attachment to an economic program that is astonishingly conventional—and, by now, rather dated—in its advancement of a strategy for economic growth founded on the notion of "flexible specialization." Unger's utopian vision is determinedly post-Fordist, and his particular bête-noir, therefore, is the defensive response of unionized workers in capital-intensive industries to the employment of temporary workers and subcontractors. Rather than use solidarity as a means of protecting themselves against this trend, he urges them to make "common cause" with subcontractors in support of schemes for decentralized access to venture capital so as to finance "the small and the new" firms which he takes to be the "vanguard" of economic growth. In face of the difficulty of giving practical institutional content to the notion of securing social control over investment decisions while preserving "the decentralized vitality of a market economy," Unger now calls for an "easier" option than any attempt to expropriate or redirect capital and arrives at nothing more radical than the public mobilization of pension funds to finance these vanguard firms.

Even in his earlier writings, his notion of skilled process workers, managers, technicians, and small-scale entrepreneurs making common cause as a "productive vanguard" by joining together to reap the advantages of flexible, high-tech production was problematic, but the general abstractness of those writings, together with their assumptions about the socialization of finance, made this less obvious. His more recent proposal, in which the "established system" of finance and corporate power is largely left alone, clearly exemplifies what Bloch meant by the premature harmonization of contradictions. Unger assumes that a legal reform which "automatically unionizes all workers, job seekers and smallscale business owners" will itself lay the foundations for a "growth-friendly" moderation of conflict between workers and managers so that they work together according to a "partnership principle" governed by "cooperation and innovation."[34] His earlier vision of solidarity that stressed the militant organization of the oppressed, the poor, and the angry to the end of developing their practical capabilities is little in evidence.

Indeed, Unger scarcely seems to notice that Social Democracy, far from being mainly concerned "to defend at all costs the historical constituency of organized labor," has long since taken up the Blairite "third way" which, except for its continuing institutional conservatism in terms of representative and administrative (if not electoral) procedures, looks suspiciously similar to his own proposals for transcending the sterile debate between state and market at the economic level through the strategy of "progressive competitiveness." Unger shows he is aware (albeit only in a brief passing paragraph) that the "language of flexible specialization and worker engagement in the planning of production . . . is ready to be captured by the managerial program."[35] But his own proposals, far from exploring the contradictions between the call for cooperation and workers' resistance to flexibility in a world where "capital has the right to move where it pleases," smother the contradictions in the verbiage of partnership, innovation, and cooperation.

What a letdown. It may be said in Unger's defense that his concern to secure growth via competitiveness for a Third World economy like Brazil is rather less obscene than is the concern of Bowles and Gintis to further enhance the competitiveness of the already rich American economy. But his full embrace of post-Fordism's commitment to "progressive competitiveness" and the unstated but consequent logic of subordinating the economy and society into an export-oriented strategy within international capitalism (structured by imperial relations, which Unger scarcely seems to notice), demonstrates how difficult it is even for someone as conscious of the problem as Unger to escape being trapped by the present in designing the future. Competition is a constraint that any project for structural reforms has to take into account; but the whole point of addressing alternatives is to liberate ourselves from the notion that it is only through competitiveness that we can address the development of our productive capacities. To accept competition as the goal—even for a poor country and even qualified as progressive competitiveness—is to give up on the project before you begin.

That so much of the contemporary literature seems "incapable of imagining any world definitively different than their own" (as Eagleton puts it), and of even going so far as some pre-Marxist utopias in projecting a social order capable of keeping going "without the spur of the bourgeois drive for acquisition" (as Bloch put it), stands as a sorry comment on the limits of the utopian imagination today.[36] This is intimately related to the failure to come to grips with the question of agency. To Scott, the question of agency is reduced to getting the state out of the way. Bowles and Gintis don't even bother to dwell on why workers would commit to a struggle for control over capital assets if the economic decisions ultimately made will still be determined by competitive markets. And in Unger, the folding of an independent working-class project into cross-class partnerships with export-oriented "vanguard" firms erodes the very possibility of the militant organization of the "oppressed, the poor, and the angry." There seems little point in worrying a great deal about agency if the transformation being considered is not really a transformation at all.

III

In contrast to the above, and much more fruitful in coming to grips with what really needs to be thought through in rekindling the socialist imagination, stands the work of Andre Gorz—starting with his primary principle of the strategy of "nonreformist reforms" enunciated over three decades ago: i.e., "one which does not base its validity and its right to exist on capitalist needs, criteria and rationales."[37] His eco-socialist critique of productivism in face of the ecological contradictions of capitalist development is obviously of great importance, as is the contribution he has made to prioritizing the redistribution of working time in an egalitarian project. But what is especially significant about his approach is his claim that workers define themselves in terms of productivism and therefore that the problem for any strategy for transformation lies in the way workers are blocked from developing their full human potential, not only by the context of ideology, politics, and the consumer culture, but by the very fact of being workers. It is notable that Gorz's critique of Marx came to rest less on the inability of Marxist thought to transcend the productivism inherent in "economic reason"[38] than on Marx's investment of the working class with potential transformative capacities—what we designated earlier as the underestimation by Marx and later Marxists of the chasm that needed to be overcome between the scale and scope of the utopian dream and the sheer extent of the stunting by capitalism of working-class capacities.

Why has socialist politics given such a special status to "work" and "workers"? Ontologically work is a stand-in for the specifically human capacity to conceive of that which does not exist and then to effect its realization. Conceived in historical terms, the use of that capacity to create our material reality through work is intimately linked to the dynamics of social change. And in the specific context of capitalism, the organization of work provides a defining contradiction of the social system and a foundation for working-class politics. It is on the basis of these ontological, historical, and sociological dimensions of work that so many socialists have concluded that the working class, in spite of surrendering its labor power, is strategically positioned to lead the struggle for universal liberation.

It is in the workplace that capitalism brings diverse people into direct physical contact, and it is here—or at least in the communities that surround these workplaces—that they first build sustainable organizations, backed to some degree by independent ideologies and resources, to overcome their fragmentation. Workers develop potential leverage on the stability of production and profits, and therefore a base for a degree of countervailing power, by regularly testing their collective strength in the workplace. But what socialists must directly address is the question of whether workers can in fact develop, on the basis of this foundation, a vision of a new society and the "all-round development" which Marx insisted was the condition for the abolition of capitalism. For the workplace is also where workers' potentials and collective hopes may be crushed.

The worker seems condemned by the very "circumstances in which the individual lives ... [to] achieve only a one-sided crippled development."[39] And although the logic of capitalism leads workers into direct conflict with employers and the state, and even though such struggles lead to the creation of new needs, it is not clear that these needs eventuate in a vision of an alternative society rather than in a pragmatic reformism.[40] It is not just a matter of a political emphasis on the need for alliances outside the workplace and the need to address the larger question of the state—as important as these issues are. The deeper problem lies in the barriers imposed by the nature of work—and also nonwork—under capitalism.

The problem becomes clearer if we consider the limits to developing capacities in the context of workers' dependency on capitalists' active role within the economy: in production, the application of science, the introduction of innovations, the economic coordination across regions, and the widest and most diverse workplaces. Capitalists are not only privileged, but *needed*; their authority as economic leaders is set against workers' uncertain ability to do without them. As long as the paradigm is the workplace, there is at least some plausibility to the idea of it being run by workers who are already familiar with its daily operations. But once we begin to address the role of competition in linking workplaces, coordinating inputs and outputs, and enforcing dynamic change, we have to confront the imposing challenge of developing an entirely new order—including an entirely new workplace.

It would, of course, be somewhat easier if our goal was simply to catch up to capitalist capacities—if we failed to question the nature of capitalist economic growth and only sought to mimic it. But the socialist project goes beyond "catching up and taking over" because the particular capacities and institutions that we face in capitalism were developed historically within particular social relations. While some may be adapted, it is not enough to simply "democratize" them to fit a new set of relations and goals. Going beyond capital requires transforming existing capacities and developing new ones, transforming existing institutions and inventing historically unique ones.

It is important to emphasize that competition doesn't just complicate the question of implementing workers' control someday, but it especially affects the political capacities needed to get to that point. The competitive process of eroding barriers to accumulation and disciplining any resistance to its logic involves a constant restructuring of all aspects of economic and social life. For capital, this can happen without disturbing their class unity: capital remains united around the accumulation project; it has the resources to continuously introduce necessary institutional innovations; the state adds its support for maintaining capital's coherence; and capital has the technological and administrative capacity to combine a sweeping degree of capital mobility with a continuity, for the elites involved, in their local and national networks. But for workers, who draw on social, geographic, and generational continuities to develop their collective capacities, capitalist competition and restructuring often undermines class unity and identity.[41] We should not therefore count very heavily on the dynamics of capitalism to do much for maintaining or building a truly independent working-class identity and culture; it can only happen *in spite of* capitalism's logic.

If the work-time realities and confusions of power, dependency, and economic complexity make it hard for the working class to develop a postcapitalist vision, can this then happen—as Gorz suggests—in the realm of leisure, in private, family, and community spaces?

If only. Gorz's inspiring utopia at the end of *Farewell to the Working Class* nevertheless still fell short of Marx's integrated and radical democratic vision insofar as it reflected the rest of that book's acceptance, in a Habermasian fashion, of the systematic inevitability of an alienated, albeit much reduced, sphere of production and another of bureaucratic planning and administration (and also confined itself to one rich country, France). And in spite of his valid criticism of an orthodox forces-of-production-determined socialism, Gorz's own argument is dependent on the assumption that the productive forces of a rich economy will sustain the liberation from work—i.e., that there is no serious ongoing economic problem to worry about in his utopia. But while work and nonwork occupy different compartments in time and space, the problem lies in how those compartments are integrated within the whole. Capitalism's world of necessity doesn't just lay the material base for less wage work; it limits, shapes, and creates specific necessities even in the realm of nonwork. Work time and the location of work determine how much leisure we have, when we have it, and how much of it is absorbed by the need for some minimum of physical and mental recovery time. In capitalism "recreation" means just what it says: re-creating our ability to work. And leisure, when it is not heavily committed to necessary and compensatory consumption, tends, as Henri Lefebvre has remarked, to be reduced to a respite from work.[42] Like a school recess or a coffee break, it is devalued by the fact that our relief is short-lived. Free time, it turns out, is not all that free. If nonwork time is to play a liberating role, this can only happen if it is part of a broader individual and social project that transcends the barrier between nonwork and work, fundamentally changing them both rather than just reducing working time.

Of the variety of social spaces that nonwork time inhabits, the household is especially important. The gendered and patriarchal division of labor within the household predates capitalism, but the nature of the household's new link to the outside capitalist world imposed a distinctive dimension to the relationships between men and women, work and family life, work and leisure, and consequently on both women and their potentials and men and their sense of what being a "whole" person entailed. Housework continued, under capitalism, to directly produce use values necessary for the household's survival and reproduction; for this it needed no external approval or market incentives. But once wages were required for buying necessities, the importance of getting and keeping a job gave wage work and the wage-earner a special importance and status within the household. The household's activities, schedules, moods, and even its (re)location were subordinated, by way of the its dependence on wage work, to the needs of the wage-earner. The corollary was a supportive and secondary role for women. A woman might make the bread, but it was the man who was considered the "breadwinner" because his wages paid for the ingredients.

The negative impact on women's options, capacities, and potentials needs no elaboration. But the issue extends beyond that of gender equality. The fact that men are generally not expected to actively deal with household and community responsibilities—such as the caring of children, daily coordination with school routines, dealing with sudden needs for emergency medical care as well as routine ones, coping with the impact of pollution to family health as well as with neighborhood crime, and the absence of community recreational space—this cannot avoid also limiting men's sense of themselves. Without the broader everyday engagements and frustrations that situate working-class men as more than just workers, it is difficult to imagine them developing the expectations of themselves and of society that are at the center of socialist consciousness: the belief in their own potential as *full* human beings and their demand for social structures to support that dream.

The women's movement has added something crucial to traditional socialist approaches to developing confidence, capacities, and consciousness. Out of necessity, as well as in reaction to male-dominated politics, it has shown a special sensitivity to the need to help people assert their rights and participate in change, and to reach out to "ordinary" people, focusing on less intimidating local issues, small group discussions rather than interventions at mass meetings, exchanges that are supportive rather than competitive, analyses that are concrete rather than abstract, and not treating work as the sum total of working-class life—"making the personal political." In going beyond the workplace, this kind of politics has also suggested routes that move the household beyond the private, to its connection with the community and to the relations between generations. No strategic debates about socialism can exclude the insights, nuances, and attention to process that the women's movement has rightfully insisted be part of any universalizing movement.

IV

We saw in the previous chapter that the trajectory of Andre Gorz's work reflected an honest ambivalence about the leadership potential of the working classes in radical change. Even though he said "farewell to the working class" in the early eighties, he could not help in his later writings like *Critique of Economic Reason* but return to the trade union movement as the core element of political change, not least through its potential as "the best organized force in the broader movement" for sustaining those varied radical social movements which had grown up "outside work."[43] Unger's suggestion, raised earlier, that unionization be mandated across the entire workforce may seem to reflect a similar recognition of the importance of unions. But in Unger's case this is less an acknowledgment of their importance than an expression of a desire to settle the issue of recognition and move on to the real vanguard of innovative firms. The focus he and others have placed on changing the nature of the capitalist firm, while more substantive than the communitarianism fashionable among philosophers today, tends toward a depoliticization of both the firm and the union.

What this approach underestimates is the social power of capital and the oppositional politics necessarily involved in changing it. We must begin not with the firm, but with changing the role and nature of workers' organizations themselves, their potential as sites of capacity-building and democratization, and especially their scope for moving *beyond* the workplace. Once we approach the issue of class and transformation as being about overcoming dependency on capitalists to the end of developing full human capacities, further expectations emerge around what unions, as the front-line economic organization of workers, might possibly do. And this in turn implies a different kind of unionism in terms of how it chooses and structures its struggles, applies its resources, defines internal democracy and participation, responds to its members as producers and service providers, and relates to the community, political parties, and the state.

The problem with unions is not, as Unger and so many others seem to think, that they have been too defensive but that in most cases they have not been defensive enough or at least not defensive in a way that allows them to get beyond merely being reactive. To be defensive doesn't mean to be static. A trade unionism committed to mobilizing its defensiveness would be committed to developing a "culture of resistance," and nothing is more important to the future possibility of socialism than the current existence of a working class that is determinedly oppositional, organizationally independent, conscious of its subordinate position, ideologically confident in the legitimacy of its demands, creatively ready to take on and lead struggles, and insistent that its own organizations be democratic and accountable so as to embody this spirit of popular activism and militancy. In addition to aggressively fighting for traditional demands, the content of union demands would take on new dimensions and be linked to generalizing, within the union, the capacity of members to participate and thereby develop their overall political and administrative capacities. Examples include pushing to take productivity gains as time off from the job and for education both at and away from the workplace; linking health and safety issues to debates and demands about how work is organized and the priorities of technology; negotiating learner-driven training; developing, through internal union educational programs, the confidence and therefore the capacity to participate amongst all members; and extending the collective capacity to discuss and disagree—to debate—*before* the arrival of those moments of crisis when external pressures reinforce tendencies to define all internal opposition to the leadership as sabotage.

In contrast to a defensiveness that is part of building a culture of resistance, there is a set of union alternatives that coopt the language of "capacity-building" and economic "empowerment" to the same ends of the supply-side defeatism we discussed earlier. They operate comfortably within the existing framework of power and their emphasis on the "progressive" in "progressive competitiveness" is expressed in proposals for "jointness" in production, partnerships for competitiveness, alliances for jobs, worker representation on corporate boards, and most discussion of the use of pension or labor funds for social investment purposes. Since they assume what labor and capital have in common is more important than any differences, they are oriented to placing worker representatives alongside management in "problem-solving." What emerges are not alternative capacities, but only practices which echo capital (e.g., learning to run businesses and funds like capitalists do); and even these are restricted to a small handful of worker representatives and officials who participate in keeping information from their members because of "corporate confidentiality."[44] The actual access to influencing decisions is, not surprisingly, extremely limited, since it isn't won through mobilization but offered to *limit* mobilization. The tradeoffs made for that access— material concessions and the symbolic distancing of the leadership from the members—carry dangerous institutional implications with regards to rank-and-file suspicions and leadership credibility. And finally, even if there is something positive that comes out of initiatives such as access to information and input into certain decisions, this can generally be achieved at less cost and with longer-lasting results through the very mobilization this approach pushes aside.[45]

While such so-called alternatives can only take us backward, they do raise the issue of responding to working-class insecurity about jobs. Although the prime function of unions has been the terms and conditions of the sale of workers' labor power, an increasingly crucial concern of their members has been that of retaining their jobs—something that unions, apart from trying to negotiate the sharing of work through reduced work time, have been ill-positioned to guarantee. Taking on this defensive concern involves the strategic challenge of unions contributing to workers seeing themselves as not just workers but producers and providers of services, and therefore capable of addressing not only how many jobs are needed, but the nature and purpose of those jobs. This would take private sector unions beyond the workplace and the single firm to thinking in terms of the whole economic sector; and it would take public sector unions beyond their role of representing "civil servants" who do things *for* others toward mobilizing *with* the people they "serve" to expand the range and access to social rights and spaces. Worker and consumer councils at the level of whole economic sectors, in contrast to single companies driven by accumulation and competition, would be better able to associate production with use values and with technological linkages across the economy and would be able to address developing the collective capacities to govern the economy democratically. Public

sector councils, for their part, would begin the difficult process of eroding the distinction between public sector workers and their clients as well
as between their work and the very different "consumption" of that work
than is involved in the consumption of commodities.[46]

The point of addressing jobs and services in this way is not so much
that this is an immediately viable strategy for the gradual encroachment
on and eventual takeover of capital and the state, but rather that it
involves a gradual development of new capacities and vision, an independent sense of how unions could be "doing-other" to the end of
"becoming-other": negotiating with employers with a new confidence of
workers' potential as opposed to demanding a voice for union leaders on
various boards; introducing demands on the state such as access to government departments in terms of expanding the range of information
they collect and provide, and state funding of unions' research; organizing meetings of workers in and across sectors to develop their ability to
analyze their situation in the economy and society as a whole; and
addressing the creation of new political and economic structures to
implement this direction, ranging from job development boards and
municipal ownership to democratic public financial institutions for controlling and allocating capital flows.

This kind of capacity building on the part of the labor movement also
opens the question of a new relationship to the community—if only, at
first, stimulated by the concern in these particular times to avoid isolation. What is involved here is the broader strategic challenge to position
unions as potential centers of working-class life. This is not simply a matter of finding support for unions in the community through linking workers to "others," but of highlighting the fact that workers are more than
just "workers" and addressing their needs in ways that value such
glimpses of their potential as their limited experience of "citizenship"
now affords, and raising their expectations of becoming fuller human
beings than their social status as workers now allows. For this relationship to the community be to be substantive rather than rhetorical (which
invocations of "the community" by many union leaders often are, no less
than by many academics and politicians), it must affect the kinds of
demands unions make on employers and the state. What this means is
that issues like the environmental implications of a worksite, reduced
work time to share jobs, and ending the inferior status of part-time jobs
must become priorities in collective bargaining; and that the nature of
union structures must change as well, for example, by opening up local

union committees to include teenagers and spouses to mobilize for changes in school education, urban and regional planning, health administration, etc. Such a new unionism, committed to enhancing local community life, would inevitably have to play a leading role in joining with other movements to engage the state at every level, from both inside and outside, to force the development of the kind of democratic administration implied by both the sectoral and community aspects of the radical union strategy outlined here.

In both their militant defensiveness and in expanding their role beyond the workplace, it is therefore clear that unions, in "doing-other," must inevitably engage the local and national state in ways that go beyond lobbying and support for electoral allies. The struggle to democratize the economy is ultimately about collapsing the distinction between economics and politics in a very particular way: one that alters the nature of the state so that the state does not stand external to everyday economic life as a bureaucratic regulator, but is integrated in the struggles to transform social relations—which is the condition for "becoming other," whereby people and institutions change themselves in the process of changing the nature of the economy.

V

Twentieth-century Marxists like Lenin and Antonio Gramsci addressed the need for restructuring the state almost exclusively in relation to what would be done *after* coming to power. But if we are to develop the democratic administrative capacities and confidence in our abilities to govern ourselves, we must find ways to constantly engage the existing state. This means that the socialist project can't advance without rethinking anew the relationship between democracy and the state. In the popular mind, the existing capitalist state embodies the democratic idea, however imperfectly, and declarations that because it is a capitalist state it is undemocratic— while true—won't change this. Analytical and rhetorical criticisms of this flawed democracy can score points, but without practical experiences that both reveal its limitations and show that something else is possible, they come up against a resigned acceptance that in a complex society this is as good as democracy can get, or mere cynicism. Our criticisms have to be tied to practical steps—aimed at changing not just what the state does, but how the various elements of the state function, showing that democratic and other gains *can* be made, instilling confidence that elements of a different and richer democracy are possible, and at the same time revealing that such gains remain limited unless we keep going further in linking democracy and economic and social transformation.

These dimensions—the need for engagement with the state, structuring that engagement so it has a socialist purpose, accumulation of the resultant capacities, the development of new means of ensuring accountability—raise all the old questions of political organization and class consciousness. But proclamations about praxis and intervention by a revolutionary party are not particularly helpful. The argument that at unique moments of deep capitalist crises and intensified struggles, a socialist consciousness and vision will explode onto the stage of history is unconvincing or, at best, incomplete. What would sustain such struggles and prevent their intensity from burning out, or prevent the severe implications of the crisis from unnerving the movement? Without a socialist culture *already* in existence—which necessarily includes, amongst other things, already committed socialists, a socialist vision, and the everyday capacity building we have stressed—there would be nothing for the militants to plug into during moments of crisis and struggle, and therefore no reason to expect these militants, through "praxis," to suddenly adopt a sustained coherent revolutionary perspective. We are therefore back to the question of the source of socialist culture.

To say at this point we need a revolutionary socialist party to build that culture again only begs the question. New parties will be needed to give political coherence to labor and other social movements as well as to get elected and to prioritize the institutional reforms and experimentation required to engage the existing state in the process of social transformation. But what exactly would such parties do to develop a socialist culture within capitalism? Developing socialist theory and clarifying socialist vision are essential first steps to building new parties capable of fostering popular strategic, democratic, and administrative capacities.

At issue here, in other words, is not only the politics of the socialist project but its theoretical underpinnings. Marx's main critique of bourgeois political economy was that its boundaries stopped at capitalism's boundaries. It created a sense of the end of history, whereas Marx wanted to open that history up. To this end, he created a better social science. But the socialist project needed something more. Because the socialist project swims in an ill-defined sea of potentialities, because it depends on nothing less than subordinate classes setting out to create a new society, it requires a more comprehensive means of integrating the science of what is to the possibilities and strategic considerations of what might be. It is not a matter of rejecting or abandoning Marxism, but neither is it just a matter of correcting or improving on Marx. It is about adding a new conceptual layer to Marxism, a dimension formerly missing or undeveloped. Amongst other things, this means a theoretical framework that is centered on the concepts of capacities and potentials. Socialism really is about the development of productive forces, but these productive forces include historically new capacities, above all the collective capacities to govern democratically everyday life, the economy, civil society, and the state. Without the development of productive forces in this sense, people couldn't run a society even if power was handed over by the ruling classes.

This means that in addition to analyzing the accumulation of capital, we also have to analyze the accumulation of capacities. This requires rethinking the units of analysis and social relationships we focus on. As long as, for example, we limit ourselves to the capitalist firm, we fail to focus on discussions about use values (what should entire economic sectors be doing) and coordination (planning links within and between sectors), in other words, about needs and our capacities to address those needs. Or, to take another example, if the unit of analysis isn't the individual worker, but the household which, through an internal division of labor produces and reproduces labor, sells labor power, and consumes, then not only do we have a better opening to address the capacities of women but we can better locate men and women in a context that bridges work and nonwork and therefore their full human potentiality or its frustration. Since both production and households are physically located within communities, this also better facilitates addressing the issue of cross-generational class consciousness and the impact of restructuring on class capacities. And the emphasis on "democratic administration" as a productive force raises questions of simultaneously politicizing the economy (rather than leaving it to the market) and thinking through what kind of state structures at every level might be involved in such a politicization if it is to conform to developing democratic collective capacities. The cognitive, strategic, and inspirational purpose of such a theory is to help us conceive how to inhabit capitalism while building bridges to those individual/institutional capacities to get socialism on the agenda. What the socialist project needs today, therefore, is not so much the details of how socialism would work or what socialists would do if they occupied the state, nor just more measures of why capitalism is not good enough. Rather it needs something transitional between these, beginning with a commitment to developing capacities to keep "the utopian goal clearly visible," as Bloch put it. To that end the motivating vision, incorporating a utopian sensibility with a concern with capacity-building, must encompass at least the following ten dimensions:

1. *Overcoming alienation.* This is not a matter of escaping work in order to fulfill our lives but rather transforming the nature of work as well as giving people outside of the world of work "the possibility of developing interests and autonomous activities, including productive activities" so that they are no longer "passive consumers of amusements."[47]

2. *Attenuating the division of labor.* The principle at the heart of the socialist project—the potential of each of us to become full human beings—cannot be achieved in the context of hierarchical structures "that obstruct participation or deny equitable access of all workers to equal opportunities for fulfilment and influence."[48] Because this won't be easy, socialists are obliged to begin this process in their own parties, unions, movements, NGOs, offices, plants, universities, etc.

3. *Transforming consumption.* Socialists must recognize that any "transformation of the relations of production and the organization of work would be conditional on a number of other, equally dramatic, changes of lifestyle and mode of consuming."[49] This is not only a matter of ecological sanity but of connecting consumers to the decisions about what is produced, the development of capacities for diverse enjoyments rather than the consumption of homogenized commodities, and the expansion of accessible and generally more egalitarian spheres of public and collective consumption.

4. *Alternative ways of living.* The household as a space where glimpses of socialist capacities are afforded suggests that experiments with more communal forms of living that have the potential of extending "intense, affectional bonds" to a broader supportive community beyond the nuclear family and other forms of household relations can provide "a compelling point of entry for a prefigurative politics which proposes new kinds of sharing relationships and new kinds of public places."[50]

5. *Socializing markets.* Bringing decisions about capital allocation into the democratic public sphere, alongside transformations in

modes of consumption and ways of living, allows us "to envision ways of reclaiming and transforming markets and money, so that they become a means of facilitating mutually beneficial exchange based on a mutually beneficial division of labour in an economy with an egalitarian distribution of economic power."[51] Only these kinds of markets and social relations will allows us to escape the steel bonds of competition that entrap so much of what passes for utopian thinking today.

6. *Planning ecologically.* The socialist project means developing the capacities within each state for the democratic allocation of time and resources and the quantitative and qualitative balance between production and consumption. The goal is to "maximize the capacity of different national collectivities democratically to choose alternate development paths ... that do not impose externalities (such a environmental damage) on other countries, by re-embedding financial capital and production relations from global to national and local economic spaces."[52]

7. *Internationalizing equality.* Envisioning this type of planning at the national level means developing international alliances and, eventually, an international system that facilitates rather than undermines these efforts. In turn, developing the consciousness and capacities that allows for the building of egalitarian social relations within states must include a growing commitment to a solidaristic transfer of resources from rich to poor countries and to facilitating the latter's economic development via common struggles to transcend the geopolitical barriers to the development of socialist capacities. This not only means recognizing the existence of contemporary imperialism but coming to terms with the "geographical conditions and diversities" of working-class existence and learning how to "arbitrate and translate" between these diversities and spatial scales in reviving socialist politics.[53]

8. *Communicating democratically.* Socialists need to give priority to developing a vision and strategy for diverse, pluralist communications media in place of the commodified market-driven media today, so as to allow for the capacities for intelligent collective dialogue to grow as well as to nurture the capacities for rich cultural development. "For a renewed collective debate about the fundamental principles of social organization to be possible, and

for a new socialist project to be articulated and get a hearing, a new media order is needed."[54]

9. *Realizing democracy.* The whole point of a socialist project conceived in terms of developing individual and collective capacities is make the deepening and extension of democracy viable. This entails the most serious commitment to conceiving and trying to establish the types of representation and administration that contribute to breaking down the organizationally reinforced distinctions between managers and workers, politicians and citizens, leaders and led, and to overcoming the barriers that separate what we are from what we might become.[55]

10. *Omnia sint communia.* Progressive intellectuals in our time have devoted enormous energy to trying to get around what was obvious to many pre-Marxist utopians, that is, that you simply cannot have private property in the means of production, finance, exchange, and communication and at the same time have an unalienated, socially just, and democratic social order; and that you cannot begin to approach a utopia on the basis of the acquisitive and competitive drive. There is no way of rekindling socialist imagination so long as this basic principle is obscured, not least because doing so avoids all the difficult questions about making democratic collectivist capacities into real potentialities.

Socialists are living through a unique period: The collapse of Communism and the complete abnegation by Social Democratic parties of any vocation for radical change has left us, for the first time in over a century, with no strong organizational focus for our goals. The political vacuum we consequently face is, not surprisingly, accompanied by a great deal of pessimism. But overcoming that pessimism is not a matter of asserting a new, yet equally short-sighted, optimism. Rather, it means drawing inspiration from the continuity between the utopian dream that predates socialism and the concrete popular struggles in evidence around the world as people strive, in a multitude of diverse ways, to assert their humanity. It means drawing encouragement from the activist Left's broadening of its political project to encompass many of the ideals we have set out above. And above all, it means apprehending what the very power of capital is inadvertently proclaiming as it overruns, subordinates, and narrows every aspect of our lives—that capitalism is "the wrong dream," and that only an alternative that is just as universal and ambitious, but rooted in our collective liberating potentials, can replace it. Rekindling the socialist imagination and finding the organizational means to accumulate the capacities to develop that alternative are not only necessary but possible. Through this kind of renewal of socialist politics, we can still discover the spirit of revolution to build a new house where freedom can dwell.

Notes

1. Arthur Miller, *Death of a Salesman* (London: Penguin, 1998), pp. 111–12. The famous Beijing production in the early 1980s, just as China's Communist capitalism was being launched, had already demonstrated the play's growing relevance.

2. Ernst Bloch, *The Principle of Hope*, translated by N. Plaice, S. Plaice, and P. Knight (Cambridge, Mass.: MIT Press, 1986), p. 198. Largely written during his exile in the United States between 1937 and 1949, the first two volumes were first published in East Germany in 1954–55 and the third volume in 1959. It is worth noting, in light of the use made here of *Death of a Salesman*, that Bloch regarded theater as a "paradigmatic institution" in terms of its ability to "influence the will of this world, in its real possibilities" (p. 424). He saw in theater proof of people's "mimic need . . . connected positively with the . . . tempting desire to transform oneself. . . . The Curtain rises, the fourth wall is missing, in its place is the open proscenium. . . . From the life we have had the narrowness disappears into which it has so often led" (pp. 412–13). For an insightful appreciation of Bloch's work by a former student, see ch. 9 of Stephen Eric Bronner's *Of Critical Theory and Its Theorists* (Cambridge, Mass.: Blackwell, 1994). Cf. Jamie Owen Daniel and Tom Moylan, eds., *Not Yet: Reconsidering Ernst Bloch* (New York: Verso, 1997).

3. Bloch, *Principle of Hope*, pp. 445–46.

4. Ibid., pp. 530, 582.

5. Ibid., pp. 519–20.

6. Ibid., pp. 148, 197–98, 209, 622–23.

7. Ibid., p. 444.

8. Ibid., p. 622.

9. Ernst Bloch, *A Philosophy of the Future*, translated by John Cummings (New York: Herder and Herder, 1970), p. 92.

10. It needs to be noted that Bloch himself tended, at least through the 1930s and 1940s, toward a "premature harmonization" of the contradictions he discerned in the Soviet Union.

11. The richest attempt to explore this lacuna ("the question before us is—why did Marx ever think that workers could go beyond capital?") is Mike Lebowitz, *Beyond Capital* (New York: Macmillan, 1995).

12. Bloch, *Principle of Hope*, pp. 232–33.

13. Karl Marx and Friedrich Engels, *The German Ideology* (New York: International Publishers, 1947), p. 26.

14. Terry Eagleton, "Utopia and Its Opposites," in Leo Panitch and Colin Leys, eds., *Necessary and Unnecessary Utopias: The Socialist Register 2000* (London: Merlin, 1999), p. 36.

15. Barbara Kingsolver, *Animal Dreams* (New York: HarperCollins, 1990), p. 133.

16. James C. Scott, *Seeing like a State: How Certain Schemes to Improve the Human Condition Have Failed* (New Haven, Conn.: Princeton University Press, 1998).

17. Scott, *Seeing like a State*, pp. 6–7, 88–89, 101–2, 342–44. At the same time Scott recognizes that "Revolutionaries had every reason to despise the feudal, poverty-stricken, inegalitarian past that they hoped to banish forever, and sometimes they also have had reason to suspect that immediate democracy would simply bring back the social order. . . . Understanding the history and logic of the commitment to high-modernist goals, however, does not permit us to overlook the enormous damage that their convictions entailed when combined with authoritarian state power." Nor does he go so far as some others do in his critique of the enlightenment and modernism which "has provided us with a knowledge of the world that, for all its darker aspects, few of us would want to surrender. What has proved to be truly dangerous to us and our environment, I think, is the combination of the universalist pretensions of epistemic knowledge and authoritarian social engineering." pp. 340–41.

18. Ibid., pp. 8, 327.

19. Hilary Wainwright, *Arguments for a New Left* (Oxford: Blackwell, 1994).

20. Erik Olin Wright, Preface to Sam Bowles and Herb Gintis, *Recasting Egalitarianism: New Rules for Communities, States and Markets* (New York: Verso, 1998), p. ix. Wright is not sure himself whether Bowles and Gintis's model is advanced "in the spirit of a thoroughgoing institutional redesign of society" (p. 87), but neither is it at all clear that the two previous volumes in this series—on a guaranteed annual income and associational democracy, respectively—would qualify by this test. In fact, by focusing on a redistribution of property rights, albeit within a competitive market economy, Bowles and Gintis clearly see themselves as challenging the limitations of those volumes.

21. Bowles and Gintis, *Recasting Egalitarianism*, p. 364.

22. Ibid.

23. To compensate for the latter (presented mainly in terms of inducing workers not be risk-adverse when it comes to borrowing and investment), the state would provide self-financing unemployment insurance (only limited payments would go to those whose "own actions"—including, it appears, failure to work hard enough to raise productivity—are "implicated in their joblessness") and bankruptcy insurance (it is unpersuasively claimed that it would be not be difficult to insure firms on a self-financing basis against "exogenous" risks like economic downturns and to distinguish these from "controllable" risks like bad management or investment decisions). Ibid., pp. 50–51.

24. See Bertell Ollman, ed., *Market Socialism: The Debate Among Socialists* (New York: Routledge, 1998).

25. An excellent early overview and assessment of this literature was provided by Pat Devine, "Market Socialism or Participatory Planning," *Review of Radical Political Economics* 24, 3–4 (Special Issue, Fall & Winter, 1992): 67–89. The most creative contributions were Devine's *Democracy and Economic Planning* (Cambridge, U.K.: Polity Press, 1988); Diane Elson's "Market Socialism or Socialization of the Market?" *New Left Review* 172 (November/December 1988): 3—44; and, especially for the attention they paid to attenuating, if not entirely transcending, the divi-

sion of labor in a complex economy, Michael Albert and Robin Hahnel's *Looking Forward: Participatory Economics for the Twenty-first Century* (Boston: South End Press, 1991).

26. All they have to say by way of elaborating on the worker-owned firms being "governed by their elected representatives" is: "We assume that workers direct the managers of the democratic firm to select investments, systems of work monitoring, and other policy options to maximize the workers' welfare." Bowles and Gintis, *Recasting Egalitarianism*, p. 37.

27. Ibid., pp. 390–91.

28. They ignore Barrington Moore's famous retort to those who relied on assumptions of cultural inertia: "To maintain and transmit a value system," he famously wrote, "human beings are punched, bullied, sent to jail, thrown into concentration camps, cajoled, bribed, made into heroes, encouraged to read newspapers, stood up against a wall and shot, and sometimes even taught sociology." And these days, we might add, supply-side economics. See Barrington Moore, Jr., *Social Origins of Democracy and Dictatorship* (Boston: Beacon, 1967), p. 486.

29. As one of their critics puts it: "Bowles and Gintis are . . . so busy making a pitch for egalitarian policies to soft-hearted efficiency worshippers that they risk inviting their readers to forget what egalitarianism is all about. It is not about Nintendo games in every home and more trips to the Mall. It is about self-respect, fairness, equal respect and fraternity. . . . The fundamental mistake is that they fail to ask what economic growth is for, and they surrender all thought of questioning, let alone controlling, the future that markets dictate to us. Even if Bowles and Gintis are right that those concerned with efficiency should support egalitarian policies, egalitarians . . . should keep their distance from supply-side economics." Daniel M. Hausman, "Problems with Supply-side Egalitarianism," in Bowles and Gintis, eds., *Recasting Egalitarianism*, p. 84. It is one of the virtues of Verso's Real Utopia series that each volume also contains such critical essays followed by a response by the main authors.

30. Roberto Mangabeira Unger, *Democracy Realized: The Progressive Alternative* (New York: Verso, 1998), p. 9.

31. Roberto Mangabeira Unger, *False Necessity*, part 1 of *Politics: A Work in Constructive Social Theory* (Cambridge, U.K.: Cambridge University Press, 1987), pp. 392–95.

32. *False Necessity.*, pp. 406–9, 438. At the time this was written in the mid-1980s, this could be seen as a theorization of the kind of political practice that had already been articulated by the activists who created the Workers' Party in Unger's own Brazil, or by Tony Benn in the British Labour Party and the activists of Greater London Council. (Unger himself was associated not with the Workers' Party but aligned with Cardoso in the formation of the less radical Brazilian Democratic Movement, PMDB. See Eyal Press, "The Passion of Roberto Unger," *Lingua Franca* 9, 3 (March 1999): 44–53. At the time he wrote *False Necessity*, Unger's hope was that the proponents of "empowered democracy" would be able to work loosely within reform, labor, Socialist, and Communist parties as well as within "the extrapartisan grassroots movements most open to their vision"(p. 409). By the time of *Democracy Realized* over a decade later, however, Unger

seemed much less confident about where to find "the missing agent of an inclusive politics" (p. 245).

33. Unger, *Democracy Realized*, pp. 1, 213–15, 263ff.

34. Ibid., p. 174.

35. *Democracy Realized*, p. 43.

36. "Those with their heads truly in the sands or the clouds are the hard-nosed realists who behave as though chocolate chip cookies and the International Monetary Fund will be with us in another three thousand years time." Eagleton, "Utopia and Its Opposites," p. 33.

37. Andre Gorz, *Strategy for Labor: A Radical Proposal* (Boston: Beacon, 1967), p. 7.

38. "The condition of post-Marxist Man is that the meaning Marx read into historical development remains for us the only meaning that development can have, yet we must pursue this independent of the existence of a social class capable of realizing it." *Critique of Economic Reason* (London: Verso, 1989), p. 96.

39. Marx and Engels, *The German Ideology*, pp. 68ff.

40. See Sam Gindin, "Socialism with Sober Senses," in Leo Panitch and Colin Leys, eds., *The Socialist Register 1998* (London: Merlin, 1998), pp. 75–101.

41. See Jerry Lembcke, "Class Analysis and Studies of the U.S. Working Class: Theoretical, Conceptual, and Methodological Issues," in Scott G. McNall, Rhonda Levine, and Rick Fantasia, eds., *Bringing Class Back In* (Boulder: Westview Press, 1991).

42. Henri Lefebvre, *Critique of Everyday Life*, vol. 1 (London, Verso: 1991), p. 33.

43. Andre Gorz, *Critique of Economic Reason* (London: Verso, 1989), pp. 231–33; cf. Andre Gorz, *Farewell to the Working Class* (Boston: Southend Press, 1982).

44. One of strongest examples of union involvement in decision making is codetermination in Germany. However, when Daimler made the decision to merge with Chrysler, this was not discussed at the board level where the German metalworkers were involved; it was deemed too sensitive, and the worker input was to ratify it after the fact. Similarly, the issue of outsourcing, which is so crucial to German workers, is not dealt with at the board level because it would be too "controversial." In Canada, there has been a mushrooming of government-subsidized "labor worker investment funds" to allegedly give the labor movement some control over jobs and the direction of the economy without the capacity to control any particular project, invest in directions which may meet criteria other than profitability, or insist that the jobs created include unionization. For a detailed critique of the latter, see Jim Stanford, *Labour Investment Funds* (Toronto: CAW, 1999).

45. For instance, demanding, through collective bargaining and legislation, reports from the company that are accessible to nonaccountants, resources for independent technical assistance in interpreting information, time during working hours to get updates and raise questions of management, union approval of work reorganization or outsourcing decisions, and input through economic sector councils as discussed below.

46. See Greg McElligott, "An Immodest Proposal, or Democracy Beyond the Capitalist Welfare State," *Socialist Studies Bulletin*, no. 52, Winnipeg, 1998.

47. Gorz, *Critique of Economic Reason*, p. 231.

48. Albert and Hahnel, *Looking Forward*, p. 35.

49. Kate Soper, "Other Pleasures: The Attractions of Post-Consumption," in Leo Panitch and Colin Leys, eds., *Necessary and Unnecessary Utopias: The Socialist Register 2000* (London: Merlin, 1999), p. 127. Cf. the debate on Juliet Schor's "New Politics of Consumption," *Boston Review* 24 (Summer 1999): 3–4.

50. Johanna Brenner, "Utopian Families," in Leo Panitch and Colin Leys, eds., *Necessary and Unnecessary Utopias: The Socialist Register 2000*, p. 141.

51. Diane Elson, "Socializing Markets, Not Market Socialism," in Leo Panitch and Colin Leys, eds., *Necessary and Unnecessary Utopias: The Socialist Register 2000*, p. 68.

52. Greg Albo, "The World Economy, Market Imperatives and Alternatives," *Monthly Review*, December 1996, p. 19. And see also Albo's ten-point program in his "World Market of Opportunities? Capitalist Obstacles and Left Economic Policy," in Leo Panitch and Colin Leys, eds., *The Socialist Register 1997* (London: Merlin, 1997).

53. David Harvey, "The Geography of Class Power," in Leo Panitch and Colin Leys, eds., *The Socialist Register 1998* (London: Merlin, 1998), esp. p. 70.

54. Colin Leys, "The Public Sphere and the Media: Market Supremacy versus Democracy," in Leo Panitch and Colin Leys, eds., *The Socialist Register 1999* (London: Merlin, 1998).

55. See Greg Albo, David Langille, and Leo Panitch, eds., *A Different Kind of State* (Toronto: Oxford University Press, 1993).

INDEX

Lunacharski, Anatoli, 45
Luxemburg, Rosa, 38–40, 94, 101, 118,
    204

Macpherson, C.B., 9, 11, 79–102
    definition of class, 86–87,
    104–105(n16)
    definition of democracy, 87–88
    net transfer of powers, 84, 90, 99
Mandel, David, 78(n18)
Maoism, 4, 19, 22
Market freedom, 16, 17, 39, 47, 54, 129
Market populism, 7
Market socialism, 46, 51, 207, 223–224
Martin, Andrew, 175, 176
Marx, Karl, 2, 4, 10, 14–15, 16, 25–28,
    50, 79–86, 89, 92–93, 98–101, 108,
    111, 116, 119, 128, 137(n56), 199,
    201–204, 214, 221
Marxism, 4, 16, 79, 80–81, 84, 88, 91,
    100, 101–103, 116, 119, 199, 221
Marxism-Leninism, 4
Marxist political theory, 91, 92–93,
    95–102
McElligot, Greg, 229(n46)
Media, 121, 125, 127, 132, 136(n44),
    224–225
Medvedev, Roy, 75
Mensheviks, 73, 74, 76, 113
Mexico, 107, 108, 123, 143–145, 190
    Chipas revolt, 145
    Partido Revolucionario Institucional
    (PRI) government, 145
Michels, Robert, 67
Miliband, Ralph, 101, 118
Mill, John Stuart, 83–90
Miller, Arthur, 197
Mills, C. Wright, 79–80
Mitterand, François, 19, 161
Mixed economy, 16, 51, 76, 117, 129,
    169, 170
Moll, Joseph, 133
Monetarism, 173
Moody, Kim, 184
Moore Jr., Barrington, 79–80, 208,
    228(n28)
Moore, Thomas, *Utopia*, 159

Movements of the disabled, 43
Mulroney, Brian, 146, 148
Multinational corporations, 108,
    175–176, 190
    See also Transnational corporations
Murray, Robin, 40–42

Nabokov, Vladimir, 66, 76
Nader, Ralph, 194(n23)
National liberation struggles, 4, 140
National Union of Metalworkers of
    South Africa (NUMSA), 190
Nationalism, 33, 38–40, 142, 149, 158
Nationalization, 35, 40, 41–42, 160, 171
Neo-liberalism, 1, 5, 8, 23, 38, 107, 108,
    111, 120, 125–129, 143–145, 148,
    154, 157, 160
    See also Globalization
Neri, Alvaro Cepeda, 145
Netherlands, 112
New Deal, 17, 147
"New Economy,9 16
New Left, 3, 7, 19, 52, 129
New Right, 2
New social movements, 5–7, 28, 110,
    131, 149, 166, 168, 202
New world order, 45, 171
New York Times, 109
Nicaragua, 13
Nigeria, 109
Nongovernmental organizations
    (NGOs), 128, 166, 179–181, 223
North American Free Trade
    Agreement (NAFTA), 143, 145
    corporate private property rights,
    144
    intellectual property rights, 144
    investor rights, 144
    side agreements, 145, 177

Organized capitalism, 16, 171

Paris Commune, 113, 127, 128
Paris 1968, 5
Parker, Mike, 185
Parliamentarism, 5, 23–24, 34, 74, 209
Parliamentary democracy, 37

Tobin tax, 182
Trade unions. *See* Unions
Transnational corporations, 122,
  144–146, 154, 178
  See also Multinational corporations
Transnational democracy, 141, 156, 161
Trotsky, Leon, 49
Trotskyism, 4, 19, 22

Unger, Roberto, 208–209, 210–211, 216,
  217
Ungovernability, 19
Unions, 9, 21, 26–28, 34, 111, 117, 154,
  166, 184–185, 216–218, 223
  industrial unionism, 7, 26
  mass unionism, 9
  new pluralism, 165, 168
  organization, 168, 176, 185, 186,
    217
  social movement unionism, 184
  Solidarity (Poland), 180
  strategies of inclusiveness, 169
  strategy for labor, 165, 172–176,
    182–189, 190–192
  union culture, 185, 188
  women and, 26, 60, 167, 168, 184,
    189–190, 193(n4), 205, 220
United States, 37, 53, 62, 73, 90,
  107–109, 112, 132, 144, 147, 186,
  190
Utopia, 115, 198, 200–203, 207–209,
  212–214, 225

Wage labor, 25, 85
Wainwright, Hilary, 111, 205
Wall Street Journal, 15
Wallach, Lori, 194(n23)

Wallerstein, Immanuel, 141–142
"Washington Consensus,9 107
Weberian bureaucratic rationality, 205
Welfare state, 5, 13, 20, 37, 117,
  124–126, 146–150, 169, 176 208
  impasse of, 169
Wilde, Oscar, 204
Williams, Raymond, 13, 17, 127
Women. *See* Gender, Unions and
  Women
Women's movement, 40, 43, 131,
  167–168, 215–216
  feminization of the labor force, 26
Wood, Ellen, 82–88, 91–92, 100, 102
Woodsworth, J.S., 23
Working class, 6, 18, 21, 24–32, 42, 93,
  94, 98–99, 109, 110, 115, 122, 131,
  132, 153, 166, 192, 202, 212, 216
  competition among workers, 27
  identity formation, 28, 31, 34–35
  organization, 21, 25–26, 28, 31, 90,
    94, 116
  "productive and unproductive,9 35
  proletariat into class, 112
  revolutionary potential of, 10,
    27–28, 44, 48
World Bank, 111, 128, 179–180, 190
World Trade Organization (WTO),
  143, 178, 180, 185, 194(n30)
Wright, Eric Olin, 206, 227(n20)

Yeltsin, Boris, 52, 53, 74
Yugoslavia, 49

Zamora, Angela, 189
Zimbabwe, 109
Zuege, Alan, 193